Theosophical Society (Madras, India)

The Theosophical Congress held by the Theosophical Society at the Parliament of Religions

Theosophical Society (Madras, India)

The Theosophical Congress held by the Theosophical Society at the Parliament of Religions

ISBN/EAN: 9783337163358

Printed in Europe, USA, Canada, Australia, Japan

Cover: Foto ©ninafisch / pixelio.de

More available books at **www.hansebooks.com**

THE THEOSOPHICAL CONGRESS

HELD BY THE

THEOSOPHICAL SOCIETY

AT THE

PARLIAMENT OF RELIGIONS,

WORLD'S FAIR OF 1893, AT CHICAGO, ILL.,
SEPTEMBER 15, 16, 17.

REPORT OF PROCEEDINGS
AND DOCUMENTS.

AMERICAN SECTION HEADQUARTERS T. S.,
144 Madison Ave., New York.
1893.

THE THEOSOPHICAL CONGRESS

HELD BY THE

THEOSOPHICAL SOCIETY

AT THE

PARLIAMENT OF RELIGIONS,

WORLD'S FAIR OF 1893, AT CHICAGO, ILL.,

September 15, 16, 17.

REPORT AND DOCUMENTS.

The following documents issued from the office of the Vice-President of the Theosophical Society and by the managers of the World's Fair Auxiliary explain themselves and give the history of the matter.

THEOSOPHY AT THE WORLD'S FAIR,
SEPTEMBER 15-16, 1893.

INFORMATION FOR MEMBERS OF THE T. S.

FOR several months prior to April, 1893, the General Secretary of the American Section of the Theosophical Society, together with Mr. George E. Wright, Pres. of the Chicago Branch T. S., endeavored to procure an assignment of the Society to a date in the PARLIAMENT OF RELIGIONS so as to present the subject of Theosophy, but was not successful until just before the Seventh Annual Convention of the American Section, April 23-24, 1893. The following letter will show the assignment made for the Society :

WORLD'S CONGRESS AUXILIARY.
COMMITTEE ON RELIGIOUS CONGRESSES.
REV. JOHN HENRY BARROWS, D.D., CHAIRMAN.

CHICAGO, U. S. A., *April 14th, 1893.*

MR. GEORGE E. WRIGHT,
212 Stock Exchange, Chicago.
My Dear Sir: It gives me great pleasure to learn that you are taking active steps to have the Theosophical Societies of the World represented in the great Parliament of Religions. I hope that when you meet your friends in New York, arrangements will be made to perfect the organization for carrying out your

plans in connection with the Parliament. I understand a local committee has been appointed by President Bonney of the World's Congress Auxiliary. I take pleasure in assigning, as days for your meeting, Friday and Saturday, September 15th and 16th.

Hoping you will have a large and important representation of your various societies, I remain,   Yours sincerely,
        JOHN HENRY BARROWS,
    Chairman Committee on Religious Congresses.

WORLD'S CONGRESS AUXILIARY

OF THE WORLD'S COLUMBIAN EXPOSITION, CHICAGO, 1893.

GENERAL OFFICERS:

President,	*Vice-President,*	*Treasurer.*
CHARLES C. BONNEY.	THOMAS B. BRYAN.	LYMAN J. GAGE.

Secretaries,
BENJAMIN BUTTERWORTH,   CLARENCE E. YOUNG.

CHICAGO, *April 18th, 1893.*
MR. GEORGE E. WRIGHT,
    Pres. Chicago Branch Theosophical Society.
    My Dear Sir: In reply to your favor of the 7th inst. I take pleasure in saying that I am advised that the Rev. John Henry Barrows, Chairman of the General Committee of the World's Congress Auxiliary on Religious Congresses, and Rev. Augusta J Chapin, Chairman of the Woman's Committee of the World s Congress Auxiliary on this subject, have recommended that the Theosophical Society be given an opportunity in the World's Congress of 1893 to set forth the Religious and Ethical aspects and relations of Theosophy, and an assignment of a proper time and place for such presentation will accordingly be made I understand that Dr. Barrows has suggested that he may be able to arrange for your presentation on Friday and Saturday, the 15th and 16th days of September, and upon that point I will refer you to him.
    The matter of what is known as Psychical Research and Phenomena having been withdrawn from your application, it is understood that the presentation to be made in the Department of Religion will be confined to Theosophy as a Religion and a system of Ethics. I am advised that some of the most distinguished members of the Theosophical Society have already accepted other engagements in the Department of Religion, and will also take part in your own presentation.
    On your return from the meeting soon to be held in New York City, I will appoint the Committee of Organization, of which you will be Chairman. Please bring with you a list of your Advisory Council and a draft of the Preliminary Address for your Congress. As the entire matter of what are known as "Occult Phenomena" has been committed to the Psychical Research Congress, I trust you will take the pains to exclude that subject from your address, and make it quite clear that the object of your demonstration is to give the Religious and Ethical world better information than they now possess of the Religious and Ethical principles of your order. This regulation I am quite sure will prove wholly advantageous to the demonstration you desire to make.
    Awaiting the further action you are to take, I am
                    Very respectfully yours,
                        CHARLES C. BONNEY,
                    President World's Congress Auxiliary.

At the Convention of the T. S. above mentioned Brother George E. Wright made report in the matter, and what follows is abstracted from his report for dissemination among members by order of the Convention.

The World's Fair at Chicago has two sides or aspects ; the first the commercial one, the second its literary, philosophical, and intellectual side. The second phase is technically known as the World's Congress Auxiliary. It takes in a great many subjects, not the least being the PARLIAMENT OF RELIGIONS. Beginning in May the different Congresses are: Woman's Progress, Public Press, Medicine and Surgery, Temperance, Moral and Social Reform. Commerce and Finance, Music, Literature, Education, Engineering, Art Architecture, Government, Law, Political Science, Science and Philosophy ; in September : Labor, Religion, Missions and Church Societies, Sunday Rest ; October: Public Health and Agriculture.

The World's Congress Auxiliary is officially constituted as follows :

1. A central organization authorized by the Directory of the World's Columbian Exposition, and recognized by the Government of the United States as the proper agency to conduct a series of World's Congresses in connection with the Exposition

2. A local Committee of Arrangements for each Congress. The Committee constitutes the means of communication and action between the Auxiliary and persons and organizations that will participate in a given Congress. This Committee of Arrangements consists of a comparatively small number of persons who reside in or near the place where the Congresses are to be held.

3. Each Committee has adjoined to it and constituting its non-resident but active branch, an Advisory Council, composed of persons eminent in the work involved, and selected from many parts of the world. The members of such Councils coöperate with the proper Committees by individual correspondence.

A further interesting and commendable feature of the organization is the recognition of Woman as entitled to equal rights and privileges in the management. There is a Woman's Branch of the World's Congress Auxiliary, and it is expressly provided that in each Congress there shall be two Committees, one of Men, reporting to President Bonney, and one of Women, reporting to Mrs. Potter Palmer, President of the Woman's Branch, the number of each being alike

The Parliament of Religions begins on Monday, September 11th, and continues seventeen days. Following is a condensed statement of the programme :

September 11th. Addresses of welcome and responses by representatives from Great Britain, Continental Europe, India, China, Japan, Australia, Canada, Africa, and South America.

September 12th. Origin and Universality of Belief in God. Primitive form of Theism as witnessed by the oldest Sacred Writings. God in History and in the light of Modern Science.

September 13th. Man, his nature, his dignity, his imperfection. The nature of Life. Various beliefs regarding the Future Life. Human Brotherhood as taught by the different historic religions.

September 14th. Religion essentially characteristic of Humanity. Expression of the relations between God and Man. What constitutes a Religious as distinguished from a Moral Life. Spiritual Forces in Human Progress

September 15th. Importance of a serious study of all Systems of Religion. The Dead Religions, what they have bequeathed to the Living. To what degree has each Religion justified the God of all the Earth in the historic evolution of the Race ?

September 16th. The study of the Sacred Books in Literature. Religion as interpreted by the World's Poets. What the Jewish, Christian, and other Sacred Literatures have wrought for Mankind.

September 17th. Religion and the Family. The Marriage Bond. The Domestic Education of Children.

September 18th. The Religious Leaders of Mankind. Incarnation claimed by different Religions. Their Historicity and Worth. The Sympathy of Religions.

September 19th. Religion in its relation to Natural Sciences and to Arts and Letters. Can the knowledge of Religion be scientific? Has the Science of Religion given aid to the other Sciences ?

September 20th. Religion in its relation to Morals. Essential Oneness of Ethical Ideas among Men. Agnostic notions of Conscience, Duty, and Right. Ethical Systems and Ethical Types produced by various historic faiths. Different Schemes for the Restoration of Fallen Man.

September 21st. Religion and Social Problems. Religion and Wealth. Religion and Poverty. Religion and Temperance. Comparative benefits conferred upon Woman by the different Religions.

September 22d. Religion and Civil Society. Love of Country. Observance of Law. Perils of Great Cities. Is Present-day Religion adequate to meet the Requirements and Dangers of Modern Life?

September 23d. Religion and the Love of Mankind. The Fraternity of Peoples. Duties of European and American Nations toward China. International Justice and Amity. Arbitration instead of War.

September 24th. The Present Religious Condition of Christendom. What Religion has wrought for America.

September 25th. Religious Reunion of Christendom.

September 26th. The Religious Union of the Whole Human Family. The World's Religious Debt to Asia, Europe, and America. What are the points of contact and contrast between the different Religions as disclosed by the preceding Conferences?

September 27th. Elements of perfect Religion as recognized and set forth in the different Historic faiths and characteristics of Ultimate Religion. What is the Centre of the Coming Religious Unity of Mankind?

I have necessarily condensed the official programme, endeavoring in the above to convey only its most salient features. But I desire now to ask all my listeners if they have noticed how perfectly Theosophical is the list of subjects presented. There is throughout no begging of the question, or assertion of dogma. Everything is placed upon the most liberal basis. In fact, the whole programme sounds as if it might have been taken from a syllabus of one of the Theosophical Branches. We ought to remember also that these ideas are to be discussed not by one set of individuals or by representatives of a single creed, but they will be taken up by the most distinguished exponents of all the world's great religions. The plan of holding a Parliament of Religions, at which the representatives of the great historic faiths shall sit together in frank and friendly conference over the great things of our common spiritual and moral life, is no longer a dream. The religious world in its great branches will be represented in this truly œcumenical conference. There will be Buddhist scholars, both from Japan and India, and probably also from Siam. Our own beloved brother and Fellow-Theosophist, H. Dhammapala, Secretary of the Maha Bodhi Society, has been commissioned to represent the Southern Buddhist Church. It is expected by the Auxiliary managers that he will be one of the greatest attractions in the Parliament of Religions, and every courtesy will be extended to him by them during his stay in Chicago. The Local Committee on the Theosophical Congress hope to secure his services also during our sessions. But leaving that aside for the present and returning to the general Parliament, I may say that at least one of the high priests of Shintoism is expected to be present. Two Moslem scholars, eminent in India, have accepted invitations. The eloquent Mozoomdar will speak for progressive Hinduism. Arrangements are being made to secure papers from orthodox Brahmins. The Chinese Government has commissioned a scholar to represent Confucianism. It is expected that Parsees from Bombay will speak of their ancient faith. Jewish rabbis of Europe and America are in earnest sympathy with this movement. The interest in the Exposition and in the approaching Congress will draw to Chicago numerous representatives of the historic religions. The Catholic Archbishops of America at their meeting in New York in November, 1892, took action approving the participation of the Catholic Church in the Parliament of Religions. To name over the list of Protestant Churches which have arranged to take part in it would be but to make a schedule of the whole of orthodoxy.

Early last winter Brother William Q. Judge wrote to me as President of the Chicago T. S., suggesting that as I was on the spot it might be well to take steps looking toward our being represented at the Fair, and to see what could be done on behalf of the Theosophical Society. I thereupon visited the World's Fair headquarters, and subsequently in conjunction with Brother Judge as Vice-President of the T. S. and our General Secretary entered a formal application in writing for representation. When Mrs. Besant was in Chicago in December we visited together the officials of the World's Congress, and on the following day the Rev. Augusta J. Chapin, Chairman of the Woman's Committee on Religions, called upon Mrs. Besant at my house. It was then practically decided that we were to secure representation, but a question that arose later caused considerable delay. That question was, where, at just what point in the Congress, ought we to be located. There never was any question as to our right to be represented. Large bodies naturally move slowly, and there was a great pressure of business upon the Auxiliary, owing to the vast amount of correspondence and negotiations rendered necessary in giving all the various religions and other organizations their appropriate places. But all was finally brought to a satisfactory issue, so far as our application was concerned.

Our assignment of dates is in every respect of a most satisfactory nature. In the first place we are granted a separate and distinct Congress of our own, which will be duly and officially advertised as the Theosophical Congress. We are not lumped in, as many societies are, among several others under some general head, thus losing much of our individuality and no little of the publicity which is sought in such an affair. On the contrary, every effort will be made by the World's Congress Auxiliary to attract attention to our Congress and to give it the most favorable auspices. In my final interview with President Bonney last Wednesday he said:

"You [meaning the Theosophical Society] are now a part of the World's Congress, and we are as much interested in making it a success as you are."

And this is in fact the case. Every facility will be extended to our people to make the best possible showing.

Then as to the dates of our sessions, could anything be better? The Parliament of Religions formally opens on Monday, September 11th, and we are assigned to the following Friday and Saturday, September 15 and 16, 1893. The Unitarian and Universalist Societies meet at the same time, and certainly we can make a showing that will compare favorably with these organizations. As a matter of fact, there is no reason why Theosophy should not make a pronounced success of this occasion. We have our philosophy which has stood the test of untold ages. All of the really great philosophers of the past have taught it. Many of the most advanced thinkers of the present day, materialistic as it is, have embraced it. The Theosophical Society includes some of the most brilliant intellects in all lands. Our orators are eloquent, our writers convincing. Where can they find a better opportunity to spread the Theosophic idea than right here in this wonderful Parliament of Religions, the meeting-place of the best minds in Europe and America, the intellectual centre towards which in this year of 1893 all the culture of the world will turn, whose proceedings are officially sanctioned by the Government of the United States, whose every act will be fully and faithfully recorded in the daily press, whose official records will be preserved in durable form, and, finally, whose sessions will form a grand historical event, marking the change from the old dispensation of darkness and dogmatism to the new era of light, liberty of thought, and religious expression, and, above all, the spirit of universal fraternity with which the Theosophical Society is animated, and of which it is indeed the standard-bearer?

All sessions will be held in the new Art Palace on the Lake Front, and during some of the time several Congresses will be in progress simultaneously. There are in the building two enormous halls capable of holding 3,000 to 4,000 people each, and besides these there are a dozen smaller halls accommodating from 300 up to 1,500 each The Art Palace is erected in a park just in front of the Auditorium Hotel, near the centre of Chicago. The Fair proper is held at Jackson Park, some distance towards the outer limits of Chicago.

In accordance with the rules of the managers of the Auxiliary, the Local Committee of the Theosophical Congress is named from citizens in or near Chicago. They are as follows: George E. Wright, Chairman; Prof. Frederic G. Gleason, Alpheus M. Smith, Mrs. E. H. Pratt, Dr. Elizabeth Chidester, Mrs. M. M. Thirds, Judge R. Wes McBride, Judge Edward O'Rourke, Mrs. Gen. M. M. Trumbull, Mrs Anna Byford Leonard.

The Advisory Council is given in the Bulletin which will be officially issued by the Fair managers. The Chairman of that Council is William Q. Judge, as Vice-President of the Theosophical Society. The necessity of having representatives in Chicago is the reason for Brother Wright's being Chairman of the Local Committee; the need of having a general representative in America caused Brother Judge to be selected as Chairman of the Advisory Council; otherwise of course Col. H. S. Olcott would have been its Chairman as President of the Theosophical Society.

On the 26th of April a cable of information was sent to Col. H. S. Olcott to Madras, India, asking for his approval of the plans so far matured and the general appointments made, and under date of April 29th he replied by cable from there that he approved if we thought the matter judicious, he being too far away to know all the facts. He thus approves, as there can be no question of the propriety of our having our days in the Religious Parliament.

The General Secretary of the Indian Section being present at the Convention April 23d gave a written approval of these plans and pledged the indorsement and coöperation of the Indian Section. A cable was at the same time sent to the European Section, and its officials replied giving their hearty approval also, and Mrs. Annie Besant telegraphed that the dates assigned were suitable for her and that she would be at the Congress and address it under one of the heads provided. Efforts are being made to have the best speakers in the T S. attend the Congress, and it may be possible to have Brothers Mead, Keightley, Burrows, and others from England, and perhaps others from the Indian Section. Precise information cannot be given on these points now, as correspondence must first be had. In the United States we can of course obtain several good speakers.

While the Fair pays for the printing of the necessary Bulletins issued by us, it furnishes no money for such matter as the present nor for other incidental expenses. Therefore, under the resolution passed by the last Convention of April, I beg to ask all members who can afford it to send to me contributions for those expenses, no matter how small or large such remittances may be, and to specify in the letter accompanying any that they are for this object.

WILLIAM Q. JUDGE,
Gen. Sec. American Sec. T. S.

144 Madison Ave., New York, May, 1893.

NOT THINGS, BUT MEN.

President, CHARLES C. BONNEY.   Treasurer, LYMAN J. GAGE.
Vice-President, THOS. B. BRYAN.   Secretary, BENJ. BUTTERWORTH.

THE WORLD'S CONGRESS AUXILIARY

OF THE WORLD'S COLUMBIAN EXPOSITION.

DEPARTMENT OF RELIGION.

Preliminary Address of the Committee of the World's Congress Auxiliary for a Theosophical Congress.

THE Intellectual Department of the World's Columbian Exposition has been planned so carefully, and upon such a broad basis, that it can not fail to exercise a vast influence in the realm of thought. In fact, by its means chiefly will the World's Fair be enabled to develop and attain to its fullest usefulness.

In the magnificent buildings of the Fair will be exhibited the choicest products of Nature and Art, all that the inventive faculty of the century has been able to bring forth.

At the same time, in the Memorial Art Palace on the Lake Front, near the centre of the city, will be shown the best developments of human thought. Under the auspices of the World's Congress Auxiliary there will be held a series of Congresses designed to represent the intellectual, moral, and religious progress of mankind. Commencing May 15th, and lasting until November, these meetings will comprise a great variety of literary, artistic, and scientific subjects.

REPORT OF PROCEEDINGS AND DOCUMENTS. 9

But no doubt the greatest interest will centre in the Parliament of Religions convened in the Memorial Art Palace, which will begin on September 11th, and continue seventeen days.

Never before during the Christian Era has such a gathering been dreamed of, much less actually proposed and carried into effect. The idea of bringing together the representatives of every historic faith, not only of Christianity but also of all the leading Oriental religions, is certainly unique, and will be fraught with tremendous results. At any rate, it marks a distinct epoch in the religious history of the world.

The Theosophical Society has been granted representation in the Parliament of Religions, thus having opportunity to set forth the religious and ethical aspects of Theosophy in the most public manner and under the most favorable auspices.

The matter was first proposed by Mr. William Q. Judge, Vice-President of the Theosophical Society, who made a formal application for representation on behalf of the Society at large. At the Convention of the American Section of the Theosophical Society, held in New York April 23d, 1893, the plan of the proposed Congress was clearly set forth, and the matter having been referred to a special committee, the latter reported, recommending that the Convention give its unqualified indorsement of the Congress, and urging Branch Societies and individual Theosophists all over the world to join in the effort to make it a success to the fullest possible extent. The report was unanimously adopted, and appropriate committees were appointed to coöperate with the World's Congress Auxiliary. At the same time, messages were received from the secretaries of the Indian and European Sections, indorsing the Congress, and promising the cordial assistance of the foreign members and on the following day President Olcott cabled from Madras, India, his approval also.

The Parliament of Religions opens on Monday, September 11th, and the Theosophical Congress will be held on Friday and Saturday, September 15th and 16th, having two sessions each day.

It is confidently expected that many of the most distinguished members of the Society, both in Europe and Asia, will be present and take part in the proceedings of the Congress.

Mrs. Annie Besant has already cabled from London her acceptance of an invitation to deliver an address. We hope to secure from India the attendance of President H. S. Olcott and several of our Hindu brothers of international reputation.

The best talent of the Society should be represented, and we hereby appeal to all Theosophists throughout the world to aid in making the Congress a splendid success and demonstrating to the whole civilized world of the West that the ideal pursued by the Theosophical Society—the Universal Brotherhood of Man—is already in considerable measure a realized fact, and that Theosophy supplies the true scientific and living basis for right ethics.

COMMITTEE OF ORGANIZATION.

Chairman, GEORGE E. WRIGHT, President Chicago Theosophical Society,
Room 48, Athenæum Building, Chicago.

Prof. Frederic G. Gleason,	84 Auditorium Building, Chicago,	Illinois.
Judge R. W. McBride, .	Indiana Supreme Ct., Indianapolis,	Indiana.
Alpheus M. Smith, . .	Chamber of Commerce, Chicago,	Illinois.
Judge Edward O'Rourke,	Superior Court, Fort Wayne,	Indiana.

COMMITTEE OF THE WOMAN'S BRANCH.

Chairman, MRS. E. H. PRATT, 425 La Salle Ave., Chicago.

Mrs. Gen. M. M. Trumbull,	614 La Salle Ave., Chicago, . .	Illinois.
Dr Elizabeth Chidester,	5910 Michigan Ave.. Chicago,	"
Mrs. Anna Byford Leonard,	4201 Ellis Ave , Chicago, . .	"

Mrs. M. M. Thirds, Secretary Central States Committee T. S., Room 48, Athenæum Building, Chicago.

THE THEOSOPHICAL CONGRESS.

ADVISORY COUNCIL.

Chairman, WILLIAM Q. JUDGE, Vice-President Theosophical Society, New York.

Col. H. S Olcott. President Theosophical Society, Adyar, Madras, India.
Mrs. Annie Besant, . 19 Avenue Road, London, . England.
Bertram Keightley, Secretary Indian Section T. S . Adyar, Madras, India.
George R. S. Mead, General Secretary European Section T. S., London, Eng.
A. P. Sinnett, . . . London, ... England.
Prof Wm. Crookes, F. R. S, London, ... "
Mrs Isabel Cooper-Oakley, London, ... "
Countess Constance Wachtmeister 19 Avenue Road, London, "
Herbert Burrows, . . London, ... "
H. T. Edge, . . . London, ... "
Viscount Pollington, . London, ... "
James M. Pryse, . . 19 Avenue Road, London, . "
C. Leadbeater, . . . London, ... "
Mrs. Alice L Cleather, . Harrow, ... "
Sidney Coryn, . . London, ... "
Mrs A P. Sinnett, . . London, ... "
Count Bubna, . . . London, ... "
Miss Francesca Arundale, London, ... "
Miss Laura Cooper, . London, ... "
J. M. Watkins, . . London, ... "
R. A. Machell, . . London, ... "
Dr. Archibald Keightley, Westmoreland, . . . "
Edward T. Sturdy, . . Dorset, ... "
J. Dick, C. E., . . Dublin, ... Ireland.
H. M. Magee B. A., . Dublin, ... "
R. B. B Nisbet, . . Liverpool, ... England.
John Hill, . . . Liverpool, ... "
F. Bandon Oding. . . Newcastle-on-Tyne, . . "
H. A. W. Coryn, M. R. C. S., Brixton, London, . . . "
Oliver Firth, . . . Bradford, ... "
Sidney H. Old, . . Birmingham, ... "
Dr. Alfred King, . . Brighton, ... "
Mrs. Herbert Crossley, . Brighton, ... "
William Kingsland, . Chiswick, London, . . . "
F. L. Gardner, . . Chiswick, London, . . . "
Dr. A. H. Guest, . . Manchester, ... "
Bartley Day, . . . Eastbourne, ... "
Mrs. A. Passingham, . Exmouth, ... "
Mrs. Archibald Keightley, Westmoreland, . . . "
Count Carl von Leiningen, Schloss Billingheim, Mossbach, Austria.
Frederick Eckstein, . Vienna, ... "
Dr. Franz Hartmann, . Hallein, ... "
Baron Leonhardi, . . Prague . . . . . Bohemia.
Mme. Cederschjold, . Stockholm, ... Sweden
Edward Coulomb, . . Paris, ... France.
The Countess d'Adhemar, Paris, ... "
Arthur Arnould, . . Paris, ... "
Marie, Countess of Caithness and Duchesse de Pomar, Paris, "
C. E. Parmelin, . . Havre, ... "
Gustav Gebhard, . . Berlin, ... Germany.
Ortho Alexander, . . Corfu, ... Greece.
Mme H. de Neufville, . Amsterdam, ... Holland.
Mlle. Immerzeel, . . Arnheim, ... "
Gustav Zorn, . . . Odessa, ... Russia.
Senor Jose Xifre, . . Madrid, ... Spain.
J. Roverolta, . . . Barcelona, ... "
Florensio Pol, . . Corunna, ... "
Dr. Gustav Zander, . Stockholm, ... Sweden,
Mme H. Sjotedt, . . Gottenburg, ... "
Herr Sven Benggston, . Lund, ... "

REPORT OF PROCEEDINGS AND DOCUMENTS. 11

Dr. Pioda,	Locarno,	Switzerland.
Count S. Frenfanelli-Cibo,	Foligno,	Italy.
Rt Rev. H. Sumangala,	High Priest of Ceylon, Colombo,	Ceylon.
Peter d'Abrew,	Colombo,	"
W. F. Wijayesecarra,	Colombo,	"
E. F. Perera,	Colombo,	"
Mrs. Musaeus Higgins,	Colombo,	"
D. O. Goonasecara,	Galle.	"
A. D. Goonewardena,	Kandy,	"
Dr. S. S. Wikaramartu,	Kandy,	"
P. R. Venkatram Iyer,	Madras,	India.
S. E. Gopalacharlu,	Madras,	"
H Dharmapala, Secretary Maha Bodhi Society, Buddha Gya,		"
Hon. S. Subramanny Iyer, late of Government Council, Madras,		"
Shrenavasa Row,	Judge City Court, Madras,	"
Dewan Bahadur. Ragoonath Row, late Prime Minister Tanjore,		Madras, India.
Norendro Nath Sen. Ed. Indian Mirror, Calcutta,		India.
Dinnanath Ganguli, Government Pleader, Berhampore, Bengal,		"
Nafa Das Roy,	Berhampore, Bengal,	"
Kali Presanna Mukerji,	Barakur, Bengal,	"
Purnendu Nath Sinha,	Bankipore Patna,	"
H. H. H. Maharajah of Benares,		"
Govinda Dasa,	Pundit, Benares,	"
Upendrath Basu,	Pleader, Benares,	"
Gyanendra Nath Chakravarti,	Prof. Mathematics, Allahabad College, India.	
M. A. Hydari,	Government Auditor, Allahabad,	"
Pyari Lal,	Judge, Agra,	"
Rai B. K Laheri,	Ludhiana, Punjab,	"
Pundit Gopi Nath,	Ed. People's Journal, Lahore,	"
Manilal Nabhubai Dvivedi,	Nadiad, Guzerat,	"
H. H. Prince Rupsinghi Harisinghi, Bhwonagar,		"
J N. Unwalla,	Bhwonagar,	"
Dr. Edulji J. Berham,	Surat,	"
Nowtarama Uttarama Trivodi, Pres't Arya Dharma Sabha, Surat,		"
Dorabji Dhosabhoy,	Hyderabad, Deccan,	"
Tookaram Tatya,	Bombay,	"
Pherozsha R. Mehta,	Bombay,	"
Rustomji K. Modi,	Bombay,	"
Khan Bahadur, Naoraji Dhadabhai Khandalawala, Judge, Poona,		"
P. Srenavasa Row,	Gooty,	"
V. Coopooswamy Iyer,	Munsiff, Sholingur,	"
N. P. Subramani Iyer,	Bangalore,	"
K. Narayan Swami Iyer,	Combakonam,	"
A. Nilakanta Shastri,	Tanjore,	"
Lieut. C L. Peacocke,	Delhi,	"
Lieut —— Beale,	Surat,	"
Jehanjire Sorabji,	Gov't Sec'y, Hyderabad,	"
Rustomji Pestonji,	Hyderabad,	"
Sidney V. Edge,	Adyar, Madras,	"
Walter R. Old,	Adyar, Madras,	"
Capt. Banon,	Kulu Kankora,	"
Gen. Morgan,	Retired Maj.-Gen., Ootacamund,	"
T. Vigiaraghava Charlu,	Adyar, Madras,	"
Bhwani Shankar,	Pundit, Bombay Presidency,	"
C. Kottaya Chetty,		"
Rama Gopal Buxy,	Punjab,	"
Rama Prasad,	Pleader, Meerut,	"
B. Keshava Pillay,	Gooty,	"
Nibaran C. Gupta,	Ranchi, Chota Nagpur,	"
Rao Bahadur A. Subhapati Moodleyer, Bellary,		"
T. G. Swaminatha Iyer,	Bellary,	"
Kewasji Merwanji Shroff,	Bombay,	"
Dadhubhai Sorabsha Moonsifua, Broach,		"
Babu Nil Comul Mukherji,	Calcutta,	

THE THEOSOPHICAL CONGRESS.

N. Anasami Row,	Coimbatore,	India.
Pundit D. Venkatachelam,	Shastri, Cuddapah,	"
A. Nunjundappa	Cuddapah,	"
H. H. the Maharajah of Cooch Behar,		"
Capt. G. Ragoonath,	H. M. Nizams Troops, Hyderabad,	"
Pundit P. Baijnath,	Gov't College, Jubbulpore,	"
Dewan Ramjas C. S. I.,	Prime Minister of Kapurtala,	"
Lala Hurrychund,	Kapurtala,	"
O. L. Sarma,	Madanapalle,	"
Bhola Deva Sarman,	Lhaassa,	Tibet.
R. Seshagiri Row,	Madanapalle,	India.
Babu Kalka Prasad,	Moradabad, Bengal,	"
Purna Chundra Mitter,	Moozufferpore,	"
Zemindar, Ragoomund Prasad Shanna.		"
Raja Sitish Chandra Pandar Bahadur, Pakur, Bengal.		"
V. Vasudeva Sastriar,	Rajahmundry,	" [India.
Prince Rajakumar Navadwipchandra, Deb Varman Bahadur, Tipperah, Bengal.		
S. R. Ramakrishna Iyer,	Tinnevelly,	India.
S. T. Krishnamacharya,	Pleader, Pondicherry.	"
Babu Shyamacharya Mukerji, Umballa,		
William Q. Judge,	Vice-President Theosophical Society, New York.	
Dr. J. D. Buck,	Cincinnati,	Ohio.
Dr. Jerome A. Anderson,	San Francisco,	California.
Edward B. Rambo,	San Francisco,	"
Dr. Allen Griffiths,	San Francisco,	"
E. Aug. Neresheimer,	New York,	New York.
Alexander H. Spencer,	New York,	"
Henry T. Patterson,	Brooklyn,	"
Miss Katharine Hillard,	New York,	"
William Main,	Brooklyn,	"
Rev. W. E. Copeland,	Tacoma,	Washington.
Dr. J. Phillip Knoche,	Kansas City,	Missouri.
Dr. J. W. B. La Pierre,	Minneapolis,	Minnesota.
J. C. Slafter,	Minneapolis,	"
Paul Henning,	St. Paul,	"
William C. Temple,	Pittsburg,	Pennsylvania.
Dr. J. H. Salisbury,	New York,	New York.
James H. Connelly,	New York,	"
Donald Nicholson,	New York,	"
Clement A. Griscom, Jr.,	New York,	"
Mrs. S. A. Harris,	Oakland,	California.
Frank Neubauer,	Los Angeles,	"
Andrew A. Purman,	Fort Wayne,	Indiana.
Dr. A. P. Buchman,	Fort Wayne,	"
George D. Ayres,	Boston,	Massachusetts.
Robert Crosbie,	Boston,	"
J. Ransom Bridge,	Boston,	"
Col. H. N. Hooper,	Brooklyn,	New York.
J. Guilford White,	Washington,	D. C.
Capt. George R. Boush,	Washington,	"
Robert Hosea,	Cincinnati,	Ohio.
Miss Bandusia Wakefield,	Sioux City,	Iowa.
Hon. Edward Drayton,	St. George's, Grenada,	B. W. I.
William Berridge,	Victoria,	British Columbia.
Miss Louise A. Off,	Los Angeles,	California.
Dr. J. H. Fulton,	Montreal,	Canada
Frank I. Blodgett,	Seattle,	Washington.
Sidney Thomas,	San Diego,	California.
Mrs. A. L. Doolittle,	San Diego,	"
Elliott B. Page,	New York,	New York.
A. W. Goodrich,	Philadelphia,	Pennsylvania.
J. H. Scotford,	Portland,	Oregon
Claude F. Wright,	New York,	New York.
John M. Pryse,	New York,	"
Col. R. E. Whitman,	Washington,	D. C.

EXECUTIVE NOTICE.

THEOSOPHICAL SOCIETY.
PRESIDENT'S OFFICE,
ADVAR, *27th May. 1893.*

THE Managers of the World's Parliament of Religions having granted us permission to present the views and policy of our Society with respect to the questions of Religion and Ethics, on the 15th and 16th September next at Chicago, the undersigned, being prevented by his Asiatic engagements from personally attending, hereby deputes Mr. William Q. Judge, Vice-President T. S., to represent him on that occasion. All steps heretofore taken by Mr. Judge in connection with the said representation, in pursuance of his correspondence with the undersigned, including the formation of Committees, are hereby ratified, and he is fully empowered as the President's substitute to adopt such further measures in the premises as may to him seem necessary. Of course it is to be distinctly understood that nothing shall be said or done by any Delegate or Committee of the Society to identify it. as a body, with any special form of religion, creed, sect, or any religious or ethical teacher or leader ; our duty being to affirm and defend its perfect corporate neutrality in these matters.

The undersigned also deputes Mrs. Annie Besant as a special Delegate from the President, to address the meetings in question on behalf of the whole Society, and to convey to them his fervent hope that this truly representative Theosophical assembly of people of all races and religions may result in the spread of that principle of brotherly love and religious tolerance which is the foundation and cornerstone of the Theosophical Society.

The undersigned most earnestly calls upon all Sections, Branches, and willing Fellows of the Society throughout the world to put themselves in correspondence with Mr. Vice President Judge, and do all that lies within their power to aid him in bringing this very important matter to a successful result.

HENRY S. OLCOTT.
President Theosophical Society.

THE PARLIAMENT, SEPTEMBER 11TH, AT 10 A. M.

The Theosophical Delegates were invited to attend, and Prof. Gyanendra N. Chakravarti and William Q. Judge, Vice-President T. S., were at the opening and sat on the platform. In response to the general address of welcome Professor Chakravarti spoke as follows :

MR. CHAIRMAN, LADIES AND GENTLEMEN—I represent a religion the dawn of which vanishes into the mists of antiquity which the microscope of your modern historical research has not yet been able to descry. I come from the city of Allahabad, the capital of the Northwestern Provinces of India, the Hindu name of which is Pryaga. It is called the Tvitha-raja, or the king of the different places of pilgrimage, as it is situated on the confluence of two of the most sacred rivers of the Hindus—the Ganges and the Jumna. From time immemorial, in various systems of religion Spirit is represented by the white and Matter by the dark color, and these two rivers, from the difference in their colors, represent Spirit and Matter, the two great factors in the evolution of the universe. And when I think that here, in this city of Chicago, the centre of material civilization, the vortex of physicality, you have the Parliament of Religions holding its sessions,—when I think that in the very heart of the World's Fair, teeming with that vast machinery which administers to the flesh, you have provided a hall for the feast of reason and the flow of soul, I am reminded of my

native home, for here once more I see the sister streams of Spirit
and Matter, of pure intellectuality and physicality, running side by
side and representing one of the grandest truths. I need hardly
tell you that in holding a parliament of all the different religions
of the world—Christian and non-Christian—you have acted in a
manner worthy of the race that leads the van of modern civilization, one of the remarkable features of which is an ever-widening
tolerance. In inviting men of all shades of religious opinions and
beliefs—aye, even a heathen like myself—you have acted in a manner worthy of the motherland of the Theosophical Society, the
fundamental docrine of which is that underneath the superficial
strata of every religion is the water of Truth, and to represent
which, as well as Brahminism, I am here amongst you to-day. I
have always felt that there is a subtle bond of unity between
India and America, and it is probable that there may be a finer
reason for the identity of our names than the theory of chance or
the mistake of Columbus can account for. It is true that I belong
to a race decrepit and bent with age, and that you form a race full
of the vigor of youth and bristling with life; and yet who has not
observed the secret sympathy that sometimes exists between extreme
old age and childhood? One of the most striking characteristics of
the Hindu race has been its longing after something vague, shadowy, indistinct, which exists not on the plane of Matter, and the
mind is therefore trained to look inward for that something which
alone could make it happy. It is this tendency that has given rise
to the innumerable schools of occultism, the various systems of
philosophy, and to the manifold grades of *sadhus, sanyasis* and *fakirs*
that flourish on my native soil. You, on the other hand, have developed such stupendous momentum on the plane of Matter, such
immense kinetic energy on the plane of the intellect, that a stranger
landing on your shores is amazed at their intensity. And yet,
amidst the glorious miracles of your steam and electricity, I could
sense in the atmosphere a certain undefined yearning toward
something not yet attained ; a feeling of disappointment and despair arising from the realization of the truth that progress in these
lines alone means but running against the dead wall of Matter,
and that through the vistas of spiritual perception alone can shine
the light that can make life happy. In all the places I have visited
I found an ever-increasing readiness to listen to and assimilate
spiritual truths regardless of the source from which they ema-
nated, and this I regard as a most significant sign of the times.
For even now I can see through the gray but thinning mists of
prejudice which are yet hanging on the horizon, the grandest event
of the future—the union of the East and the West. As the sun
rises from the East, so the dawn of truth heralds from the East.
To the East is given the sacred satisfaction of having given birth
to all the great religions of the world, and to the West belongs the
proud privilege of having supplied the world with all that can
make physical life comfortable and even luxurious. But as perfection cannot be attained in humanity or in the universe (for
what is true in the microcosm must also be true in the macrocosm)
without a harmonious blending of Spirit and Matter, it is my fervent

hope that the East and the West may join hands, each giving to the other what it needs,—the West supplying the East with energy, vigor, and power of organization, and the East opening up for the West its vast treasures of spiritual lore locked up in treasure boxes grown rusty with age. And I hope that with the opening of this Parliament of Religions to-day will begin the work of unsealing that great Fountain of Truth from which will flow perennially living waters of peace and joy to comfort the millions of thirsty souls in the century to come.

THE CONGRESS T. S.

First Session, September 15th, 10 a. m.

The President of the Parliament being occupied at the time, the local chairman, Brother George E. Wright, took the chair in order to open the meeting and give the gavel to the Vice-President, making the following address:

BROTHERS AND SISTERS—It affords me great pleasure on behalf of the organization to call the meeting to order and to inaugurate the Theosophical Congress. Can we or do we fully appreciate the importance of this occasion? We who participate in this great Congress of Religions are makers of history. No event in ancient or modern times has been of such direct benefit to the human race as a whole, as will be this. What makes the case peculiar is that we are standing on the threshold of a new era, an era of liberality in thought, in investigation, in religion, of calm and unbiased comparison. As Theosophists we should be profoundly moved by this great change that has come over religious thought, and especially thankful should we be that we are permitted to take part in this grand reformatory movement. Our dream is indeed realized; what we hoped for, but hardly dared expect, is coming to pass. The Theosophical idea takes its place along with the other religious and philosophical concepts in the World's Parliament of Religions, and appeals equally with them to the consideration of all thinking people.

So far as our position in the Parliament is concerned, nothing more could be desired. Every courtesy has been extended to our Society and to our Committee by the General Committee of the Religious Department, and in addition to the two days' Congress to be held in this room, we have been assigned the great Hall of Washington on Saturday evening for a general presentation of Theosophy. On that occasion it is expected that several of our most eloquent speakers will be present. The name of Annie Besant is alone sufficient to arouse public enthusiasm; and besides we will have our respected Vice-President, Mr. Judge, and our beloved brother, Chakravarti, from India. It is one of the great features of Theosophy that it appeals to the reason instead of to the emotions. Nothing could be more absolutely logical than the doctrines of Karma and Re-birth. Hence, during our meetings in this room the Theosophical ideas will be carefully and religiously announced, and all will be invited to give them due consideration.

Each paper to be presented has been prepared with the greatest pains, and every word that could be deemed superfluous has been left out. Indeed, so wide is the scope of the topics involved that only with the greatest difficulty could the entire programme be condensed into the five sessions allowed for our Congress. But on Saturday evening, in the Hall of Washington, will be given what might be termed a general review of the topics treated of exhaustively in the Congress, and the speakers whom I have named will prove that Theosophy is not necessarily a dry system of metaphysics, but has in it all elements requisite for the most interesting narrative and the most thrilling eloquence.

I now have the pleasure of introducing the permanent chairman of the Congress, one who is known the world over as an indefatigable worker in the cause of Theosophy, a lover of truth and a hater of religious shams, the friend and coadjutor of the founders of the Theosophical Society, and, I may add, the leading organizer of the Society, William Q. Judge.

Brother William Q. Judge took the chair, and addressed the meeting as follows :

BROTHERS AND SISTERS—It is a very high honor to me to be allowed to preside over this Congress. It is a triumph for the Theosophical Society to be permitted to hold this Congress after eighteen years of violent abuse and ridicule continued up to the last moment ; and we may consider that the Theosophical Society, after all these years of persistent work, has at last got a footing in the West. It always has had it in the East, but now at last we have it here. And I think the best thing to do to-day is to proceed at once to business. More is done and accomplished by work than by compliments and speeches one to another. We are all supposed to be brothers and sisters together and not to need flattery, or at least we ought not to need it ; we ought not to ask it. I only have to say that I am very glad personally to be able to preside over you, but I should be just as well pleased if any of you were selected to have this position.

Mr. Wright has given you an outline of this Congress. Perhaps it may seem to some singular that the Theosophical Society should be in a religious parliament, because we have no creed and have always said that we were not a religious body. But we hold that religion and science and human life cannot be separated from each other, and for that reason when the Parliament of all the Religions of the World comes together it is very proper that the Society, the only one in the world which represents the union of science and religion, should be represented in it, and we were very fortunate in being allowed to be represented on that basis and on no other.

This Congress has been sanctioned by the President of the Theosophical Society. That sanction was necessary because we should not go into a Parliament of Religions without the sanction of our own President, who has deputed Mrs. Annie Besant to represent him as special delegate. He has deputed me to represent the Theosophical Society throughout the world, as he himself, being so far away, could not come here. The other delegates whom we have here, as already mentioned, are Brother Chakravarti, from Allahabad, India, who is in a peculiar position in this Congress. His position is that he is a delegate from the Theosophical Society, not particularly from India: he comes from India, requested and brought here by the whole Society to represent his form of Theosophy before us, but he is the delegate of the entire Society. Mrs. Annie Besant is the delegate of the European Section, together with Miss F. Henrietta Muller and Mrs. Isabel Cooper-Oakley of London. These ladies were appointed delegates by the European Section at the last Congress, which was held there in July. Mrs. Cooper-Oakley, who is one of our leading members and who has been traveling all over the world in behalf of the Theosophical Society, has also been especially delegated by the Australian Branches. In addition to these particular delegates we will have as speakers a member of the Chicago Branch, Mrs. Thirds; a member of the Cincinnati Branch, Dr. Buck; a member of the San Francisco Branch on the Pacific Coast, Dr. Anderson; and a member who has come from London, Mr. Claude F. Wright. Thus we have representatives and speakers from almost every part of the world to take part in this Congress. I have asked my brother Claude Wright to relieve my voice by acting as my secretary at this meeting, and after Mrs. Besant shall have read to you a message, he will read to you some credentials which we have and Colonel Olcott's executive order, so as to make this meeting perfectly regular. I now ask you to give your attention to Mrs. Annie Besant, who will read a message sent to us by Colonel Olcott, President of the Society, from Adyar, Madras, India.

MRS. BESANT—I have in my hands from Colonel Henry S. Olcott, the President-Founder of the Society, a message of greeting to all assembled here and of congratulation upon our gathering, which has been received by cable in code form. Being translated, it is:

PRESIDENT T. S. TO CONGRESS.

To WILLIAM Q. JUDGE, VICE-PRES. T. S.:

Across seas and continents your Asiatic brethren salute you; mingling their congratulations with yours for this auspicious opportunity to tell the representatives of many nations and of the world's great faiths the fraternal message of Theosophy. From ancient temples and rock-cut fanes the voices of the ancient Teachers once more utter the words of wisdom that showed our ancestors the true path to happiness, liberation, and spiritual peace. May the blessing of the Sages be with you all, and may the truth prevail. H. S. OLCOTT, P. T. S.

Headquarters T. S., Adyar, Madras, September 15, 1893.

MR. CLAUDE F. WRIGHT then read the President's Executive Order and the various credentials of delegates, which are found in the Appendix.

Mr. Judge—You will please now give your attention to Brother Gyanendra N. Chakravarti, of Allahabad, India, who will speak to you under the head of the programme which you have. I would like to ask you to be as quiet as possible, because this hall is a bad hall to speak in at any time; and with these trains constantly running, it is worse; so if you will all keep very quiet you will reduce difficulties to a minimum.

THE THEOSOPHICAL DOCTRINE OF THE UNITY OF ALL SPIRITUAL BEINGS; THE ETERNAL UNITY OF SPIRIT AND MATTER AS TAUGHT IN THE BRAHMANICAL SCRIPTURES.

PROF. GYANENDRA N. CHAKRAVARTI, OF ALLAHABAD, INDIA.

The Professor began by reciting the following Sanscrit verse:

Nayamatma pravachanen labhyas na medhya na bahuna srutena yamebaishavrinute ten labhyas tasyaiva atma vrinute tanum swam.

Ladies and Gentlemen, Brothers and Sisters—That is a sloka from one of the most sacred of the world's sacred literature. It is from one of the sublimest books of India's bibliography, a book which was ever the guiding star of the life of one of the greatest of Europe's thinkers—Schopenhauer—I mean the Upanishads of the Hindus. It means that the Atma, the Spirit, is something which cannot be understood either by words or by hearing or by intellect. They alone who resort to the spirit have the light of the spirit brought to their own spirit. This being the view of things, and the Theosophic spirit in the West being but another name for the Atma of the Vedas, the high essence of spirit, I need not tell you that this is something which cannot be brought down on the plane of a speech, or even on the plane of the intellect. True Theosophy in its esoteric aspect is the eternal, the undying truth, the sun of that permanent verity which shines always, from the beginning of things to the end of things, and from the end of things again to the beginning of things. True it is that in different ages and in different times men of high spiritual culture, born with a mission in their breasts, have taught this truth on the plane of intellect, but the spirit, as the verse of the Upanishads says, can be cognized only by the spirit. Once in the plane of intellect, it ceases to be spirit. The different religions of the world, the various teachings which now supply the spiritual pabulum to the world, are not the sun of which I have talked to you. The religions represent but one ray of but one aspect of that sun of truth, passed through the lenses of several glasses, and having thus the light more or less destroyed in passing to the plane of the intellect, the plane of thought and the plane of words. The different teachers of the world, according to the necessities of the times, according to the conditions of life with which they are surrounded, according to the light which glows in them, have given to the world but one side of the truth, a mere sign-post, a finger-post to lead one on the path at the end of which alone you can find the eternal truth. In the East, in the West, and all over the world such men have been born. Call them by whatsoever name you choose, prophets and seers, martyrs and saints, Buddhas and Rishis have lived in this world to give expression to this truth, goaded on, impelled by something within them to leave some material representation of that which is unrepresentable, to serve as a help for men to get behind the physical universe.

Theosophy, then, in its highest aspect is unrepresentable, is ineffable, and can be realized by the spirit alone, not by mind or thought. And yet the fact remains that Theosophy is to-day a living thing, a thing that is now sinking into and permeating the most advanced thought both in the East and West. What is that Theosophy, then? It is again an attempt made to bring that truth in some form down to the plane of intellect, the attempt of modern Theosophy, and a most glorious attempt in my opinion it is, to once more bring home to the minds of the people that behind the more or less translucent veils of every religion shines the glorious sun of truth. It is attempted once more to make the followers of every denomination of religion to realize and feel that spiritual knowledge as spiritual composition, as spiritual inspiration, as spiritual revelation, is not the birthright of one particular set of people, of one particular part of the earth's surface. And need I tell you that if Theosophy has stopped at this very point, if it stops merely with the formulation of this one doctrine, its aim would be as grand as can be conceived. Why, look only at the reddened pages of history, how religious warfares have marred and stained the history of mankind because of the non-realization and non-perception of this one grand truth. Religions which are supposed to teach charity, brotherliness, divine love, have been set one against the other like the roaming fierce tigers of the jungle. They have pounced upon one another. Instead of extending love, they have torn men to pieces. Bear in mind what history shows you, what misfortune has been wrought by the elimination of this principle, and you will cease to wonder when I claim for Theosophy that even if it stopped at the initiation of this one principle, it is entitled to the admiration and to the reverence of the whole world. But it does not stop there. It does not stop merely by laying down an axiom as to which you may inquire and inquire rightly: where is the true evidence? It tries to give to the world certain methods by which they can more or less rend asunder the veil in their own religion which hides that eternal light; it serves as a pioneer to persons treading the dreary path of life, telling them that below these many colored superficial strata of their own religions, which may differ in external composition, if they dig deep enough they will find the living waters of truth. And it does more. It teaches you how to dig; it supplies you with the axe and spade with which you can cut the surface of every religion and see yourselves and show the world at large that the living waters are no fiction; they are a reality, having in them power and capacity to quench the thirst of the human race. It thus not only gives you an axiomatic truth, but puts forward a body of doctrines, in an imperfect way it may be, because all on the plane of intellectualism which will make you see your own religion offers to you the same fundamental truths which you can find in every religion in the world ; and this, I say, is one of the important factors of the Theosophical organization.

Theosophy is following the time-honored and the sublimest doctrines of the Brahmans of India, who, as you know, have never from the very dawn of their ancient religion tried to persuade men and the followers of any religion to give up their own and take up another. Brahmanism to-day stands as it did thousands, millions of years ago, the only religion in the world which is non-proselytizing. It does not try to bring men away from the paths which have been indicated by the sages that have been born among them; it does not try to draw them away from the principles which have been enunciated for the particular benefit of particular countries and particular surroundings. It says that in your own religion, if you dig deep enough, you will find the truth. And it is laid down most emphatically in one of the most sacred works of the Hindus that (Sanscrit)

Swadharme nidhanam sreya paradharma bhayavaha.

" It is best to die in one's own faith ; the faith of another is full of dangers."

Starting, then, with this principle of exoteric and esoteric Theosophy, you will understand that Theosophy is at once a religion and not a religion. In its higher aspect, as I have just now defined it, it is at once the final source of all religions. In its lower and popular aspect, it is no religion at all, because it is the congeries of all religions. It shows, as I have told you, that every religion has its place in the universe and every religion has its particular functions to perform. This view of religion is almost a necessary consequence of some of the fundamental doctrines which Theosophy tries to press forward on the views of the world. You are aware, very likely, that the first principle of Theosophy, or, at least, the first rule which every brother is bound to be guided by in the organization of the Theosophical Society, is the principle of Universal Brotherhood. Why Theosophy requires that each man stands to every other man, never mind where his home may be, across oceans and continents, it may be, still distance is nothing to spirit ; each man stands to every other man in the relation of a brother, tied together by a common chain of gold, coming out of one eternal spiritual source, working hand in hand and side by side through the course of evolution, and finally returning hand in hand again, to that eternal source from which he came. Nor does the idea of brotherhood restrict itself to the human kingdom alone. Theosophy extends its idea of brotherhood very much further. It teaches that in every animal, from the very highly developed organism to the merest protoplasm in which the current of life is just starting, which is just emerging from the state of vegetation, there is the ineffable, the all-pervading spirit which beats in the breast of every man. It regards every animal that walks the jungles or adorns the domestic hearth as one which is merely waiting its time to reach the same amount of advancement and progress that has been made by the paragon of animals—the human being. Nay, it goes farther:—that every animal is a candidate for those diviner perfections, for those higher states of existence, to which humanity has not yet attained. This law proclaims to you that every animal is to you a brother pilgrim, belated, behind, it is true, but deserving of greater pity, greater consideration from the mere fact of its being an animal. (Applause.)

One step further and where do you go? There are no walls hiding the spirit of brotherhood and Theosophy. The walls that exist in art, in science, in society are all down ; the spirit of love expands, and where does it go, think you ? Why, it pervades the universe, becomes co-extensive with every atom that you can or cannot see, every insect that breathes, and beyond. Where is the importance of that grand doctrine which has been taught from time immemorial in the East to man : Man, thou art not alone, thou art one of the several thousands of millions of beings co-existing, one with them ; because thou art God and they are God. God pervades the whole universe, and the universe itself is God. That is the doctrine which Theosophy teaches, that is the doctrine of the glorious teachers which I stand here to-day to bring to you, to the Western homes of the people.

The principle of evolution, according to the Indian Shastras, is that there is but one eternal reality, one outbreathing spirit, from which all that exists has come and into which all that exists will go back. At the beginning of time, forth from the bosom of Parabrahm, which, according to our notions, is the highest spirit, came two different aspects—the Purusha and the Prakriti. Purusha is the name of spirit, and Prakriti is the name of matter. We Hindus recognize no difference between spirit and matter ; we regard them as but two different facets of the one which alone exists behind all illusions ; we regard them as two poles of the same magnet ; we regard them as two points of electricity—that electricity that America revels in to-day—the electricity of the positive field and the electricity of the negative field. Both are electricity, but exhibiting different functions. One attracts the other, and then from the point of contact passes the spark. There is Purusha exhibiting one kind of electricity, the positive, and there is Prakriti exhibiting another kind of electricity, the negative. Attraction issues between these two ; lo ! forth comes the spark of the universe. That is the theory of evolution according to our Shastras. These are the two male and female principles which have been recognized in every old system of religion, wheresoever it may have flourished ; this is the doctrine that is represented in the various symbols that you see everywhere in the world ; and I venture to say, although it may not be believed in the West, that your cross upon which the divine Jesus is said to have been crucified represents that very truth, the pole of the spirit acting on the pole of matter, giving rise to the universe. The Egyptian tau, the cross on which is represented the serpent, represents the same truth ; it represents the evolution of the universe in transit, of which the snake is a representation. And this doctrine is the foundation of the whole structure of Brahmanism, which I am here to-day to represent on the platform of the Parliament of Religions. Thousands of thousands of pages I could quote for proving the soundness of my position, but it is for evident reasons perfectly useless. I shall quote only one, again from the Upanishads, which will show that what I have been stating to you is really the sound position.

Anoraneean mahatomaheean atmasya juntor nihita guhayam tum akartu pasyati vitsokah dhatu prasadan mahimanatmanah.

This spirit of which I have been talking, the smallest within the smallest atom, is greater than the greatest universe. It is, it is said, in the heart, in the nervous centre of every man and of every animal. This spirit is revealed to him who, having subdued the passions of the flesh, seeks to stand in its light. This, I think, will prove to you the soundness of my proposition.

And now I pass on to give you a beautiful illustration from one of our sacred works. It may be said by some of those who are present here, or by those who may read what I have said : " Why, you have been quoting this doctrine from the Upanishads, admittedly the most sacred of your books, and it may be that this is only an isolated gem in the vast rubbish of your theological literature. I am now going to relate to you a story from the Puranas, which are regarded by others than Hindus as mere theological twaddle, the source of nursery tales and fables concocted in the brains of the baby race of humanity. Yes, I am going to quote to you a story from one of these Puranas, which are composed, as I conceive, to represent the same truths which are in the Vedas and Upanishads, but clothed in a separate garb, in allegories which are meant for the people, which gives them attraction and impels the people to listen to them and thus follow those truths.

In the old times there was a great Adwaita king. By this Adwaita is personated materiality. This king, from wealth and luxury and pride, had forgotten there was any spiritual being greater than he was himself. He had, by the strange irony of fate, also explained in the Puranas, a son who, as chance or fate may have it, was a very devoted follower and worshiper of the god Vishnu. What an irony ! A being in the home of a monster of infidelity and crime, a saint, this ornament of the Hindu world ; on the heap of ashes and rubbish around him shines forth a diamond of unparalleled lustre. From the very beginning this divine being lisps his first syllables in grammar in the name of Hari. The father learns of it and gets angry ; he calls his son's teachers to him and says: " How dare you teach my son this blasphemy? How dare you tell him of any being with power greater than myself? Dare you destroy my own idol and tear it from his heart, and set up there some one else ? " They swore they had done nothing of the sort ; the boy was the most peculiar in the world ; they wanted him to recite syllables from the grammar for pronunciation and accent, but, inattentive and deaf to all their trainings, he would again recite the name of his very beloved Hari, the god whom he so loved. By his persistence in repeating the sacred name in the presence of his father, who could not bear that sound to be spoken in his presence, he got the boy hurled from the top of a precipice. Down he went from the precipice with a joyous heart, faith in his eternal Hari, and, lo! he was in the lap of his god, not a scratch on his skin, safe and sound he sat at the bottom. Other means were tried. He was taken in front of a mad elephant, with the object that the huge animal would make short work of him and tear him from flesh to bone. But the mad, ravenous elephant acted mildly with the devoted boy. It put forth its trunk, wrapped it around him, raised him and placed him upon his back, whereupon he rode triumphant upon the back of the elephant. Various devices were tried to kill this infant son of this wicked king, but firm as the rock of India did he remain. Never for a moment did fear enter his heart; his faith was unflinching, his devotion warm and firm; and who could destroy a boy like that? Finally, driven to the last resources by his anger, the father got the boy to stand in his presence and said: "It is all an illusion; it is all untrue. Where is your Hari? if there is that Hari, can you show him?" The boy replied: "Yes, I can, even before you, although you have defiled his holy blessings and his great name." The king said: "Well, if Hari can come, I want him to come forth from this stone pillar here," and, lo and behold! with a crash of thunder, the stone, unshaken and immovable, was rent in twain, giving way, and out leaped forth, in form majestic, the god Hari, before whom the whole world bows down.

Now, I ask you, brothers and sisters, if you really regard this story as a necessary emanation of idolators, as some would have you believe? Does it not convey even to your minds a truth which, though clothed in fable, it may be, still is burning in its vigor and in its energy? And, ladies and gentlemen, here I stand to-day to talk to you, drawing from our matchless manuscripts in which is found the basis of religion, craving justice at your hands. I know you are liberal, you sons of America, sons of the land of freedom, the land of liberalism, the land of justice! I crave no indulgence on the score of the religion's being old; I crave no charity! All I want is that you should not allow your minds to be prejudiced, to be poisoned and abused by the thousands of defamations and slanders that are cast at our religion. Let your own mind work, and then pronounce your dictum. I am here to-day to abide by it. (Applause.)

THEOSOPHY IS A SYSTEM OF TRUTHS DISCOVERABLE AND VERIFIABLE BY PERFECTED MEN.

THESE TRUTHS ARE PRESERVED IN THEIR PURITY BY THE GREAT BROTHERHOOD OF INITIATES, THE MASTERS OF WISDOM, WHO PROMULGATE THEM MORE AND MORE FULLY AS THE EVOLUTION OF MAN PERMITS.

MRS. ANNIE BESANT.

You have heard from our brother Chakravarti that fundamental teaching of philosophy which you may find, as he also told you, in every religion, be your religion what it may, that of the fundamental unity of all lives, of the fundamental unity of spirit and matter, shown to us in the West in the writings of his own land, just as you might yourselves show it in the scripture that you in turn revere as divine. To my lot in these opening speeches of our Congress it falls as my duty to deal with Theosophy as a system of truths discoverable and verifiable by perfected men; truths preserved in their purity by the great brotherhood, given out from time to time as the evolution of man permits the giving; so that we are able to trace in all the religions the source whence they flow, the identical teaching which underlies them. Our position then as Theosophists is this: The truth is attainable by man—the truth as to the universe, as to man's nature, as to the relationship that exists between man and the universe that surrounds him; that this is a matter, not of faith, but of knowledge, not to be simply accepted on authority, but capable of discovery and capable of verification; that religion loses much of its rightful force in the world if it is not regarded as a reality and a fact, a truth which men may in due course of time verify for themselves if they are willing to take the appropriate means, if they are willing to make the requisite endeavor; so that we stand as believers in, and as very elementary exponents of, the mighty system which, as our brother told you, is the ancient religion of India, or science as well in his own land. And not in his land only, but in every land where man lived and aspired and yearned after knowledge and truth. For there is no land where the Spirit does not speak, there is no land where the voice of the Divine may not be heard; and if to-day the speech be somewhat clearer, it is not so much the difference in the speech as the difference in those who hear. The voice of the Spirit can be heard by no one save by him in whom that Spirit has become developed and able to understand. Now with regard to this system of truth, we allege that truth exists on all planes of the universe and may be studied on every plane. Without at this stage going into the enumeration which belongs to the later part of our exposition, it may suffice to make our position clear if I remind you that in the world generally you would admit the possibility of truth under a threefold division: truth as to the physical universe, of which the exponent is what we are apt to call in the West "science"; truth in the region of the intellect, which is regarded as philosophical; truth in the region of the spiritual, which is put as especially belonging to religion. With us there are no such divisions, as Brother Judge told you in his opening words. To us there is one truth with many aspects, one truth manifesting itself on many planes. Religion is not apart from philosophy, nor philosophy from science; nor is there antagonism between them, nor possibility of contradiction and denial. They are, as it were, the three facets of truth, but one and the same, while the true aspect may be different, and to us Theosophy includes religion, philosophy, and science, truth attainable by man and verifiable by him over and over again. This truth we allege exists complete. A perfect knowledge of spiritual things, a perfect knowledge of intellectual verities, a perfect knowledge of scientific facts. This great body or system of truth has been discovered by perfected men, not only discovered, but verified over and over again, building that great system of truths, spiritual, intellectual, and material; and nothing has been allowed to stand as a part thereof except such things as have been verified, experimented upon, redemonstrated by generations of seers, by one after another of this brotherhood of perfect men; so that the very truth itself should lack no means of demonstration — demonstration more complete than anything that is dreamed of by Western science, arriving at certainty with regard to this great body of truth. Now in science we are accustomed to a definite statement of certain facts. Those we call scientists are fitted for their work. They have apparatus to aid them in their researches. When a discovery is made by one, then others try to reproduce it. The utmost skill of intellect and ingenuity is exerted in order that the most crucial experiments may be applied to test the value of the new discovery; and only when the discovery, taken for a while as an hypothesis, has been reverified over and over again, is it permitted to rank as a part of scientific truth. But as every one must admit, such a body of truth obtained by struggle and endeavor, verified and reverified by trained and experienced scientists, the value of such a body of truth cannot be appreciated by the first comer, nor must anyone venture to say, merely because he is ignorant, "This or that cannot, I feel, be true." In the scientific world knowledge is the one authority; ignorance has no right save the right of silence. But when men go out of the scientific world they seem to make their own ignorance the measure of truth (applause), and to take the right of the most dogmatic denial of all that does not come within the narrow limit which they have never really striven to extend. And with regard to spiritual truth the conditions are fundamentally the same as those which are necessary for the discovery, the verification, and the understanding of scientific truth. In the one case the scientist, with his delicate apparatus of lenses and of balance, with his careful fashions of analysis, with "the sublime patience of the investigator," as Clifford rightly called it; and in the spiritual sphere sages work whose spiritual nature has been perfected, who have made for themselves the apparatus for spiritual investigation, not of lenses nor balance, but of the open eye of the spirit. And if for many a year a scientific man will struggle to perfect his instrument, if generation after generation the scientists of the West will give hours, months, years of patient trial to make but one tiny improvement in some piece of apparatus, that so great an exactitude may be established and truth more clearly seen, do you expect that in the sphere of the spiritual, as much above the intellectual as the intellectual is above the sensational, do you expect that less pains are needed there than are needed on the physical plane? and that man without endeavor, man without toil, without self-sacrifice, and without self-abnegation, can gain knowledge mightier than the intellect, can dream of and perfect the spiritual faculties necessary for an appreciation of the truth? Science has her martyrs in every clime, science her pioneers, her pupils, her fighters; and in the world of the spirit there is indeed a devotion vaster than science can inspire, dangers to be faced before which the dangers of earth are trifling, and only those whose heart is pure, only those whose will is strong, only those who for life after life have learned to conquer the material and the intellectual and gradually developed for themselves the spiritual faculties, only such men have power to discover, only such men have power to prove and verify. But in that every man is divine; in that divine love is your heart and mine as much as the heart of the sage; therefore we also can feel, if only temporarily, the pulses of that spiritual life urging us on always towards the realm of Spirit. And just in proportion as we feel them the vision begins to open, until we know of very certainty that spiritual truth is real and not a fable. (Applause.) But if this be not so, there is no such thing as religion. Unless the spiritual world be a reality, religion is the most terrible of hypocrisies. There has not been one great teacher, go back to the antiquity of Hinduism, come forward to the teacher who is most revered in the West, who has not, asserting his mission, justified it by the fact that he was the son of man, and that the fact of the sonship of humanity was the essential heart of divinity within him. Nay, in the lips of your own teacher the argument is found, "Greater works than mine shall ye do." And he claimed that they could follow where he had trodden. So that this underlies your faith as such, as it underlies any true faith in the world; for the Christ is but humanity perfected, the first fruits of the promise of what every child of man may be. And this mighty heritage of truth, discovered and verified in long past ages in order that the child race of man might be shown the road along which it was to travel; that great heritage of truth, preserved by the brotherhood of perfect men, has been the basis of every religion. In Hinduism, the most ancient religion of our own fifth race, you find it, if you search for it carefully in the scriptures which have been the guide, the sustenance, the help of millions upon millions of the most acute brains as well as the most spiritual hearts that our race has produced. In all the ages there have been the teachers holding out the truth and giving it out just as far as man was able to receive it; and as the careful mother, the careful teacher of the child guides the feeble steps along the path of learning, so that, at each step, clear knowledge may reach the child, and that with each new step, still clearer the light may come; so these elder brothers of our race who have perfected their own natures live in the world in order that their younger brothers may have the advantage of their guidance. Take the scriptures of the world—Brahmanic and Buddhist, Hebrew and Christian—take what you will, every one of them has the same teaching, and whence the identity if the source be diverse? Not only so, but in philosophy and in science, if you will read your history with eyes opened instead of closed, you will see before each great impulse of philosophical and scientific thought the coming of some one who suggests possibilities, who throws out hints, who works marvels, and so gives new impulse to the advanced thought of the world. You have had it in the great philosophic schools, in the schools of Egypt, the schools of Greece; and then you may trace it downwards and find scholars continually repeating great spiritual, philosophic, and scientific truths; and so we begin to understand how our evolution has been guided. We begin to realize why it is to-day there is this anxiety to know something more of truth, something clearer and more definite of this science of the soul. The science of the soul in Hindustan, later in Greece named Theosophy, now again proclaimed under the Grecian name as more easily familiar to our Western ears, proclaimed to-day newly, indeed, but only the old brought forth anew, for in our teachings there is nothing new; in our teaching there is nothing save that which has been proclaimed over and over again wherever the human heart was ready to listen, wherever the eyes of the soul were open to see the light. And if to-day these truths are more widely spread than ever, which is true, for the veil between the esoteric and exoteric has been made somewhat thinner, it is because the point has been reached at which the spiritual soul is becoming more manifest in man, and so with less of allegory and fable the same old truth may be proclaimed in the ears of men. Therefore in the end of the nineteenth century the same old Masters of Wisdom, who had founded Hinduism, who had founded Buddhism, who had founded Christianity, who had founded the other great religions of the world, have in these later days again initiated a spiritual movement to give further impulse to spiritual knowledge and to call men nearer to the home where alone their souls will find eternal peace. It is the same ancient home, it is the same birthplace of our race; but we have forgotten our birthplace, and so the words that again speak of it sound strange. They send once more their message to proclaim these same old truths, to initiate once more a movement in order that that movement may attract all who are ready to take in its real and spiritual form. They proclaim the old message from the lips of one whose name will be familiar to many here present — Helena Petrovna Blavatsky — to whom many of us owe our very knowledge of the life of the soul, and whose memory we therefore reverence as more than the memory of a mother; for the mother gives life to the body, but the spiritual teacher awakes the soul. And therefore while we claim for her no authority, while we ask no one to accept her save as she herself may win acceptance by the word she utters; while we do not ask that any shall take her as authority, for authority lies in the message and not in the messenger, and the recognition comes from the soul and the memory, and from nothing in the life without—still we pay that fitting reverence and gratitude to the channel which those of us have a right to do who have found it has brought to us the very waters of life. And so, thus regarding her, we carry on the reverence to those who sent her and who have not forgotten their younger brothers nor grudged to them the help they need. And thus we stand to-day witnesses for the existence of spiritual truth; witnesses to the possibility of the understanding of that truth by men; witnesses of the existence of these perfected sages who help humanity on its upward climb and show the light to all who are willing to see. And to you of different faiths, to you of different modes we say, You are not different, for your spirit is one with ours. Our language may sometimes differ from yours. What is language? It is that which divides, while the spiritual truth unites, and thus it applies to any other race and any other creed. Our religions in their names are different; in their essence they are one. We have on our platform men and women also who are one in our recognition of the truth. We know no division; we have learned to transcend it. We have no separation; the spirit is one only. And those who have been taught, those who have learned, they are all one mighty body for the service of the world; and in truth those we speak of as Masters, those we speak of as Initiates, they claim as a far nobler title to be the brothers and the servants of men. (Applause.)

HEVAVITARANA DHARMAPALA, F. T. S., OF CEYLON.

BROTHERS AND SISTERS—A philosophical exposition of this grand subject of Theosophy is not within my province. Abler minds are here to give a Theosophic exposition of that beautiful subject. I am here as a Buddhist. I come to attend the religious Congress as such; but I am here to-day to express my deepest sympathy, my deepest, I should say, allegiance to the Theosophic cause, simply because it made me to respect my own religion. And now look: there are Brahmans here on this platform, and here are my sweet sister, Mrs. Muller, and my brother Chakravarti, one a Brahman and the other a Christian, and by the study of Theosophy she loves it just now more than she used to do. I was in school and read the name of the Theosophical Society, and when the Theosophical Society arrived, especially the Theosophic founders, we welcomed them and Mme. Blavatsky to Ceylon. They came there with a message of peace and love. They said, "Study your own religion; abuse not the religions of others, and try to find out the truth: but lead a pure life." That was the message they brought to Ceylon, and it was so sweet and so nice I accepted that common teaching, and here I am to-day as evidence of that fact. Beyond that I am not prepared to speak to-day.

THEOSOPHY AS FOUND IN THE HEBREW BOOKS AND IN THE NEW TESTAMENT OF THE CHRISTIANS.

MISS F. HENRIETTA MULLER, OF LONDON.

Religion is to be defined as "the Culture of the Soul"; *Revelation*, whether written or traditional, is the knowledge requisite for such culture.

The aim, therefore, and the intention of all Scripture is the instruction of the Soul; therefore, also, Scripture addresses itself directly to the soul and not to the senses; its meaning can be apprehended fully by the soul alone, its language is spiritual and veiled as the Soul's own language and Being are spiritual and veiled. The key to the inner meaning of Scripture must be sought through and beyond the outer in which Revelation clothes itself, every interpretation of the intuition being sifted and modified, and rejected or accepted on its own merits by the Mental Faculty.

Again, Revelation may be defined as an Intuition of the Kosmos, which reveals itself in and through the Primeval Consciousness of Mankind. It is distinctly traceable in the history of nations; its sign and symbol may be observed appearing at various times and in various forms; like a golden thread it may be seen running through the life history of a race or people, now shining clear in full light of noon, now temporarily lost in the gloom of night. Such Kosmic Intuition reaches down to and is the voice of Deity. It is One and Eternal, Undivided, Homogeneous. It is untouched by its own manifesting activities, or by its own assumption of heterogeneity, thus differentiating only in its manifested form, not in its essential Being. Now the measure of manifestation in a given direction or time, since it varies not with or by Kosmic Intuition or Being, necessarily varies only with and by the nature of its medium or channel, and it follows that, all Revelation being one *per se*, the measure of the truth of any given religion is solely regarded by the *receiving capacity* of a given people at a given time.

The capacity to receive Divine Truth varies greatly with different nations, and even with the same nation at different periods of its growth. Compare, for instance, the condition of the Jewish people in this respect with the races and peoples who surrounded them, or their condition at the time of Christ and that of the American people to-day—the Jews bound fast by the chains of a degraded tradition, enslaved by material or sensual tendencies, blinded and misled by their own corrupt priesthood, who riveted their chains only too securely by enforcing the fulfilment of the letter of the law and denying the spirit; compare that period of their history with this epoch-making event which gathers us here together from all parts of the world, which exhibits the people of America as ready to hear and to learn the truth from whatever country it comes, as seeking its common basis in all the religions of the world. This occasion may be taken as a portent of the future religious history of America, as a measure of their capacity to hear and to receive Divine Truth. Am I taking too sanguine a view when I say that America may one day accept joyfully the head cornerstone which was rejected by the builders in Palestine 2,000 years ago, that *the Christ* whom the Jews crucified is the Christ whom the sons and daughters of your land are seeking?

The Divine Idea develops itself and the Pathway of God may be known—sometimes through the permanence and unfolding of a great national ideal, sometimes constructively in the history of a people, sometimes through their discipline or dispersion; it exhibits itself often in and by the lives of their great men. The ideal of Abraham was to build up a people of *strength*, to mould the national character on a lasting foundation; and his Thought or Idea implanted there on the plastic nature of the undeveloped race has endured throughout the ages and distinguishes the Jews to-day. Moses sought to construct a great and free nation. *Liberty* was the leading characteristic of his scheme. The Divine Idea thus manifested always involved a constant reciprocal influence between the Great Personality embodying it and the community receiving it. Through all the line of Jewish Prophets the same theme runs; it can be traced in their language, science, art, culture, and mythology of the people, more distinctly, perhaps, in the lives of the Great Personalities of Jewish history, Abraham, Moses, Elijah, and Jeremiah.

To any Theosophist the identity of function and nature of the Jewish Prophet and Indian Rishi are undeniable. What the Rishis were to the Indian peoples whom they ruled and taught, that the Prophets were to the Jews,—Sages endowed with gifts of prophecy and other spiritual powers, holding communion with God, living amongst the people, giving them spiritual teaching, possessing and exercising temporal power as rulers and kings, creating and moulding the national character, and imprinting upon it in all its purity that Divine Idea which they had themselves received of God. Both Prophets and Rishis were sent to the nations who needed them in their infancy as the child needs the guidance and personal care of its parents; both were withdrawn from it when their task was done.

The definitions given above of Religion and Revelation are fundamental; they involve no less than seven principles generally accepted by Theosophists, which in their *full* meaning and in the main are denied by orthodoxy.

(1) They involve the belief that it is *not* in the external form, nor in the literal meaning of scripture, that Divine Light is to be sought, but that the letter conceals a profundity of inner Truth requiring an esoteric key for its interpretation. Without this key which the intuition alone can supply there is danger of grave error. Of the early Christian Fathers, Athanasius was not the only one to utter a note of warning that by a literal, *i. e.*, non-esoteric or purely rational understanding of the Bible, one may be led to form an almost blasphemous conception of Deity, as a cruel and false god.

(2) They involve the oneness of Deity in that it underlies immediately all manifestation, that in it all opposites are united and the independent existence of evil as a principle is denied.

(3) They exhibit the duality of Deity as at once and eternally the unmanifest and noumenal, and the manifest and phenomenal.

(4) The absoluteness of Deity in that it is untouched and unchanged by its own manifestation.

(5) The Divinity of Man and the Humanity of God. "God's highest revelation is Man." "Perfect Man is Highest God."

(6) The Law of Analogy or Correspondence, which by postulating the simultaneous unity and duality of God enjoins us to seek below that which is above, and above that which is below, to learn to know the Macrocosm by and through the Microcosm, to attain universal wisdom through individual self-knowledge.

(7) All scriptures are therefore true esoterically, and falsified only exoterically by the imperfect nature of the personality through which they are revealed. All saviours of men are "Christ," although they may not even know his name.

Professor Buchanan of Boston says:

"I have a profound reverence for the Mexican god Quetzalcoatl, for the Indian Krishna, and for Jesus, but the man of Nazareth is the one who comes nearest to *us*, my soul goes out to him in love. I look upon these three great systems (the Mexican, the Hindu, and the Christian) as three distinct earthly evolutions of *our religion*, inspired by and sustained from heaven."

Which is to say that Christian Theosophy in Palestine, in India, and in Mexico are all substantially the same thing—all are revelations of God through the Divine Teacher who is Christ.

Were it not so, the Parliament of Religions would be impossible.

It is only because the intuition of our humanity is now no longer, as formerly it was, under the Mayavic sway of the *false appearance of difference between religions* that it has at last attained the power to dispel Maya, to penetrate the illusion, and to perceive the inner truths essential to all religions; this precious ray of wisdom, hitherto the possession only of the elect, the Seers, Prophets, or Rishis of the race, is now becoming the heritage of all enlightened persons.

Thus it is demonstrable that it is only by virtue of the development of spiritual light in the West that this Parliament is realized; it is only because progress in the inner planes of our being has moved forward along with progress on the outer planes that it has become possible and practicable. Each member of this Parliament is contributing to the onward movement which will ultimately reach its climax in a recognition of the spiritual kinship of the race; each one is drawing humanity nearer to a common centre of Light and Leading. Let us take our stand in the brighter radiance of to-day, on the bedrock of our religious liberties, let us with exceeding joyfulness glorify that God within us who is teaching and guiding us individually and collectively; from all quarters of the globe we come gathered here together as Architects and Builders of a larger Temple not made with hands.

I am privileged to make my contribution to this glorious Home which we are creating. I come as a Christian woman and a Theosophist, as a disciple of our teacher H. P. Blavatsky — may her name be for ever blessed!—and as a loving servant of our Masters.

The symbolism of the Bible is to be sought in its history and its allegory. Yet the symbolism is not to be taken as evidence of the incorrectness of the history as history, which must be judged on its own merits. A key to the interpretation of its symbolism is offered by one of the greatest Kabbalists who says : " The more unreasonable the story of the allegory, the more profound is its occult meaning," and the more widely may its application be extended. Thus the first chapters of Genesis are *first*, an account of the creation of our earth ; *second*, an account of the first four races, our ancestors who inhabited this globe as described by H. P. Blavatsky. *Third*, they describe the generation and emanation of the soul from and by the Seven Potencies or Hierarchies of God.

They it is who say " Let us make man in our own image," who implant in each man the nature of the whole Kosmos, thus producing a perfectible entity, one which may in its completeness touch and ultimately rule the seven planes of Kosmos. Moreover, these three keys to the interpretation of these chapters show that they are not so much an account of the creation of our earth as an exposition of the laws of creation generally.

Again, the Hebrew Books, besides being an historical account of the rise and growth and decline of the Hebrew nation, are also a symbolical history of the Soul, its origin, birth, nature, powers, growth, and destiny. These are all pictured in the story of the people Israel ; their trials and journeys represent the manner of the soul's evolution. Egypt is materiality, Canaan is the passional and sensuous nature which Israel, or the Soul seeking spiritual regeneration, must subdue before the " Promised Land " can be entered. The " Promised Land " itself is " the Kingdom of Heaven," or the liberation of the Soul from the thraldom of mind and sense.

The Prophetical Books exhibit the high prophetic power of the Jewish Seers and holy men, and mark a narrow but deep occult metaphysic—a metaphysic which prominently distinguishes the Divinity of the Soul and the Oneness of God, without, however, daring to analyse it. Fear is a strong characteristic of the ancient Hebrew.

The Gospels are, as much as the Hebrew Books, a revelation of the soul typified in the birth, life, suffering, crucifixion, and resurrection of Christ. These events in His life represent the inwardness of the Soul, its divinity, its evolution, regeneration, and reincarnation.

"Christ and the Gospels are the key to the Creation of Man, of his past, present, and future eternal being. His nature. why and when created, how and for what purpose, they show us who and what is God—the everlasting, self-existent, and glorious— what His nature and how he manifests Himself in man through love, life, and light. What the *word* is, that is truth, and how all this mighty power can effectually operate in love and gentleness on the spirit and being of man. How man is redeemed from the Fall, what that Fall was, what Life and Death are, what these are intended and made to bring about, who and what is the Principle called Satan, and how all this seeming antagonism works together to make manifest the hidden power and wisdom of God." (*Buchanan*.)

Of the two main doctrines which are prominently brought forward by Theosophy, both Karma and Reincarnation receive confirmation, although the time was not yet ripe for the completer enunciation of them which H. P. Blavatsky gave forth. There is nothing either in the Old or the New Testament which is contradictory of them, and there is much scattered evidence esoterically given. Nor could this be otherwise: the writers of the Bible Books would not be permitted to teach exoterically doctrines which were still only revealed to the esoteric student.

A paper on "Fire Worship," by Nasawanji Billimoria, of Bombay, was then read by title only.

MR. WILLIAM Q. JUDGE—I have been asked to say a few more words on the subject of Theosophy in the Christian Bible; that is, I have been asked to show what Theosophical doctrines can be found in the Christian books.

One of the Theosophical doctrines is the doctrine of Karma; that is, exact justice ruling in the spiritual as well as in the physical; the exact carrying out of effect from cause in the spiritual nature of man, the moral nature as well as in the physical world. That is, that every man is ruled in his life, not by a vengeful and partial God, but by justice. This life is just; whether one is miserable or happy, whether he is poor or rich, it is just. Where is this doctrine found in the Christian Bible, this doctrine that as ye have sown so shall ye reap? That is, having lived before in this world you have made causes which bring about to-day the life you lead now, which have made the characteristics that you have, which made you what you are now, and have plunged you into a living hell or into a happy heaven to-day. We say this doctrine has not of late been taught in Christianity; but it is in the books of the Christians and it ought to have been taught, it would have been profitable had it been expounded. Now, where can it be found?

Does not Jesus say, among other things, you should not judge others? Why? Because if you do you will be judged yourself. What you mete out to others will be meted out to you. That is, what men do to others will be done to themselves. Where and when is this to be done? When is the measure to be meted out if not in this life or some other? St. Paul says: "Brethren, be not deceived, God is not mocked, for whatsoever a man soweth that shall he also reap." Do not these quotations prove that in St. Paul and in the words of Jesus can be found this doctrine of Karma: that as you sow so shall you reap? That your circumstances now are the result of your own acts? This is the doctrine which is the most prominent in the Theosophical field. I call it Theosophical, not because the members teach it, nor from its presence in our literature, but because it is found in the religion of every nation; that is why it is Theosophical. But you have been taught that you must be good or you will be punished. In the West you are told you will be rewarded and punished in this life and in the next. But men are not punished in this life. To-day thousands of men live lives of luxury, strife, and crime, but they are not punished here, and, according to the teachings of Christianity, they stand a pretty good chance of escaping punishment hereafter if they only believe. We see that many are not rewarded who are good, but are often born into misery.

The doctrine of reincarnation is taught in the Christian Bible, that is, that you will be born over and over again in this world according to your destiny, to follow the effects of causes you yourself have put in motion in whatever life. Where is that found? In the mouth of Jesus; and certainly if Jesus, the founder of Christianity, has stated this, has any man or any body of men, has any person any right to say that it is not true? I deny their right, and I say that Christianity has been deprived by theologians of a doctrine which Jesus himself declared, when reincarnation is taken away from it. We say that the doctrine is in the Gospels. One day they brought to Jesus a man who was born blind and asked him why was this man born blind; was it for some sin he had committed or those his parents committed? Now, how could a man be born blind for a sin he had himself committed unless he had lived before that time to commit it? This was a doctrine believed in at that day. The Jews believed it and Jesus was a Jew. He did not deny the doctrine on that occasion. He only said, "Not for that reason." If the doctrine were wrong, certainly Jesus, as the Son of God, would not only have denied it, but he would have said, "The doctrine you enunciate is false." He said nothing of the kind. At another time he himself declared the doctrine, and he asked his disciples, "Whom do men think that I am?", meaning and referring to what was believed at that time, that great sages were born over and over again for the enlightenment of mankind. They call them Avatars in the East. They had an idea great sages and prophets would come back. Will you tell me how such men then could be reborn at all unless under natural law and unless such law governs every man? So Jesus, referring to this idea, said to his disciples: "Whom do men think that I am?" And they said: "Some men think that you are Elias, who was for to come." St. John had been killed just then by the ruler of Judea, and Jesus said to them that Elias had already come back in the person of John and the rulers had killed him, not knowing he was a reincarnation of Elias. So in one case he did not deny and in the other he explicitly asserted the doctrine. And if we take this view we know what he meant when he said to Nicodemus that a man must be born again. He meant not only the regeneration of the soul, but reborn into the body again; that is, that man is a soul who comes into a house to live life after life, and he must go from house to house until he has learned the whole architecture of human life and is able to build a perfect house. In Revelations, the last word of all the books, we find the great speaker writing that he heard the voice of God saying to him that him who overcometh the flesh and the devil, the world and sin, "I shall make a pillar in the house of my Father and he shall go out no more." Does not that mean he had gone out before? The old fathers in the early ages of Christianity taught that if we triumphed over the flesh and the devil, the world and sin, God would make each one a pillar in the house of his father and he would not have to go out again. That is the doctrine of reincarnation.

Then if you will look at the history of the Christian Church you find that the doctrine was taught for five hundred years, and not until the Council of Constantinople was it rejected. At that time it was turned out by ignorant monks, and since then it has not been taught by the teachers, but it is in the Christian books, and to these Christian books we appeal. I say these very doctrines are in many other places found there. Another doctrine is that man is not merely a body, but is a composite being of many divisions. St. Paul taught we have a spiritual body as well as a material body, that we are a spiritual body and a physical body and spirit. That will bring in every one of the seven principles of the Theosophical category. So we say, all through the Christian books, in the Old Testament and in the New, we may find the great doctrines of Theosophy, by which I mean the great universal ideas of unity, of universal brotherhood, of strict justice and no favoritism, of reincarnation, and of the composite nature of man, which permeate every religion as well as the books of the Christians, both old and new.

Adjourned until 3 p. m.

FRIDAY AFTERNOON, SEPTEMBER 16TH.

MR. JUDGE—I inadvertently this morning forgot to state that Mrs. Cooper-Oakley is one of the delegates from the European Section. She is a resident of London, and has been appointed by the Australian Branches also, because she has just come from there. The next session after this will be this evening in this hall, unless we shall be able to secure a larger one, as a great many persons have gone away because this one is so full. This evening we shall have addresses from Mrs. Besant and others on various important doctrines of Theosophy. I understand that many persons who are not fully acquainted with Theosophy and suppose that in one short meeting we could describe it all, go away with the impression that Theosophy is too high a philosophy for the common people. Theosophy is exactly the reverse. It is not for the parlor merely, and it has never done much good through the parlor. The parlor does not like it. It is an everyday religion, and if those who had any other idea will remain for all our sessions, they may be able to find out how Theosophy may be of use in daily life. The next session after this evening will be to-morrow, when we meet again here or in some other hall. The evening session on Saturday will be in the Hall of Washington, which is a larger hall, and which has been given to us for the purpose of enabling three or four of us—Mrs. Besant, Professor Chakravarti, probably Mrs. Oakley and myself— to make a general presentation of Theosophy to the Parliament. Of course that means you, because you constitute the Parliament. I wish also to state that there is also an overflow meeting in the next hall, which, if it grows to sufficient size, will be addressed by Bro. Claude F. Wright on some Theosophical subject. You will now please give your attention to Dr. Buck of Cincinnati.

THEOSOPHY HISTORICALLY CONSIDERED AS UNDERLYING ALL RELIGIONS AND SACRED SCRIPTURES.—ESOTERICISM IN RELIGIONS AND PHILOSOPHIES.

DR. J. D. BUCK.

No history of either philosophies or religions would be complete or intelligent that lost sight of the mystic element, that supersensuous realm from which all unseen causes emanate; that ideal world, the existence of which the thinking, reasoning mind perceives, but which man has never yet realized in the outer life of the world. Neither do we find such histories as exist ignoring this mystic realm. On the contrary, they all treat of it, and either, like Enfield, frankly confess their inability to understand the subject, or, entirely misapprehending the doctrines, represent them as foolish or fraudulent. In *The Gnostics and their Remains*, the learned author makes the following remark:

"The Christian writers who have treated upon the origin and nature of these doctrines were (Origen excepted) ignorant ecclesiastics, who could discern nothing in any religion beyond its outside forms, which they construed in the worst possible sense, even seeking for the most unfavorable interpretation of which such outward appearance was susceptible."

If this shall seem a severe criticism of these critics, a very little examination of the works under question will convince any candid reader that it is but the simple truth. It follows, therefore, that these doctrines have very rarely had a fair hearing, and that to the present day they are entirely misunderstood because so continually misrepresented. The real doctrines have seldom been heard of in modern times. Beliefs that are as old as human thought, and which number among their adherents more than half the human race, possess a novelty to the average reader that is strange indeed, and for the reason above stated.

They have been distorted out of all resemblance to their true intent and meaning. The time has come in the progress of modern thought when these old truths are being restated, and they will have a candid hearing. To accomplish this result constitutes one object of the Theosophical Society.

There is a certain body of doctrines designated as Theosophy, and while they embody many truths, are designated by many names known to all history, and underlie all great religions and philosophies, they concern also the very foundations of all real science and all true knowledge, no less than the basis of ethics.

It would be difficult to trace these doctrines in detail through the religious and philosophical history of man since the beginning of the Christian era, for two reasons. *First*, on account of the misapprehension and consequent misrepresentation already referred to; and *Second*, for the reason that they have been held sacred and secret, requiring a key for their interpretation. The reasons for this secrecy need not here be entered into, for no one at all conversant with the subject will deny the fact. The author of the *Gnostics*, to whom I am indebted for many valuable suggestions, says :

"Secret Societies, especially that one of which the maxim was, as Clemens tells us, the truly wise one, 'Learn to know all, but keep thyself unknown,' erect no monuments to attract the public attention; they deal in symbols to be privately circulated; or else they embody their tenets in mystic drawings like the Ophite Diagramma, and in papyri, long since committed to the flames."

Now in view of these facts, viz.: the misrepresentations derived by the ignorant from the outer form and symbols on the one hand, and concealment by the initiated on the other, it may very naturally be asked: How can any one in modern times, or since the decline of the Mysteries in Greece and elsewhere, determine what these doctrines really are? Certain it is that mere curiosity or idle and ignorant speculation can never discern them. To such as these they are forever a sealed book. But just as all great religions have had their inspired teachers, their seers and prophets, so has the Secret Doctrine had its wise interpreters in all ages. What music was to the intuitive genius of a Beethoven or a Mozart, and what it became under their interpretation—a revelation of beauty and harmony—such has the Secret Science ever been to those who know, and such their revelations to "the listening ear and the faithful breast."

In order to be able to trace these doctrines, in outline at least, through the ages, one must first know what they are.

"The Secret Doctrine establishes three fundamental propositions" (p. 14 Proem) :

(a) "An Omnipresent, Eternal, Boundless, and Immutable Principle on which all speculation is impossible, since it transcends the power of human conception and could only be dwarfed by any human expression or similitude." This fundamental idea must be grasped and followed through varied forms of expression and under many names, and no other proposition can be entertained that is inconsistent with it. The second postulate is :

(b) " The Eternity of the Universe *in toto*, as a boundless plane, periodically the 'playground of numberless Universes incessantly manifesting and disappearing,' called the 'manifesting stars' and the 'sparks of Eternity.' " "The appearance and disappearance of worlds is like a regular tidal ebb of flux and reflux." Herein is postulated the Law of Cycles, alike applicable to atoms or suns, to individual man as to solar systems. The third postulate is :

(c) "The fundamental identity of all Souls with the Universal Over-Soul, the latter being itself an aspect of the Unknown Root ; and the obligatory pilgrimage for every Soul—a spark of the former —through the Cycle of Incarnation (or necessity) in accordance with Cyclic and Karmic Law, during the whole term."

From these three fundamental propositions the entire philosophy unfolds or emanates, just as Cosmos issues from the One Eternal Principle. I am not aware that the doctrines thus clearly formulated can anywhere be found outside the writings of H. P. Blavatsky. The philosophy of evolution thus set forth furnishes a key by which the mysterious chambers and secret crypts of antiquity may be opened and explored. "The pivotal doctrine of the Esoteric philosophy admits no privileges or special gifts to man, save those won by his own Ego through personal effort and merit, throughout a long series of metempsychoses and reincarnations." Bearing these fundamental ideas in mind, we may briefly consider a few among the almost innumerable number of their representatives and embodiments during the past twenty-six centuries.

It is a familiar saying that all our great religions and philosophies have come from the far East. If this be true in a general sense, it is true in a special sense regarding the Secret Wisdom. King says that "so long as philosophy was cultivated in Greece, India was ever regarded as the ultimate and pure source of true wisdom."

Pherecydes, the first preceptor of Pythagoras, is said by Josephus to have derived his doctrines from the Egyptians, and his illustrious pupil and founder of the Italic School of Philosophy went also to Egypt to complete his studies. Neither of these philosophers is known to have committed his doctrines to writing. Egypt was at that time the seat of learning, with colleges at Heliopolis, Thebes, Memphis, etc.

After spending twenty-two years in the schools of Egypt, Iamblichus relates that Pythagoras went to the far East to converse with the Persian and Chaldean Magi and with the Indian Gymnosophists. The real source of the learning of Pythagoras being thus clearly defined, the doctrines he taught but confirm their source. In a form more or less veiled by symbol and allegory, he taught the Secret Doctrine. Following Pythagoras came Buddha, the great Indian Reformer of Brahmanism, whose entire life and doctrines were but an expression of the traditions and philosophy of the old Wisdom Religion. The Socratic doctrines as expounded by Plato constituted the very soul of the Greek philosophy, and the influence of the Porch and the Academy not only constituted the glory of Greece and later of Alexandria, and largely influenced the early Christian philosophy, but influence the world to-day, as they have entered into the thought of all great thinkers and writers for the past twenty-five hundred years. Plato was an Initiate, and the core of his philosophy is the three postulates already quoted.

The Essenes, whom Philo Judæus and Josephus describe as existing in Palestine at the time of Christ, King declares to have been "Buddhist monks in every particular," as proved by the Edicts of Asoka. The word Essenes or Hessenes is derived from the Arabic *hessan*—pure. One has only to read the accounts given by Philo and Josephus to learn the identity of the doctrines of the Essenes with those of Jesus, bearing in mind that both the Essenes and Christ speak of a Secret Doctrine not to be revealed to the multitude.

Some twenty years ago De Quincy took the position in a popular essay that "unless it can be shown that the Essenes were the early Christians, it must be conceded that there was no need of a revelation through Christ, as his teachings were all anticipated by the Essenes." The Essenes were sworn not to speak of their doctrine except among themselves, and they were sworn also not to write of it, except in allegory and symbolism. This is expressly stated by Philo; and upon this and other statements, Eusebius, as late as the fourth century, gives the opinion that the Gospels and Epistles of the New Testament were the secret books of the Essenes. In proof of this Eusebius cites the exercises, festivals, and rules in vogue among the Essenes as recorded by Philo, and declares them to be the same as practiced by the Christians of his own day. Eusebius was anxious to show that the Essenes were the early Christians, when the fact is that the Christians were the later Essenes, added to their number "from without," in other words, the "uninitiated," who possessed a portion of the Secret Wisdom, or Gnosis, revealed to them by Jesus, preserved by the sages of the Jewish people before the time of Christ, and derived originally from the *hessan* or pure Buddhist monks. Buddha originated these doctrines no more than did Jesus, for we find them taught by Plato, Pythagoras, and Zoroaster, if we but follow the key for their interpretation.

Of the many schools that flourished during the first three centuries of the Christian Era, there were two of paramount importance to our present study. These were the school of the Gnostics, and that of the Theosophists founded by Ammonius Saccas. "It is a noticeable fact that neither Zoroaster, Buddha, Orpheus, Pythgoras, Confucius, Socrates, nor Ammonius Saccas, committed anything to writing." Whatever we now possess of their teachings has been derived from their disciples or from their contemporaries. For the best record of the Gnostic teachings we are indebted to the church Fathers, through their attempts to refute and destroy them. King declares himself most indebted to *The Refutation of all Heresies*, a work composed by Hippolitus, Bishop of Ostia, who was himself put to death A.D. 222. Irenæus and Origen, with the same purpose in view, contributed largely to the same result. The Gnostic teachings seem first to have been promulgated by Simon Magus, then by Menander and by Basilides at Alexandria, who died about A. D. 138, and was followed by Valentinus, who was born of Jewish parents at Alexandria, and who was styled "the profoundest doctor" of them all. "The fundamental doctrine held in common by all the chiefs of the Gnosis was that the visible creation was not the work of the Supreme Deity, but of the Demiurgos, a simple emanation and several degrees removed from the Godhead."

This doctrine of emanations may be traced in the earlier teachings to which we have referred. It was derived jointly from the Zendavesta and the Kabala, and was thus of Chaldeo-Persian and Indo-Egyptian origin. It was taught in the mysteries of Initiation, and was then, as it is now, a Theosophical Doctrine. The Magi and the Kabalists were Initiates and Theosophists, and the Gnostics taught the same philosophy. The sevenfold form in which all emanations proceed, the seven planes in nature and the seven principles in man, were more immediately derived from the

Kabala, of Chaldeo-Persian origin, under the form of Angels, Principalities, and Powers, the same as the Gods of the earlier Greek writers, the "Creators" and "Builders" of the Secret Doctrine. This septenary teaching was especially pronounced with the Ophite sect, a branch of the Gnostic School. Against this doctrine of emanations the church Fathers waged a continual warfare, and the so-called heresies of the early church arose through these discussions and the attempt to establish the doctrine of a personal God and the bitter disputes concerning the nature of Christ; and though many a church Father was tinctured with Gnosticism, they were overruled or destroyed by the more ignorant priests with the rabble at their backs, resulting in giving to the Christian world a personal, male Deity and vicarious atonement in place of the more beneficent and philosophical doctrine. Antiquity shows no worse type than the Jewish Jehovah, and no worse confusion than the theological disputes regarding the Docetic Gnosis.

The school of Theosophists founded by Ammonius Saccas arose about the middle of the third century. His followers, Porphyry, Plotinus, Proclus, Iamblichus, and many others, were styled neo-Platonists.

Their motive aimed, it is true, at a revival of the philosophy of Plato, but Ammonius undertook to bring order out of chaos, agreement out of fierce controversy, and so to bring about the reign of Universal Brotherhood among all classes. He undertook to show that the fundamental doctrines were the same among many sects. Among the Gnostics the severest penalty for those who refused to listen or to believe was want of knowledge and subjugation to Matter; and with Ammonius and his followers, ignorance was considered a misfortune, and disbelief no crime. Both Gnostics and Theosophists taught Reincarnation and Karma, as did, in one form or another, nearly all philosophies and religions of antiquity. Indeed, even a superficial examination of the history of Gnosticism and neo-Platonism will show, provided it be intelligently made and without prejudice, that the movement inaugurated in 1875 by H. P. Blavatsky was almost identical with that undertaken more than fifteen centuries ago by Ammonius Saccas. The teachings are substantially the same, and the motives identical. Here, then, is a direct line of descent. From Pythagoras to Plato, with the teachings of Buddha laying more stress on ethics than on philosophy, and so as a reformer founding a new religion on that already growing corrupt; thence through the Essenes and the Alexandrian Therapeutæ, in the time of Christ. Jesus taught the same doctrine and instituted the same reform in Judaism as had Buddha in Brahmanism. The Gnostics and Theosophists kept alive the old philosophy of the Vedas, the Zendavesta, the Kabala, and the Egyptian Secret Wisdom—always Theosophy—the Secret Doctrine —till the sublime philosophy received a check under Constantine, and with the Mohammedan conquest and the burning of the Alexandrian Library the dark ages began.

Divine philosophy was compelled to yield to brute force and ecclesiastical supremacy. These same Theosophical doctrines found a home in Arabia with the Alchemists of the Middle Ages, and for centuries were known to the Western world through the alchemical nomenclature. They may also be traced in the songs of the Troubadors and Minnesingers, as these wandering minstrels roamed over Europe in the Middle Ages. Like the Beatrice of Dante, the "Lady-Love" of the troubador was often the "Divine Sophia," while many a legend and fairy-tale, like "Collin Clout" and the "Redbook of Appin," was the same secret disguised.

Roger Bacon in the thirteenth century, and Paracelsus in the fourteenth, stand as Theosophists and Initiates in the Secret Doctrine. Time will not permit points in comparison, nor even the naming of all authors or writings that bear direct testimony to the Theosophical doctrines. The Society of Rosicrucians, originating, it is supposed, in the fourteenth century, might be classed as Platonic, Gnostic, Theosophic, Kabalistic, Masonic, or Alchemic, for the simple reason that it embodied, philosophized upon, and yet concealed, the Secret Doctrine.

The philosophical systems of Newton, Des Cartes, Leibnitz, and Spinoza all embody postulates and principles found in the Secret Doctrine, and can on this basis be reconciled with each other. There would be little difficulty in establishing Sir Isaac Newton's indebtedness to the writings of the "Teutonic Theosopher," Jacob Behmen, by both historical and philosophical evidence, as Andreas Freher and William Law were contemporaries of Newton; and for the further reason, that copious translations from the writings of Behmen were found among Newton's posthumous papers. No principle embodied in the philosophy of Newton is absent from the writings of Behmen. What Newton did was to give to these philosophical principles a scientific expression and a mathematical formulary, so as to fit in with the advancing scientific thought of the age. Newton's first law, that attraction and repulsion are equal and opposite, is but a mathematical formulation of the old Hindu doctrine of the "Pairs of Opposites," or the dualism of nature as taught in the Kabala and in all Mysteries.

Tracing these doctrines in the oldest religions, whether in the Vedas, the Egyptian, Chaldean, or earlier Greek Mysteries, or in the Kabala, and comparing them with the secret teachings of the Essenes, the Gnostics, the Alexandrian Theosophists, the Rosicrucians, and the mediæval Alchemists, we find not only general agreement and substantial harmony, but far more consistency than among scientists from the days of Newton in regard to the estimated heat of the sun ; or between theories of the present day regarding the constitution of matter or the nature of the atom. If modern science can be called exact, these older doctrines cannot be called fanciful. There is contained in these old teachings a science more exact and profound than is yet known to modern times, for the ancient Initiated were not only the most subtle metaphysicians and the most correct reasoners, they were in the truest sense Philosophers.

The three postulates of the Secret Doctrine are to be found in all these old philosophies. They have been compared and annotated through H. P. Blavatsky and the authors of her *Secret Doctrine*. Such comparison will show that revelation and inspiration are not the exclusive possession of any one religion, least of all do they belong exclusively to the youngest of these religions, the Christian. It can be demonstrated that every religion has an underlying esoteric basis, and that basis is the Secret Doctrine.

If the history, rituals, and glyphics of Free Masonry be examined with such knowledge of the Kabala as is furnished by Mr. J. Ralston Skinner, not a shadow of doubt can remain as to its origin and significance. Its Ancient Landmarks are but the outer form, the dead letter, of the most ancient initiation into the Mysteries of Occult Theosophy. More than one Masonic writer, like Dr. Oliver and Dr. Mackey, trace Masonry to the Secret Society of the Essenes, and the most common traditions of Masonry claim Zoroaster and Pythagoras as ancient Masters in Masonry.

The entire philosophy and Rituals of Masonry cluster around the Legend of Hiram Abiff, the "Widow's Son," who lost his life in the defense of his integrity. The Mystery of Christ, who, like Christna before him, was the "son of a Virgin," deals with the same Secret Wisdom. The "son of the widow," and the "son of the Virgin," are alike fatherless. This is the Great Secret; The Mystery of the Ages; one and all, from beginning to end, these mysteries—old and forever new—conceal the knowledge of the nature of the Soul and its journey through matter. The Essenes held this secret under oath of perpetual concealment, as did every ancient Mystery. Jesus partially revealed it to the Gentiles, and therefore the Jews, who knew the secret, conspired with the rabble to put him to death, in conformity with the prescribed penalty. Socrates before the time of Jesus, and Paul afterward, suffered the same penalty. All three may have been rather self-taught than formally initiated. Those who possessed the secret through the process of initiation had in each case abused their power and prostituted their knowledge, and yet they refused either to reform or to permit any outer revelation. Neither Ancient nor Modern Mysteries or Secret Societies have, or ever had, anything to conceal from "him who knows" the mystery of the human Soul; its origin, nature, journey through matter, and return to Paradise or absorption in Nirvana.

The self-taught mystic, who derives his knowledge through his own spiritual intuitions or by subjective illumination, without a knowledge of the philosophy of the Secret Doctrine, is usually a religious enthusiast or a Mystic. He may even found a religion or a school, but he can never become a hierophant of Initiations. He may possess the "Doctrine of the Heart," and perform apparent miracles, but is not likely to become an Adept in all the Occult forces of nature. The perfection of man requires the complete at-one-ment of body, soul, and spirit; or universal consciousness with perfect knowledge; and hence the power to use for the highest good.

John Reuchlin, the head of the "Humanists," the preceptor of Luther, and called also "The Father of the Reformation," was a profound Kabalist, and undertook to reform the abuses of his times on Theosophical lines. He resisted successfully the raid of the Dominican Monks and other bitter assailants, but failed to engraft the wise and pure Theosophical doctrines on the gross ignorance of his times. A glimpse of these doctrines under theological dress may be found in a little anonymous volume called *Theologia Germanica*, supposed to have been written by a member of a sect called "The Friends of God." This book was a great favorite with Luther, as was Reuchlin himself, as shown in Luther's letters. The abuses of superstition gave place to the dogma of Faith, and knowledge and light derived through Theosophy fell to the rear. The age was too materialistic, the ignorance too gross and dense. The Protestant Reformation might otherwise have been a very different affair indeed.

A single conclusion remains to be drawn. So far as outer records go or inner meaning has been revealed, this old philosophy, this ancient science, this Wisdom Religion, was as perfect and as well known in the days of Pythagoras as at any later period. Plato added nothing to it. He but transmitted, or concealed, that which he had been taught in the mysteries of Initiation.

The conclusion is obvious. This Secret Wisdom dates back to the building of the Pyramids and is embodied in the Vedanta of old India; and not only were the most ancient sages and Rishis Initiates, but the true wisdom has been preserved and transmitted from age to age, and the Masters spoken of by H. P. Blavatsky, the real authors and inspirers of her *Secret Doctrine*, exist to-day as the Theosophical Mahatmas. The evidence may be found along the lines I have so imperfectly sketched, and is confirmed for all but the ignorant and the scornful in H. P. Blavatsky's great work. To the student who is really in search of the truth, the evidence is convincing and overwhelming in favor of the existence of a core of truth, represented in numberless forms and running through the countless ages, preserved and transmitted by genuine Initiates, and this core of truth is THEOSOPHY.

Theosophy has, therefore, a history and a literature but little known and seldom even suspected in these later times. No discovery of modern science, no well-defined and well-authenticated principle of modern philosophy, exists to-day that was unknown to the genuine Initiate of old. The "great secret" was never fully revealed except as a matter of experience of the Soul. One must understand this fact, and its bearing upon the process of obtaining real knowledge, in order to be able to follow understandingly even the outer text, or those general principles embodied in the language of Symbolism. The deeper mysteries are incapable of other expression, as they pertain to the soul's experience. Initiation is, therefore, in the truest sense an evolution. The great secret is taught theoretically and philosophically, and put in practical demonstration by the neophyte under guidance of his instructors. This is the meaning of the travesty among Masons on "Practical" and "Symbolical" or "Theoretical Masonry."

Language is therefore inadequate to convey these deeper secrets to the ignorant. Symbolism conceals them from the profane and records them for the knowing. Concealment may be considered necessary where revelation is impossible except through long training and experience. To "conceal" and "record in symbols" are therefore synonymous. Herein lies the key of the Secret Doctrine, and the Esoteric basis of all true Religions. To experience is to know, the foundation of all Wisdom. The Secret Doctrine and the Wisdom Religion are therefore the same, viz.: THEOSOPHY.

LINKS BETWEEN RELIGION AND SCIENCE,
AND
REVELATION NOT A SPECIAL PROPERTY OF ANY ONE RELIGION.

MRS. MERCIE M. THIRDS.

Whatever our religious or our scientific preconceptions may be, we are mutually convinced that he best understands a subject who is familiar with all its parts. We distrust conclusions based on partial knowledge, no matter how exact that may be, for experience has taught that the value of any fact can only be properly appreciated when it is considered in its relation to other facts. What in separation seemed important may be an insignificant part of the whole. What seemed trifling may, in its proper place, link all our facts together into harmonious unity.

It seems evident, too, that in any correct generalization all concurrent truths must have their place. Not one may be omitted, but, grouped as we find them in our investigation, they must together build up the reality we know. Then do we behold Truth. Order succeeds chaos. Instead of disjointed fragments, from which only partial knowledge can be wrested, we have an intelligible whole. However dissimilar, its various parts supplement each other, and for the first time disclose their real character and value.

Now, may we not reasonably regard Nature as such a unity? And as mind, no less than matter, is an aspect of nature, is it not possible that all facts of experience and observation are not merely congruent, but mutually complemental? If so, knowledge gained by experience should be related to observed facts, synthesis aiding analysis in search for truth. That our modern method is different we are well aware. Analysis alone is relied upon. Investigation is specialized, each seeker following his clue in a separate domain. Grandly useful as this system undoubtedly is for study of details, it leaves facts of one kind unchecked by corresponding facts of another nature. So long as it is followed merely to collect details, no fault can be found; but when, in the absence of synthetic unity, each department is left to theorize on independent data, we may fairly question their conclusions.

It could hardly be expected that a method which accepts analysis alone as sufficient basis for generalization should regard subjective and objective realms as necessary complements of a whole. Still less could it heed a world confessedly beyond the range of mind and sense. Faith and knowledge, sharply sundered, lose all sense of relationship with each other, and the inevitable result is an antagonism which reason is powerless to overcome. Religion, resting upon revelation, affirms the existence of a Divine Intelligence from which creation proceeds. It declares that life is from God, and that man possesses a soul which is immortal. Science, trusting only the senses, delves into matter, collecting a splendid array of facts. Assuming that there can be no reality with which it cannot come into physical contact, it dismisses as valueless all evidence of a subjective kind. Forced, therefore, to regard life and intelligence as phenomena merely, it seeks their cause in matter itself. We are told that force is a property of matter, and that, conjoined, they are sufficient to produce a world. Finally, the origin of man is referred to evolution from lower forms of life, while belief in Deity and the human soul is branded as superstition.

Between these contradictory hypotheses no reconciliation is possible. If one is right, the other must be wrong. It is idle to claim that no conflict exists between religion and science so long as their teachings are mutually subversive, and nothing can be gained by an attempt to believe irreconcilable theories. The task before us, then, is not to weld religion and science into an unsympathetic union. We are merely called upon to consider if there are not gaps in the testimony given, and to find, if we can, additional evidence.

A slight examination will suffice to show that the evidence upon which conclusions have been based is not complete. Let our witnesses themselves confirm this statement by their own admissions. Although religion offers practically nothing in regard to other than spiritual states, it explicitly declares that man is a triune being, composed of spirit, soul, and body. Well, what is the spirit? and what is the soul? If told they are one, what becomes of the triple classification? If they are dissimilar, what is the difference, and what the function of each? To these questions no answer is given.

Science, on the other hand, even while contending that matter is the one reality, is forced to postulate some unknown medium in order to explain such familiar phenomena as light and heat. Although agreeing to call it ether, eminent scientists disagree radically in opinion concerning its nature and constitution, proving that these still lie outside the limits of actual knowledge. Moreover, according to their own hypothesis, it must differ from any of the three known states of matter, solid, liquid, and gaseous, in order to meet the requirements. We are only assured that it is a subtile substance of homogeneous character, so tenuous as to elude chemical test and to pervade all the molecules of matter.

And if a gap in knowledge of things spiritual and things material is immediately betrayed, no surprise should be felt when we discover that recognized facts are not always satisfactorily explained. For example, if mind is, as science tells us, a material essence evolved by molecular activity in the brain, why is it not most keen when the play of physical forces is most apparent? A comparison of student and athlete clearly indicates another rule. Memory, which is truly called the basis of individuality, is ascribed to unrecognized impressions in cerebral substance. How, then, shall we account for its continuance when that substance is periodically replaced by new tissue? In what can it inhere during these changes, and how can such mysterious impressions be transmitted from one molecule to another?

It is not necessary to multiply cases of inadequate scientific explanation. A few of such fundamental character suffice to prove that acquaintance with nature is much less thorough than is generally supposed. In lieu of complete demonstration, speculation has boldly dealt with fact in an effort to bridge gaps which have so far successfully resisted accepted methods of research. Is it, then, audacious to reflect that the term science, a synonym for knowledge, has been usurped by many still-unproven theories?

That a new domain has already opened before us can hardly be disputed. Experiments of the late Dr. Charcot and his colleagues in France, added to the earlier testimony of Mesmer, Braid, and others, have pretty conclusively shown that the mind is able to exert marvelous powers. In the hypnotic state, itself a mystery to science, subjects are made to obey the unexpressed commands of the operator. Their thoughts follow his suggestion. Their emotions are played upon like strings of an instrument, responding exactly to the performer's touch. Even the will slavishly exerts itself to enact his thought. Stranger than all, perhaps, to those who so confidently rely upon their senses, the subject sees, tastes, or feels as he is silently bidden, regardless of external stimulus. Or, if the operator so wills, his senses cease to act, though all outer conditions for their exercise are present.

Facts like these inevitably suggest that the mind is not a mere phenomenon of matter. Indeed, if granted, they prove that it exerts force itself, and is able to exercise that force beyond bodily limits. What acts as compelling cause cannot be classed as mere effect. Neither can we define force as a property of matter when it is displayed as a property of mind. Whatever may be its nature *per se*, it is lifted beyond physical causation.

Now, as an energy acting outside the body, thought must have some appropriate medium of transmission. Concerning the hypothecated ether, Dr. Richardson of the British Royal Society says: "Without the ether there could be no motion; without it particles of ponderable matter could not glide over each other; without it there could be no impulse to excite those particles into action. Ether connects sun with planet, planet with planet, man with planet, man with man. Without ether there could be no communication in the universe : no light, no heat, no phenomenon of motion."

But with this subtle medium provided, we can comprehend how mind force can travel through space. Vibration aroused in this sensitive substance would flow outward reaching another brain, where we have only to postulate a translation of ethereal vibration into physical to have it registered upon that brain. Now, it is evident that if mind acts in an ethereal medium it cannot itself reside in brain-tissue. A centre from which force emerges must always lie behind, or within, the plane of its operations. Otherwise, although responsive vibration might be induced, there could be no direct transmission of force.

To account for sensation Dr. Richardson found it necessary to assume the existence of a different, or varied, ether. He calls this nervous ether, and says: " The evidence in favor of the existence of an elastic medium pervading the nervous matter and capable of being influenced by simple pressure is all-convincing. In nervous structure there is unquestionably a true nervous fluid, as our predecessors taught. It occurs to my mind, however, that the veritable fluid of nervous matter is not of itself sufficient to act as the subtile medium that connects the outer with the inner universe of man and animal. I think—and this is the modification I suggest to the older theory—there must be another form of matter present during life; a matter which exists in the condition of vapor, or gas, which pervades the whole nervous organism, surrounds as an enveloping atmosphere each molecule of nervous structure, and is the medium of all motion communicated to and from the nervous centres." According to his view this is an individually-evolved medium, and therefore distinct from the ether of space.

Recent experiments in what is called the externalization of sensation corroborate this opinion, for such a substance seems to have been actually extracted from living bodies. Subjects in a trance state have been insensible to pinching and pricking of the body, while at the same time they have felt pain when these operations were repeated upon the air about them. Moreover, wounds, such as pin scratches, inflicted upon this invisible envelope, have promptly duplicated themselves upon the physical body, proving an interrelation of substances and an unbroken continuity from mind to body.

It appears from these facts that ethereal, like physical, matter is of different grades, permitting varied functions and making possible diverse activities; and as spatial ether must pervade the body also, we are led to infer that the subtile form within the physical links together, or unites into one composite body, these various ethereal substances. Enshrining the mind, therefore, and, through sense avenues, gathering impressions from the outer world, this invisible double spans all the gaps existing between mind and its physical manifestations. Moreover, it furnishes a basis for all allied psychological phenomena, such as thought-transference, telepathy, clairvoyance, clairaudience, etc., all dependent either upon thought transmission or upon internal sensation. Memory, too, is explained by its presence, since it offers a continuous medium in which impressions may inhere during molecular changes.

In addition to all such evidence, the existence of an ethereal double is confirmed by a mass of objective proof which in any other department of nature would be accepted as incontrovertible. From every age and race we may glean testimony to the occasional appearance of ghosts, apparitions, shades of the dead, or whatever else they may have been called, down to the present when they masquerade as spirits of the departed. Under all names these vapory forms answer a common description, which applies equally to our hypothecated double, for it is substantial yet unlike the matter of our plane. We are evidently in a borderland between mind and matter, where disclosures already made may serve as clues to regions often called unknowable; for prove that mind acts in an ethereal medium, and the possibility of its continuance after death becomes clear: demonstrate that consciousness is separable from the body, and its existence in other states is made certain.

Religion and science now stand side by side before the mystery of mind. Again the question arises: What is spirit? Ancient wisdom answers: Spirit is life, it is consciousness, the one reality that through all changes of evolution remains ever the same. Its manifestations differ according to the various vehicles in which it is embodied, but its essential nature continues forever unchanged. Sleeping in the vegetable, dreaming in the animal, it awakes in man. Mind is consciousness unfolded to this stage of active thought, and therefore man, who perceives the relation between subject and object, becomes the only self-conscious denizen of earth, the only ego among its myriad creatures. Soul is the eternal basic medium in which life resides, a sublimated essence to unfamiliar thought scarcely distinguishable from spirit, but which is, nevertheless, a clothing, or vehicle, of life *per se*. Mind, therefore, is spirit in its essential nature, but in its manifestation it is soul.

Now, if we remember that although matter is eternal in its basic nature, its present constitution has been evolved from primal element, or elements, it becomes evident that soul is a missing link in our old explanations. Over a gulf that seemed impassable it stretches force and substance. Creation by the energy of mind becomes at least thinkable, and evolution, upon the bosom of invisible space, unrolls a visible world.

Certainly, with such an origin, man's history should tell a different story than would be possible had he sprung, by ever so slow degrees, from an animal ancestry. In the latter case, steady unfoldment should be the rule, savages passing through barbarous states onward to civilization, and leaving forever behind them outgrown conditions. All our facts confute this supposition. The persistence of savagery, and even its recurrence in regions where civilization long since flourished, puzzle the Darwinian school. Men little higher than the brute still exist, while history points, even in its dawning, to noble civilizations. Archæology tells the same story of even a more remote past. Numerous vestiges of prehistoric civilization are found on our own continent, those of Yucatan especially leaving no doubt of the high development of its people in some forgotten epoch.

The mystery vanishes, however, when we regard man as a spiritual being, developing by contact with matter his intellectual nature, and thereby, by a reflex process, evolving a correspondingly better bodily instrument. By the gradual development of physical structure consciousness passes through as many changes of manifestation, and with every radical change of its embodiment must rouse anew its native powers. It follows, therefore, that mind develops in cycles, as history shows; also, that it is most active when it has freed itself from material conditions. By this freedom is not meant lack of a body, but its subjugation and training by the mind. It is for this reason that physical tendencies must be subdued before spiritual powers can be awakened.

Some indication of what these may be is afforded by the phenomenon of genius, a very different thing from normal mental action. Genius may labor, but it never plods. Swift as an arrow to its mark, and over a pathway apparently as traceless, it leaps to truth. It knows, because it sees deep into the real nature of things. Spurning the senses, it uses mind itself to fathom nature, and spans the chasm between seen and unseen realms. Genius, then, is the unfettered power of mind, a flash of spirit itself, which offers us another link between man and his immortal soul.

From the occasional flash of genius to full illumination is but a step in the process of unfoldment. Triumphing over the sluggish opposition of matter, which it has finally moulded into harmony with its requirements, mind has expanded into consciousness of the all. Veil after veil of matter has been lifted, each, in turn, revealing its own secrets and making clearer all the knowledge gained in lower realms. That the same process should continue into soul regions may logically be supposed. The mounting vision then would scan the world of spiritual causes, and see truth at last revealed.

Revelation, therefore, is the natural insight of a perfected soul. As reason crowns man now, knowledge will reward him then. By an impartial law of spiritual growth it is attained, prophet and seer transmitting to unillumined minds truths needed for their guidance. The pure soul, seeing God, stretches a helping hand to weaker brothers, and writes for them upon some sacred scroll the laws of life and duty.

So religions are founded when they are not merely versions of an older faith. Their fundamental identity is a necessity, and the strongest possible evidence of the truth of revelation. "God is no respecter of persons." At all times and with all races he has dealt impartially. Everywhere the story of man's spiritual origin has been told, and the hope of immortality implanted. Arrogance and egotism may claim a special favor, but the bibles of all races offer confutation. Their teachings may be differently expressed; one or another aspect of spiritual truth may be emphasized; but each reveals the Fatherhood of God, the Brotherhood of Man, the sacredness of duty. Each forbids selfishness and inculcates love; and finally, through aspiration, all point to possible perfection of the soul.

THE COSMOS SEPTENARY IN ITS CONSTITUTION; MAN THE MIRROR OF THE COSMOS AND THINKER; INNER AND OUTER MAN A SEVENFOLD BEING, THUS CORRESPONDING TO THE COSMOS.

MRS. ISABEL COOPER-OAKLEY.

The chairman has given me twenty-five minutes in which he wishes me to say what I have to say, and therefore I hope that all those who intended to go out a few moments ago, will kindly sit still for twenty-five minutes longer.

A little while ago, when our brother Dr. Buck was speaking, he spoke of the *Secret Doctrine* and the wonderful way in which Madame Blavatsky had gathered together in that book the Secret Doctrine and the Wisdom Religion of the ages. Now a great deal I am going to say is taken directly from that book. You must remember I shall not pretend to prove to you in the short space of twenty-five minutes all that I am going to put forward, but the book is there. It is the source from which we draw our light, all those of us who are spiritually alive to Madame Blavatsky's teachings. It is the source from which we have learned. It is equally open to you yourselves. I am going to put forward an outline of the septenary classification, as given in the oldest systems in the world.

Now, I want first to say one word as to why 7 is one of the most occult teachings. The septenary classification was the oldest division into which all the different differentiations—spirit, mind, intellect, the physical, were divided, and that number 7 was taken from the natural laws of life. It had been seen and noticed by the ancient sages of the world that 7 was the governing principle of all the functioning powers of this manifestation of ourselves. 7 is the number which rules the moon. The moon changes four times in twenty-eight days; 7 is the number of colors of the spectroscope; there are 7 notes in the musical scale; 7 comes out in nearly all physiological conditions, in the functions of illness and health; 7 is the number classified, arranged, and studied by the most ancient philosophers in the oldest times; therefore, it is by going back to these oldest sources that we are able to take up the number and study this number which they have put forward as standing at the back of this physical manifestation of ours. The cosmos is septenary in its constitution; that means that the unity of which Brother Chakravarti was speaking this morning has 7 different ways of manifesting itself to us, and that 7 is the only way by which we can really sense and arrange it. Now Madame Blavatsky says in the *Secret Doctrine* that this number 7 extends through the cosmos, in the planetary chains, in the earth, in all the conditions of life, both in the consciousness and physical senses and everything else. And she says that if we watch it from the material atom to the element of spirit, we find this number 7 making itself manifest.

The 7 fundamental principles of our constitution are classified as follows: God; it is what is called the absolute; it is that from which everything has come and to which everything has to return, and in which everything is done; the next aspects are those of spirit and mind and matter, which make up four. Then you come to will, the creative impulse in the forms of intellect and energy, sometimes called the Logos of the Greeks, the universal ether and life. Within the septenary classification, as the law variously energises, is the cosmos manifested to us, and thus do all the manifested forms of life come to us in their conditions of manifestation. That, of course, is upon the cosmic plane. The planetary chain we are told is under the same septenary condition of differentiation. Standing in the planetary chain is our earth, and here we come again to the septenary classification, here we come to the principles and conditions of energy and form which we ourselves know something about. We have here on the earth, water, earth, air, fire, and ether; that makes five elements, so called, which are now made known to us. Ether is very gradually being known at this present moment, and behind ether are two more which we shall gradually come into touch with as man's own senses evolve up to that point. Then we shall be able to understand these finer conditions of matter; for remember we are speaking of matter under these conditions, we are talking of matter of which we ourselves at the present moment have no knowledge, a matter so tenuous, so fine and subtile in its properties, that it really stands to us as spirit, while spirit lies far back of it. We are taught that the septenary correspondence runs in a perfect and exact way right through the whole of this differentiation; and man is sevenfold in his constitution.

Now, we have in Theosophical teachings what are called the seven principles of man, and I will run very briefly through these for you, because it will make some of the other speakers more understandable when they speak of these principles under the terms of conditions of consciousness. The first principle, starting from the spiritual pole, is spirit or *Atma*, as it is called in Sanscrit terminology. The second principle, counting downwards, is what is called *Buddhi*, the wisdom, the soul, the entity, the intelligence. The third principle, counting downwards again from the purest spiritual pole, is what is called *Manas*, the mind, that is in connection and in correspondence with the universal mind in which all is contained, that universal ideation from which we all come out. The fourth, coming still downwards, is what is called *Kama*, which means the whole of our nervous, emotional, sensory nature, the whole man which may come under the mind—the emotional and sensitive man. Next we come to the fifth principle, counting downwards again, and this is called in the East, *Prana;* it is in the whole world that principle which we might call cohesion. It is the life principle which holds the whole of the man together, and when that principle departs from a man, he breaks down, he has passed to another condition of subjective consciousness on another plane beyond. The next principle, counting downwards still, is what we call the astral body, the *doppel-gänger*, the double of a man, the actual man in a finer, more tenuous condition than the material man as we know him. You must remember that there is a great deal of evidence of this astral man, and you can find it if you choose to look for it for yourselves. You have only to read D' Assier's *Posthumous Humanity*. He has collected together a record of the appearances of this astral man. The next in the list, what you might call the seventh counting still downwards, for often we count the other way—it does not matter which way you take these principles—the seventh is the physical man, which we Theosophists look upon simply as the shell in which we live, in which we have temporary being, which we use as a vehicle for evolution and for making ourselves known during the condition we call earth-life. This condition is in touch with the earth condition, and there is a perfect correspondence between all these conditions in man and the conditions of earth-life or the elements outside; because correspondence is at the very basis of the whole of the Theosophical method of classification. Now, you must remember one thing, please, that when we talk about the principles of man, we do not mean to speak of things that are put one over the other like the skins of an onion, that you can take apart or put together in little pieces. All these are different conditions of consciousness which interplay and intertwine within each other. There is a very good illustration given by a writer in *The New Cosmos*. The author gives the following illustration. He takes a bottle and fills it with steam and stops the bottle so that none of the steam can escape; then he puts into the same bottle as much alcoholic vapor as he has already put steam, but as the latter is finer it interpenetrates the interstices between the molecules of the steam. Why? Because they are each governed by their own laws and conditions of matter. He then puts in addition into this bottle still other vapor. Why can he do this? Because these vapors are governed by their own laws belonging to their own conditions of matter, and they do not interfere with each other. You may multiply that out to seven, and you will understand what we mean by the interpenetration of the seven principles of man. We mean that man is made up of these different conditions, essences of matter, matter being an essence according to the Theosophical interpretation. These principles are inseparable from man; they make up the sum total of man, and each is governed by its own laws and each belongs to its own part of this wonderful cosmos of ours. So, then, this man is a sevenfold being.

Now we come to the inner and the outer man. The four lower conditions or principles of which I am speaking now, the last named, made up of the physical man, the astral man, *prana*, this cohesion, and *kama rupa*, or our desires, these form the lower quaternary, the four impermanent principles. That is, these four lower conditions of matter are what we change with each birth and life; these four conditions of matter in the vehicle, the body in which we live, are the impermanent principles. The other three above are called the inner man, the permanent individual, and are what are called *Manas*, *Buddhi*, and the Spirit, which is that portion of the divine *Atma*, that portion of the divine Spirit, we share with the whole cosmos.

Brother Judge speaking just before luncheon said we come back and back into this world to live and to work out the conditions started by us in other lives. It is this triple portion of man, this permanent part that includes the spirit and the soul of man, that comes back and back to earth-life ; for that is what is called the real, permanent man, and in the oldest Eastern philosophies it is looked upon as the only permanent part of this life at all. That is called the reality of life, while the physical body, which we Westerns look upon as of so much importance, is looked upon by them as the gross, the lowest part of man. Why ? Because that which furnishes the only permanent part of us is that part which remains from one earth-life to the other, and through it we carry on that string of spiritual experience which makes us grow up to the perfect evolution of the future, because it is really ourself.

Now, the next part of what I want to say—I am condensing what I have to say into a very brief space—the next point is, man is a creator of the cosmos and the thinker. So at the present moment we have had the sevenfold classification outside in the whole cosmos ; we have had the sevenfold classification in the planetary chains ; we have the sevenfold classification in this earth-life, and finally you come down and down and down, in form, size and amount until you come to man himself, man who has mirrored in himself and in his soul the whole of these wonderful powers of the cosmos without. We can mirror in our minds the whole of the universe, the whole of the energies, and the whole of the manifestation that lies in the great cosmos without us. That is really the point of view from which we are bound to look at man and to look at ourselves. We have to look at ourselves as mirrors; not passive mirrors, but as active mirrors, as reflecting and bearing in ourselves every power, and every force, and every energy that is in the cosmos without. As one of the speakers this afternoon told you, you stand as the Microcosm to the great Macrocosm, and it is through the unity of life and manifestation we get the idea of our responsibilities. We have within us the potential energy of the whole divine life, that spiritual unity of which Brother Chakravarti was speaking this morning, that spiritual unity which belongs to the whole physical and cosmical system, which is focused, so to say, when it comes to the life of man. There is no energy, force, matter, nothing in the universe without us which is not within us at the present time, mirrored in us in a potential and latent condition, waiting for us to bring it out, waiting for us to evolve ourselves up to that point at which we may come into touch with the higher forms and conditions of the universe. As spirit is the basis of the whole of these manifestations, what we call matter is only one aspect of spirit. What we call the material aspect of our body is only one aspect of that divine spiritual life which is really at the back of the whole of this manifestation. I said just now that mind is the mirror of the universe. You must remember there is one great difference between mind as it is now, between this earth as it is now, and the cosmos of which I was speaking a little while ago. There is such a thing in man as free will, and although the will of the cosmos is perfect, is in a perfect condition, the will of man is not yet perfect. Each one therefore is dealing with a different set of conditions altogether from others. Man has that amount of free will in him that he can make the conditions surrounding him in this earth-life either perfect or imperfect, and the continued selfishness of man, counting from one age to another, from one generation to another generation, has resulted in what we call evil. You must remember according to the oldest teaching in the world, there is no evil *per se*, but only such as we, as men and women, have made by their own selfishness. And what we have now to do is to reduce this to a minimum, to draw it back again into goodness.

The whole of evil is the outcome of separateness or selfishness. It is looked upon in the East as the very greatest evil, this evil of separateness. What we are trying to get back to in the moral, mental, and spiritual world is that fundamental unity concerning which you have been spoken to to-day. Speaking of man as a mirror of the universe, we have within us therefore the possibility of being mirrors both for good and evil. We may either carry out these ideas mirrored in us through appropriate conditions of matter, as at this moment, and hand them on with a hardening, growing selfishness, or we may try to cultivate our lower natures into what is higher, purer, and less selfish, and so try to bring back the whole of its differentiation to that one unity of divine unselfishness. You must remember it depends upon ourselves entirely whether we will mirror what is good and unselfish, or what is bad and selfish. We can make ourselves of all that is pure, good and true; we may draw from this great cosmos around us all of its divinest principles by making ourselves one with it, or we may draw to ourselves to focus and mirror in ourselves the whole of this selfishness of the world, the whole of the narrow thought for our brother man and our sister woman. And so we can again accentuate it and send it out again to the world, making a little more selfishness and a little more harm in the world. Therefore our responsibilities are great, since we do contain within us the whole of this great force. We are ourselves in our hearts the very centre of this divine life; it circles without and it circles within; it is mirrored without and it is mirrored within; and we by making our mirrors pure and clean, we by living up to and trying to reflect that divine light and life without, may extend through the whole material world as we are now dealing with it, that divine life and principle. This is that purer condition of tenuous matter I was speaking about a little while ago, instead of the gross conditions of material existence we are now putting up for ourselves in our Western civilization. Only by struggling against this material condition can we make ourselves that perfectly pure mirror of that divine life without. This you must remember was the teaching that H. P. B. has left for us to hand down, this was the teaching of her to whom earnest Theosophists owe the whole of their spiritual life; this is the teaching she has given us to hand down to every man and to every woman who feels inclined to make themselves in this way mirrors of the divine life without, to hand it on to future ages unbroken as it came to her, unbroken as it was kept by those great Masters, to mirror it and focus it and send it out with pure unselfishness and love. It has a moral aspect, a mental aspect, and a material aspect. The seven steps through which we must pass to reach that divine life belong to the moral world, and they are equally as real and as true as the whole material manifestation without. If you want to read of the septenary classification in the moral world, if you want to read of the septenary classification in the spiritual world, there is one book written by H. P. B. called *The Voice of the Silence* for those who want to mirror what is most divine and pure and true in this life; and we recommend that book and those words of devotion she has written down for us.

STATES OF CONSCIOUSNESS; EVOLUTION OF THE SOUL.

PROFESSOR CHAKRAVARTI.

LADIES AND GENTLEMEN: This morning I had the pleasure of quoting for you from the most sacred books of the East—the Upanishads. In India the Upanishads are compared to the cow, the holy animal of the Indies, the giver of life and prosperity to the people, and it is said that Shri Krishna, one of the gods of the Indians, milked the milk of divine wisdom from this cow and put it into another equally holy and sacred book, the *Bhagavad Gita*. This book is the very sacred treasure of the Indies, this is the blessed bible of their nation, and this is the book which has called forth so much admiration from men like Schlegel and others, so that they have burst out in unbounded terms of ecstacy. From that book I will quote one sloka which puts in a nut-shell, in the language of the gods, the Sanscrit, which language alone is capable of condensing so much inspirational matter within such a small space. [Here the speaker recited in the Sanscrit.]

This means that the senses of human beings are great, but greater than the senses is the mind; greater than the mind is *Buddhi*, by which is meant the higher intellect (the pure reason of Kant); and above *Buddhi* is "That." The first classification, that is, of the physical senses, includes the various organs of perception, and of touch, and of feeling, which are called in Sanscrit *jnanendriyas* and *karmendriyas*, or organs of action and organs of perception. The second is the mind with which all of you are exceedingly familiar, the *organum* through which you sense, the field upon which we have perception, sensation, and intellection. With these two I do not propose to trouble you, because these are familiar to the ordinary run of human beings in the present age.

The mind constitutes part of the entity we call man. But there is another, a higher and a nobler self, the very existence of which we are oblivious of in the every-day, common-place hurry and endeavor of life and material existence. It is only when our physical senses, and the mind, which is the product of those senses, are lulled to sleep by the harmony of Nature, we find coming to us a voice mellifluous and divine, from that self which sleeps within us, telling us that we are not base, groveling creatures, limited and powerless in our capacities, but that we are the very angels of Heaven; that our capacities are infinite; that our future is a future which is inconceivable and has no bounds. Verily, thou art an angel of Heaven, fallen in the mire of matter, although thou dost not recognize thyself. Therefore we hear the voice from the paradise we once inhabited and the denizens of which we once were; and we hear the voice of the bird, which is represented poetically in one of the finest conceits of the Indian philosophy. In the philosophy of India man is represented by two birds sitting on a tree. The tree is the body, the physical encasement; there are two birds—one is the bird which sits on one of the boughs and eats the fruit of the tree and enjoys it; but there is another bird which sits higher up at the top of the tree, and eats not, enjoys not, but witnesseth only. This represents the two selfs in man, one the lower, which is always hungering for gratification, for satisfaction, for physical desire, and eats of the fruit of physical existence. But the other one is above and higher, and cares not for the gratification that comes from the senses, but is silent in its purity, watches what is going on, extracts the essence of the lower, and reigns supreme in its profound silence. These two selfs have to be realized before you can realize that there can be two states of consciousness besides our own usual state. But before coming to that I shall complete my explanation of the *sloka* I have quoted.

The fourth thing that is mentioned in the *sloka* is not given any name. Let me call your attention to the fact that in translating the *sloka* I told you that above the plane of this pure reason is—no word can say what it is—"That." The mighty poets, the Rishis, the sages who claim to stand in the burning presence of divinity itself, have not the courage to put in words the majesty of that existence. It is, as has been already said, the thing from which mind and intellect and words come down. [Here the speaker again recited a verse in Sanscrit.] You do not find "That" anywhere and come back baffled. It is the burning bush in the presence of which one of your Jewish sages said: "Take off thy shoes; the ground which thou treadest is sacred." Yes, no shoes can be permitted in the region where only spirit reigneth supreme. All personality, all thought, all self, all thought of separation, all thought of the vehicle must be given up, parted with forever, before we can come within these sacred precincts. That is the *Atma* of the Hindus.

Corresponding to these four states, or rather the various parts of man, are the four states of consciousness, of which I have to speak now. According to Sanscrit psychology they are called by four different names. The first is called the *Jagratha* consciousness, by which is meant the waking consciousness, the consciousness with which all of us are familiar. The second is called the *Svapna* consciousness, or the consciousness of the dream plane; it means not only that with which you are familiar as dreams, but climbs on to the plane of the Astral light, on which seers can see so many things not ordinarily visible to the ordinary man; it is the plane of the clairvoyant, thought-reading, and all phenomena of a similar nature. Above that plane of consciousness is the plane of *Sushupti*, the literal meaning of which is "dreamless slumber." That plane of consciousness is one in which there is neither dream nor waking consciousness; that is the plane into which people of the ordinary run sometimes fall when they sleep and do not dream, but of the nature of which they have no remembrance, because their intellect is incapable of bringing down any realization of that sublime existence. And above this state of *Sushupti* is the greatest state, called in Sanscrit *Turya*. *Turya* is the state in which there is no matter, nor mind, nor time, nor space, nor virtue, nor vice; it is that state into which the greatest seers have now and again risen; it is that state the fire of the glimpses of which have made those who enjoyed it burst out into *mantrams* of mighty potency; it is that state into which your divine Christ himself used to fall and in the ecstasies of which he uttered: "Father and I are one." Yes, it is then, and not till then, that man can consider himself divine. When once in front of that altar of truth he realizes no difference, he is once more back to the source of his existence—the stream has gone to the ocean, the drop has dropped into the bosom of the lotus, and then there comes peace, harmony, joy, a sense of unity, which the poor struggling words of human beings must strive in vain to represent. That is the higher condition of consciousness—the *Atma*. We run up into these conditions by gradually working up, by easy gradations, from the physical plane of existence in which man considers himself as apart from every other human being. For here his eyes reveal to him that the body is a house of clay which parts every individual from every other. Not so in the plane higher. In the Astral plane man sees certain subtle forces emanating from the body of every individual, affecting every individual; he sees the thoughts imprinting themselves on the cosmic light, working for good or evil, and he realizes that man is not the isolated being he is supposed to be.

One step higher and we come to the plane of spiritual consciousness. There he is face to face with one of the grandest realities of existence, that which I postulated to you this morning. He sees for himself and realizes that what appears to separate one individual from another are but emanations like the rays of the sun; that each is bound with the other, that each has the same consciousness, each has the same source, each the same home. The evil of separateness therefore is killed out until he reaches the condition which is ineffable, unutterable, immeasurable. The union of the lower with the higher self is really the object of the aspiration of every religion that has been pronounced on the surface of the earth. It is because we have allowed this hydra-headed monster of the lower consciousness to divert our very existence that we know nothing of the higher self, because we have tasted the sinful fruit of physical knowledge that we are thrust out of the Paradise which is ours by birth; it is because we never look to the centre of our being and are immersed in matter, in physical pursuits, in the gratification of the senses, in the enjoyment of luxuries, that we never get one breath of the sweet balmy air of our home. Exiles we walk upon this earth; exiles shall we remain until we can open the gates of our hearts to the light, and let at least one ray of that divine sun penetrate into the dark crannies of our constitution. (Applause.) The spirit is the real, the one great reality, and all the other states of consciousness are nothing compared to the reality; they are but illusions cast by our senses. The moon which shines resplendently in a dark night projects itself betimes into the body of a cloud when it rises above the horizon, and it grows dark. It is the sun that gives light to the moon. The consciousness which you consider now to be the only reality, the physical consciousness which you have allowed to divert your whole being, resides only in the background, is unreal, and is to be seen shadowy and vague in the presence of that sun of spiritual consciousness which, when it dawns, bedims all light, because all the other states of consciousness are but reflections of that one glorious light. [Here the speaker recited a verse in Sanscrit.]

This means: "By Him is everything brightened; by the touch of his hand is every article lightened." You have therefore to pass from these lower states of consciousness by subduing your passions, by conquering all the desires of the flesh, by making your gaze look inward rather than downwards. These are the two birds indicated in the Shastras; one is the material, physical body, the other is divine. You have to choose between these two birds. You may have all the luxuries of the flesh, but how long can they help you? Your physical body, this poor house of clay, is all illusion, destined to die, existing only on the stem of the spirit. To-day it blooms, te-morrow it withers and is cast away. Choose, if you like, these ephemeral pleasures of the senses; but the wise man, resisting all temptations, knowing their temporary and transitory character, tramples them under his feet, conquers like the warrior the lower temptations, and mounts up the perilous and majestic ladder of truth on which is the divine, where he finds eternal peace and harmony.

Again in the Shastras: [Reciting in Sanscrit.]

"Pleasures of the senses are those that are felt only by the child. The wise know the lessons of truth and the nature of existence; they condescend not to seek the permanent among the impermanent." It is therefore essential for man, who has to evolve his soul, to try to conquer temptation; he should try to live up to the very highest ideals of life, and then he may be able to enter as time goes on into that sanctuary of praise where the sun shines and no clouds of sin or sorrow can intrude upon the sacred heights.

Adjourned until 8 p. m.

FRIDAY EVENING, SEPTEMBER 15.

MR. JUDGE:—Brothers and Sisters: We have made a slight but probably a grateful change in the program. We have taken nothing out, but we have added something to it without increasing the length of the session. By some inadvertence in making up the printed program we omitted a paper from its proper place, which should have been read by Dr. Anderson, on "Reincarnation as applied to the sex problem," and we have injected Dr. Anderson's, which will take fifteen minutes, into the proceedings of this evening. We have made another change also, and Mrs. Cooper-Oakley, whom we heard this morning for a very short time, will take up this evening one-half' of my subject; that is, instead of myself dealing with the Theosophical view of death, Mrs. Cooper-Oakley will deal with that subject. Then the evening will be ended by Mrs. Besant's taking up the subject which is assigned to her, that is "Karma." Please give attention to Dr. Anderson.

REINCARNATION AS APPLIED TO THE SEX PROBLEM.

DR. JEROME A. ANDERSON.

The differentiation of sex, as seen in the Vegetable, Animal, and Human kingdoms, at a first glance might seem to be only a method adopted by Nature to ensure the perpetuation of form and the preservation of species. Traced from the apparently asexual cell up through all the slight variations of form and function with which it is associated, it culminates in the human race in two distinctly marked types of character, in which the merely physiological question of procreation has become of secondary importance. We are therefore compelled to look more deeply into the problem, and in doing so, it is quickly seen that sex is but an example upon the material plane of that mysterious Duality in Unity which is at the basis of all differentiation, and hence of all manifestation in the universe.

This Duality in Unity which makes philosophically conceivable the necessary postulate that everything in the universe is resolvable into an ultimate, absolute Unity; of which Unity the infinite manifestations of Nature are but infinite aspects, may, perhaps, be best studied on this plane by a study of its purest type—electricity. Here we have one fluid exhibiting two opposite states, both necessary to the existence of the fluid—or, at least, to its manifestation —apparently ever seeking equilibrium, yet never attaining it; causing bodies dissimilarly electrified to madly rush together, only to be as violently repelled when the object of the union has apparently been accomplished; exhibiting in these ceaseless attractions and repulsions a giant energy which, when chained by man, makes all other forces yield obeisance to it, and when chained by Nature holds stars and worlds in harmonious motion. For it is the attraction and repulsion of that mysterious energy, whose action on earth we see manifested as electricity, which are the centrifugal and centripetal forces holding the planets in their orbits, and of which the "gravitation" of modern science expresses but one mode of its dual action. If gravity were a single force, causing material bodies to "attract all other portions of matter with a force directly proportional to the product of the mass, and inversely proportional to the square of the distance between them," which is the statement of Newton's law, and which also expresses the law of magnetic or electrical attraction—then would those bodies known as comets surely fall into the sun upon their startlingly near approaches to the latter, in describing the perihelion of their orbits. Their mass is almost infinitely lighter than that of the sun, and if Newton's law of mass and distance governing the "pull" of gravitation were true, no amount of accelerated motion due to momentum could prevent this result—a fact startlingly apparent when they pass perihelion and recede from the enormous attraction of the sun—an attraction which, at the comparatively immense distance of the earth, represents a force acting upon this planet which would snap in twain a steel rod 162 miles in diameter as easily as a cobweb. In the fact of their being so nearly on the same plane of substance as the sun that their close approach permits an actual transfer of electricity, thus causing them to become similarly electrified, and bringing the repulsive energy of the electric fluid to bear, is to be found the reason for this otherwise inexplicable phenomenon—their escape upon these near approaches.

Applying this electrical law that similarly electrified bodies attract one another, while those dissimilarly electrified are repelled, gives us a clue not only to the infinitely small question of the manifestation of sex, but also to the infinitely greater one of the eternal manifestation of worlds or universes—a reason, scientific and logical, for the alternate periods of objective and subjective life which Eastern Philosophy has recognized and describes under the beautiful metaphor of the "Days and Nights of Brahm." For this endless Motion or Breath, which is at the origin of all life, and which by the very law of its own existence can never cease its eternal action, stands revealed as to its mode of motion, however incomprehensible its origin may be to us. We can perceive that this law of electrical attraction and repulsion, thus forever striving to restore equilibrium only to utterly destroy this equilibrium when attained, is one which, even if it acted blindly and mechanically, would forever forbid inaction, death, or rest taking place in all the unthinkable cycles of eternity. Physical science declares, and apparently with justice, that all physical forces tend towards a state of final equilibrium—one which Flammarion terms Absolute Death, and when all the suns and worlds shall have died, this scientist speculates upon a possible new origin of force and consequent evolution by the collision of two dead, wandering suns! Yet the law of attraction and repulsion shows us that when electrical equilibrium shall have been established the terrific repulsion of bodies all similarly electrified will rend every molecule asunder, and that there cannot remain one single molecular combination of matter within the universe. By such steps, requiring almost eternal periods of time for their enactment, will all the matter of the universe seek more and more ethereal, or—to us—subjective conditions, and when some equally incomprehensible limit of motion is reached in this direction, in the course of still other immeasurable eternities, a universe of matter as it now is, will reappear. In the descending sweep of this mighty Motion of the Great Breath, as each plane of substance approaches a state of equilibrium, there will be formed connecting points between this and the plane towards which the electric vibrations are driving matter—Laya centres, the Secret Doctrine calls them, points which are dissimilar in their electrical condition to all the matter driven to a lower plane, and which points, therefore, attract the matter of this lower plane under the law of the attraction of dissimilars, and around which are thus built slowly and after many "wars in heaven," suns and worlds. Such Laya Centres, positive to all molecular matter, and in the state of suns, pour, in the descending arc of evolution, mighty streams of life and energy which are thence reflected upon and give life and energy to their planets as well as all matter upon such lower planes. Yet this stream, pouring light, heat, and life upon our planetary system through our sun, carries with it the certainty of the sometime destruction of that to which it now gives life, when the state of equilibrium which physical science prophesies shall have been approximately attained. The very measure of time during which our solar system will endure is given, had we but skill to compute it, in the motion of the pith balls which dance between the poles of the electrical toy. For the fraction of a second required for equilibrium to become established in these is in strictly accurate proportion to the time required for the same condition to obtain throughout our solar system.

All this may, no doubt, seem a digression, yet a proper conception of this law of opposite poles or opposing states of the same force, of Duality in Unity, as exemplified in the electrical law of attraction and repulsion, is absolutely necessary to the proper conception of the relation sex bears to the human soul. We can perceive that as the electrical energy thus vibrates from plane to plane of substance in its efforts to establish an Universal equilibrium—an equilibrium which the very law of its own being makes possible only in infinity, or never—the whole Universe will thus gradually became differentiated into great planes, each of which will be negative to that above, and positive to that below. We can also perceive that on any plane where the process of electrical equilibrium is in active progress that the process of evolution is of necessity also in active progress. Such is the condition of our Universe at present, in which there are no two molecules exactly similarly electrified, and in which the matter, in a state of unstable equilibrium, is electrified, controlled, and ensouled by electrical or life energy from the higher one which, compared to the lower, is infinitely more stable. Now Consciousness, Force, and Substance are three hypostases of the One Absolute or Unknowable, and are eternally associated. Therefore, the human soul, being easily demonstrable as an ego or entity occupying a plane of consciousness far above that of the molecular cells of its body, is, when compared with the unstable condition of the latter, on a plane of stable, controlling equilibrium. On its own plane, the processes of evolution or of equilibrium having been completed for the cycle, the opposing forces of duality are at rest. It is therefore stable and positive to its body; is a conscious Laya Centre, so to speak, through which flows consciousness that ensouls, experiences, and controls evolutionary modification of the eternal life-energy seeking equilibrium on the plane below, or that of the body. Hence, the Human Soul, or that which in Theosophy is technically known as the Higher Ego, the Thinker, the true Individuality, the Reincarnating Ego, and so on, is sexless. It has after an almost infinite cycle of duality rebecome Unity on its own stable plane, and that differentiation which would correspond to sex upon this is unknown. But as the soul, the Pilgrim in the Cycle of Necessity, descends by incarnating in these human-animal forms, in order to consciously conquer this plane where the dual action of the One Life, or evolution, is in active operation, it has of necessity to incarnate in bodies having now the preponderance of the negative and again of the positive manifestations of the One Life. Hence, though being itself sexless, it incarnates now in a series of male forms, and again in a series of female forms, in its necessarily alternating efforts to bring about conscious harmony or equilibrium upon the molecular plane. It can never know all the possibilities of life or of consciousness here without touching the two poles, without thus experiencing here the two aspects of the One Life.

Looked at from this higher view-point, the sex problem is solved. Reincarnating now as a male and again as a female, the human soul symmetrically widens its conscious area and stores the results of these experiences in both the poles of existence upon its own stable plane. Therefore is all the talk and all the hope of man and woman becoming similar mentally, or in any other way, except as countless ages of evolution shall have rounded out and equilibrated both aspects of life, but childish babbling. They are at the opposite poles of conscious being upon this plane—poles which can never meet nor merge here, but which can only be unified when the sexless, passionless human soul shall have acquired all necessary or possible experiences; when it shall have completed its conscious partaking in, and supervision of, the processes of evolution now in active operation.

Thus by recognizing and teaching the true relations our souls bear to our bodies, that upon its own habitation the soul is sexless and passionless, Theosophy offers but another view-point from which to obtain a broader, more philosophical conception of human life and its duties, responsibilities, and opportunities. The recognition of the law of Karma, or the law of Cause and Effect, which compels the further recognition of the fact of the necessary reincarnation of the human soul under this law, will restore the relation of the sexes to the pure and holy condition from which it has been degraded by ignorance.

All churches unite in declaring marriage to be a sacrament, but which of them knows or teaches why this is so? The very term "sacrament" has been debauched by sensual philologists into a phallic significance. The mental attitude of the West toward the sex relation is simply appalling. Instead of being regarded as the solemn, sacrificial avenue through which a human soul—a future god—returns to take up again its life tasks; instead of being limited solely and religiously to procreative purposes for thus furnishing holy and pure tenements for those bound to us by the tenderest ties, the most loving associations, in past lives—for those for whom we would have died then and would die now after they join us—how do we regard it? How have our very priests and ministers taught us to regard it? Let the recommendation of St. Paul, let the classic couplet of Martin Luther—holy monk and Founder of Protestantism—be the answer!

Marriage in the West is but little better than legalized prostitution; its high and holy office unrecognized; its pure, creative passion brutalized, sensualized and entirely perverted. It is the duty and the mission of Theosophy to correct and reform all this. It can only be accomplished by and through our deeper philosophy of human life; our sterner, higher code of human ethics. No time-serving Martin Luther nor specious pleading St. Paul can ever distort or pervert ethical conceptions founded upon demonstrable laws of nature, together with the most satisfactory logical and philosophical deductions and inductions therefrom. We must teach the West to recognize in woman not the weak, passive vehicle, created as an avenue to a sensuous Paradise, but a soul transiently at the opposite pole of material existence, and a pole which, of necessity, has in it as deep a significance, as god-like potentialities, as that which our ignorant, brutish egotism has caused us to regard as superior. It must be recognized that the sex which is her's in this life may be ours in our next—must be ours in many future lives ere we attain a symmetrical evolution of character. The law of Karma, ever restoring disturbed equilibrium, is omnipotent and inviolable; and by our very attitude towards the opposite sex, be it that of man or woman, we are creating character traits which may have to be sharply corrected by unpleasant experiences in that opposite sex during our next life.

By the light thus afforded from the standpoint of the true soul must the sex relation be comprehended; and, once rightly understood, few teachings are capable of a more quick, more sure amelioration of a vast amount of human woe. In this relation we consciously take at least a minor part in the creative processes of nature; we claim a portion of our future heritage as gods and guardians of lower worlds. Its abuse, therefore, reaches to the very depths of our spiritual being in its karmic effects. Let the gibbering inmates of insane asylums, let the wan sufferers from nameless, shameful, terrible diseases, testify whether this is true or not upon the physical plane; let our Police records, our Divorce Courts answer upon the moral plane. Let us restore marriage to its pristine purity; let us recognize that sex is of this plane only; that the soul ought to—is entitled to—live far above the unreasoning desires of the animal kingdom below us, to which and even lower than which we descend when our motive is but sensuous desire. By conquering this tyrant which we have invited to occupy the throne of our mind, we shall be free to use the creative energy, now perverted and wasted, upon intellectual and spiritual planes. So shall we re-enter the Paradise from which we have been expelled; so shall we reclaim once more our lost heritage.

"What is the flaming sword but sin,
   Which blinds our eyes at Eden's gates?
Lo, purity shall enter in,
   Nor fear all adverse gods, nor fates!"

And we shall re-enter; not clothed with the raiment of innocence, which is but the garment of ignorance, but with those infinitely surpassing them; with robes whose web is the shining threads of perfect knowledge, and which is crossed by the woof of purified passions, of slain desires, of upward strivings, of toilings for others, of daily and hourly sacrificings of the lower to the Higher Self.

THE THEOSOPHICAL VIEW OF DEATH.

MRS. ISABEL COOPER-OAKLEY.

Within twenty-five minutes I have to say what I can on the Theosophical view of Death. If there is any one subject more than another which appeals to the whole human race, which comes equally to us all, be we rich or poor, be we high or low, it is death.

Theosophy has very large and decided teachings about death, and as my time is limited I shall divide it into two sections. I will deal first with the practical or technical teaching of Theosophy upon death, and secondly with the Theosophical view of death. Those of you who were here this afternoon will remember that when I was dealing with the sevenfold classification of man—the seven principles of man—I divided them into what are called the permanent and the impermanent. Theosophy teaches that the four that are called the lower principles are the impermanent part, and the three higher principles—the divine, spiritual, mental—are the permanent part which comes back and back to this earth-life. Now those four lower principles are the four conditions of consciousness, the four conditions of life, because you must remember that Theosophy teaches that everything is life. The *Secret Doctrine* teaches us that every atom is full of life, that there is nothing but life, and that what is called "dead matter" is full of life and full of consciousness on its own plane, working under its own laws. Now "death," as it is generally called, only touches these four lower principles, these four grosser or transitory conditions of consciousness. And death is simply the withdrawal from the without to the within of that consciousness which is the pivot and the focus upon which the whole point we call man is built. Mind is enveloped, so to say, that is, this mental portion of man that is divine is enveloped with these four lower principles, enveloped with the *kama*, or passional, or desire elements, enveloped with *prana* or the life principle, enveloped with the astral body, which is the finer reflection of our physical body and is more finely developed than our physical body. Now, death is simply the withdrawal from the outside portions, the grossly physical, to the inner plane of what we call life. Life, instead of being differentiated in the usual way in the physical body, instead of remaining outside, instead of being distributed throughout all the principles, withdraws itself to act for a while under certain other conditions of consciousness.

We will divide them again into the objective and the subjective. The first division that takes place is when life steps back from the grossly material into the astral body and the first differentiation takes place. To the ordinary Western world that is death. It means less to our Theosophical friends. It means less to us who are only living on the physical plane of that one where touch, taste, seeing, handling, hearing was what we were made up of through life. But a person is alive just as much without that as with it, just as much as he was five minutes before, only he is on another plane. The reason we feel the loss is simply and solely because we do not understand how to throw our consciousness into that more subtile, subjective condition of consciousness at the back of the material one. The next condition of disincarnation, the next withdrawal that takes place, is the disincarnation of the astral body. It is what is called in the bible, the second death. The *prana* or life is all withdrawn. The third condition of death is when disincarnation takes place in the body of desires or emotions, when a person's sensations, emotions, wishes, desires are for the time being in a condition so subjective that they are not any longer passionally energetic on the material plane. Then what is called the spirit, its vehicle Buddhi, and the soul pass on into its own condition of rest. It has never lost its own consciousness; the vivid consciousness which it has then depends entirely upon the way its earth-life has been led. Now the place to which this pure triad goes for a certain time is called *Devachan*, which stands in the same position with regard to us in earth-life, as what is termed Heaven does to Christians in their teachings. *Devachan* means a place of angels, and there it is that the higher ego passes on to rest after earth-life, to gather into itself all experiences through which it has passed in its earth-life, because it is not dead. The experience it has passed through, it has been gathering into itself and assimilating before it returns once again into this earth-life to garner up for itself future knowledge and future experience.

Now look at it from the point of view of the West. When a person has once passed out of the physical body, he is to us to all intents and purposes dead. But you must remember, friends, that this is only the view of the West. The other is the view of the East. And when you turn to the physical features of death, you must remember that out of the whole of the peoples of this world the only people who dread death, who fear death, are those people who do not understand the subjective life, those people to whom the Eastern teachings are a sealed book. You do not find many persons in the East who mind death. The poorest coolie out there will lie down and die easily, every man and woman there passes out of this earth-life in a perfect condition of calmness and confidence. Why? Because they have made the subjective life a reality; because to them this material life is not everything; to them they have a thing of study, they have a thing of history, they have a law of philosophy regarding that subjective condition which is called death. They have those who have tested it in their own knowledge and in their own consciousness; they have now living amongst them people to whom the passing from conditions of consciousness is a noble and a practiced thing. And once put yourself outside of this body, once that you can have any knowledge and sensations apart from this body, the whole fear of death will have passed away. Where is the people in the world in which there is so much fear of death as in the Christian peoples? You can take the Eastern peoples right through, and you will find their attitude towards death is very different. Why? You must remember, as I said before, there is all this subjective knowledge, there is the whole philosophy and a whole series of experiments with regard to this. And now in the West we are coming into touch with this subjective philosophy from a different standpoint altogether, and a good many Western scientists are helping us with regard to it. There is a very good book written by a German, Dr. Carl Du Prel. He has gathered together under the heading of *The Philosophy of Mysticism* a very great many facts with regard to the abnormal consciousness, the subjective consciousness, and he proves the mind as being apart from matter. The moment you have proved to yourselves, be it in ever so small a way, that you can have one spark of consciousness, one spark of your mind act apart from your body, the secret of death is solved for you. Therefore it is worth your while, men and women in the West, it is worth your while if you want to pass that portal with free security and knowledge, it is worth your while to throw your time and a little thought into the study of the subjective conditions of life. It will repay you in the end; because there must come that time when we do cross the bridge. Now Du Prel, in his *Philosophy of Mysticism*, has gathered together all these abnormal states of consciousness in which he proves that the mind can act apart from the body. Not only does Du Prel do it, but you can turn to the whole of your scientific scholars who have proved it by a series of investigations in hypnotism, and so on. Then if you choose to turn to the East, and if you will study those old books in which they have put forward all that has been gathered together with regard to this very study of which we here know so little, you will find there is a whole philosophy, nay, more, a whole knowledge proved over and over and founded upon experimental facts over and over as carefully as any Western scientist can do his work. There is an authority in England, a man who is very well known, Mr. Edward Carpenter; his book is by no means a philosophical treatise, but it is very full of a certain kind of facts which he himself gathered together in India and put together in a very light and pleasant book. The title of the book is *From Adam's Peak to Elephanta*. He went out with an object to the holy land of India, and puts forward the value to him of the ideas given by an Eastern teacher he met there. That teacher proved to him that by a certain process mind and thought can be trained to act entirely apart from matter, and that mind and thought can be brought under our control; and when I say under *our* control I mean that eternal ego, that divine ego, which stands at the back of the lower mind ; I am speaking of that higher mind of which our brother, Professor Chakravarti, spoke this afternoon ; proving that within us is a permanent brain that is not lost in death, and that it is which goes from one life to another, bringing with it its experience.

Now you must remember that when you once look at life and death thus, they are but different conditions of consciousness in which we ourselves live and may learn and function. It is worth while to take a little time to study it. You must remember this, friends, and take a little time to study it and think about it; you cannot learn all this in a few moments; you cannot study the subjective conditions of consciousness in a few hours; if you think it is worth while to know something about that life to which you must pass, in which all must live in the future, you must withdraw some of your energy from the material plane; you cannot have the same amount of energy working in two planes at once. In a short time you may know nothing about death, though you must go to meet it. Faith may be a very beautiful thing, friends, it may be a very poetical thing, but when you stand face to face with death, knowledge is a great deal better. And we are short-sighted out here in the West in the sufficiency we are building up here. Here you are in one of the leading cities of America, nay, in one of the leading cities of the world, and the whole of your energy and the whole of your thought, your wishes, desires are thrown out into material building and in the material working of different sorts. If you should desire ever to sit down and think about that future life into which we must all pass, you should begin. Now, in the East it is made such a careful study that, as I said before, you may know how to pass out of this life with a knowledge of what you are going into, of what is going to happen in all these conditions in yourselves.

As we go out of this earth-life, so shall that lower material part of mankind also, and we will take it up with its causes and use them again, work up again, work out again the same faults with which we go out of this life. The lower part of our nature, all our faults, all our characteristics, all that we have not perceived and got rid of in this earth-life now, all that remains waits for us in essence until the ego returns again from its resting in heaven. You have been told that, by the law of cause and effect, we have to work out for ourselves every effect which we have started. And considering that one-half of the causes were started in this world, in this world we must work them out. One-half the causes are started here by our desires, by those material wishes, by material longings; all this garment of life into which we throw our energy, all that energy, belongs to our ego, and until we have transmuted it and turned it into the higher life, we must come back and back and take up that same garment again. Therefore, friends, even from a different point of view it is worth while to study a little about the subjective arrangement of death. It is a wearisome task to put on old clothes again life after life ; and every old fault we have had in this life, every weakness we do not conquer here, we come back and have to conquer again. Why? Because outside of the portal we call death it remains waiting for us, the skeleton garment of ourselves, the skeleton garment of our wishes, of our desires, and all that we have been in this life. It is only the outward material garment that changes; it is only the outward matter that ever alters; and according to Theosophical teachings we bring this back, all that we have really impressed with our own individuality, our own faults, our own weaknesses. It is a part of ourselves, and until we have regenerated it and lifted it up and perfected it, all the deaths in the world will not do away with it. That is the reason that in the life here the work is to be done. Death is a different condition of consciousness, and the work that was started in the consciousness of life is to be worked out also in the consciousness of life. Another quality of consciousness into which we pass then is *Devachan*, and our appreciation of it, our being able even to understand it, depends upon the way we have lived here; the whole of our subjective condition as that passes out and as we live in it there, depends absolutely upon the way we live here.

You must remember, friends, that in Theosophy there is no atonement; there is no one bearing your burdens for you. We have to pay our own bills and work out our own salvation through one life after another. (Applause.) And so it is that according to the Theosophical teaching of death, the responsibility of human life is enormously greater than it is in any Western teaching here. It means that we cannot get any sort of salvation that we do not gain ourselves. And now when I say, Go to ourselves, I do not mean the external plane; I mean to withdraw into ourselves and try to live that eternal, divine life which is the real life-principle of us all. As Dr. Chakravarti told us to-day, when we have this ideal mind in us, if the whole of our energy is turned into this ideal mind, how can we give so much to material life. We are bound to make as careful a study of death, what we call death, the processes of death, as we do of life, and the whole of life would grow much purer, much grander, and much more noble if we would once take up the responsible position of understanding that every day and every hour we are paving our way to that subjective condition which we call death. Every hour and every day are telling upon us for this reason, that unless we put into action this higher mind, unless here in this earth-life we withdraw into that higher mind and make the higher mind active, when we go into death we can have no consciousness of it at all. I mean by that that a person who has put all his energy into the lower quaternary must pass out of death without reaping the influences in it as do those people who have made a study of the subjective consciousness here in the earth-life. We can only do this by our own will, by our own desires at the present moment, and by turning our attention to the study of it.

Now, there is a simple little book which will give you more details upon this subject, written by Annie Besant and called *Death and After*. I refer you all to it to study, because it gives in the plainest way the whole Theosophical view with regard to the subjective conditions and the subjective entities. There is one view of death I must speak of before I stop. The whole of the subjective conditions of life are full of entities, beings working, acting on their own plane; it is full of life; nay, and as full of energy and as full of knowledge as we are in ours; and we do not pass there into a condition of nonentity at all. We pass into a condition of entity there in which there are laws, in which there is life; where are beings full of energy and full of life, working as you all are at the present moment; that the laws of that condition are just as carefully worked out, just as carefully arranged and governed, and that the whole of these different conditions, or rather I am speaking just now of the subjective consciousness, have all the conditions in which we live, in which we may be entities, in which we may have intercourse with other entities; and yet unless we have knowledge we are liable to make as many mistakes there, that is, in the earlier conditions of our progress through what we call death, as we should in this world. You must remember that just outside of this earth-life all the people who pass out are not perfectly good. Do you suppose that this earth-life is not surrounded with all the souls of those men and of those women who have been so earth-bound in their moral natures that they cannot pass on to anything else? There is a great mass of evil spirits just as there is a great mass of good, and we are bound to meet all these different entities at some time or another, and that is why I say that knowledge of subjective conditions and subjective life, as it has been put forward and studied in those Eastern literatures, is a thing that the public is sorely in need of at the present moment.

Now, one more word and my time will be up; that is, one from the Theosophical standpoint and from the technical standpoint. There is one more point of view from which to look at it, and that is from the emotional standpoint. There is no person amongst us who does not dread the moment when he will feel that those who are nearest and dearest to him have to pass out of this earth-life. And whether you study it for your own knowledge only, whether you study it simply for the sake of what you want to know for yourselves, you may at least study it from the point of view of what you want to know about those whom you love; because not all the love in the world, not all the tenderness in the world, not all the brotherly feeling in the world, can take any one of us across that portal with our nearest and our dearest. Every soul has to walk alone across that portal, and what we can do to help them is by telling them where they can find these teachings, where they can find that comfort which alone can help them when they come to change conditions; because true Theosophists do not believe in death at all. From a Theosophical point of view it is no longer saying good-bye to those who are near and dear to us who pass through the portal of death; it is not a parting with them or a going of them out into the unknown, because we have the road shown to us by which we may know, and those we love may know it too. We know what road they are going, where they are going, and what their condition is to be. And if you only, as I said before, study it for yourselves, at any rate you may look at it from the point of view of knowing something of those you love, desiring to know where they are, in what conditions they are, under what change they have come, how they are graded. Surely that must be a comfort, this knowledge about every human soul, and it must be learned some time or another. We know perfectly well that although that body may be lying in front of us, that that person who a few moments ago was full of life, though that person seems dead, we Theosophists know he is not dead, but still alive, and that to them and to us, while there is a division between us apparently, we know that between us and them there is no division at all, that it is only a different condition of molecular life. Friends, there is comfort in it, and that comfort we are feeling ourselves with regard to this, that comfort is what we want to hand on to all the rest of the Western world ; because that is the great one reality of life we have to face, and it is only in this Eastern teaching that you will find that knowledge and that truth about the condition called death. (Applause.)

UNIVERSAL BROTHERHOOD A FACT IN NATURE.

WILLIAM Q. JUDGE.

I have been requested to speak on the subject of Universal Brotherhood as a fact in nature; not as a theory, not as a Utopian dream which can never be realized; not as a fact in society, not as a fact in government, but as a fact in nature. That is, that Universal Brotherhood is an actual thing, whether it is recognized or whether it is not. Christian priests have claimed for some years, without right, that Christianity introduced the idea of Universal Brotherhood. The reason the claim was made, I suppose, was because those who made it did not know that other religions at other times had the same doctrine. It is found in the Buddhist scriptures, it is found in the Chinese books, it is found in the Parsee books, it is found everywhere in the history of the world, long before the first year of the Christian Era began. So it is not a special idea from the Christian Scriptures. Every nation, then, every civilization has brought forward this doctrine, and the facts of history show us that, more than at any other time, the last eighteen hundred years have seen this doctrine violated in society, in government, and in nations. So that at last men have come to say, "Universal Brotherhood is very beautiful; it is something that we all desire, but it is impossible to realize." With one word they declare the noble doctrine, and with the other they deny the possibility of its ever being realized.

Why is this the case? Why is it that although Christianity and other religions have brought forward this doctrine, it has been violated? We cannot deny that it has been. The history of even the last few years proves it. The history of the last forty years in America, without going any farther back, proves that this doctrine has been violated in the West. How could it have been a doctrine that the Americans believed in when they had slavery in their midst? How could it have been believed in by the French when they stretched out their hand and demanded of Siam, a weak and powerless nation, that it must give up to them its own property? How could it have been believed in by the Germans and French when they constructed engines of war and went into battle and destroyed each other by the thousand? Does not the American War of the Rebellion and the vast amount of treasure wasted and the thousands slain in that civil war prove conclusively that Universal Brotherhood has not been practiced? It has been professed but not practiced. Now, go further back, go back in the history of the nations in Europe, without going to any other country, and what do you find? Do you not find sectarian prejudice? Their view of Universal Brotherhood has for years prevented the progress of science. Is it not true that only since science became materialized—a most remarkable thing, but it is true—I insist that since then only science has made progress. If Universal Brotherhood had been a belief of this nation, then we would not have had the burning of witches in America; nor in other countries would we have had the burning of Catholics by Protestants, nor the burning of Protestants by Catholics; we would not have had the persecutions that have stained the pages of history; and yet we have always claimed that we have had Universal Brotherhood. We have had the theory but not the practice. Now, then, has there not been something wanting? It is a beautiful doctrine. It is the only doctrine of the Theosophical Society, the only thing that any man is asked by us to subscribe to. What, then, is the matter with it? Why so many men who say that it is beautiful, but it is impossible, simply impossible? There are even some branches of the Christian church which say, "There is Jesus; why, the altruistic, noble teachings of Christ are beautiful; but no State could live three months under such doctrine." The reason that it has not prevailed in practice is that it has been denied in the heart.

The Theosophist who knows anything about life insists that Universal Brotherhood is not a mere theory. It is a fact, a living ever present fact, from which no nation can hope to escape; no man can escape from it, and every man who violates it violates a law, violates the greatest law of nature, which will react upon him and make him suffer. And that is why we have had suffering; that is why you have in Chicago, in London, in New York, in Berlin, in all the great cities of the world, masses of people who are claiming with violence what they call their rights and saying they must have them, and that another class is oppressing them; and danger lurks in every corner because men are insisting on Universal Brotherhood. This noble doctrine has already become a danger. The reason of all these things is that men have denied the fact. Now, we propose to show you, if we can, that it is a fact.

If you will notice you will find that when it rains over a certain area vast numbers of men are affected similarly. The rain has to fall on the fields in order that the harvest may grow, so that afterwards it may be gathered, and all the farmers are affected together by the rain. If you examine society you will find that at the same hour every day almost all the people are doing exactly the same thing. At a certain hour in the morning thousands of your citizens are going down that railway or rush all together to catch the train, and at another few moments afterwards they are rushing out of the train to get to business, all doing the same thing, one common thought inspiring them. That is one of the proofs—a small one—in social and business life that they are affected together, they are all united. Then in the evening they will come home at the same hour, and if you could see, at the same hour you would see them all eating together and digesting together, and then later on they are all lying down together at the same hour. Are they not united even in their social life? Brothers even in that? And what do we see here in business? Lately I have felt it; every man has felt it, and many women; doubtless all have felt it; lately we have had a financial crisis, perhaps have it yet, in which dollars have been scarce, during which men have discovered that there are only just so many dollars and half dollars to each person in the country, and we have altogether been suffering from that panic all over this vast country. Suffering, why? Because commercially we are united and cannot get out of it. China even is affected by it, and Japan. India, they say, was the cause of it. Some men say the reason for this panic is that India put the price of rupees down, and we who produce so much silver began to feel it. I do not know that that is the reason. But I think there is another cause. I think the American nation is so fond of luxury, so fond of fine clothes, so fond of having a heap of money, that it has gone too far and there was bound to come a reaction, because it is all united together with the whole world, and when it spread itself out too far the slightest touch broke the fabric. That is the reason, and that is another proof of Universal Brotherhood. We are all united, not only with each other here, but with the entire world.

Now, then, go further still materially and you find that all men are alike. We have the same sort of bodies, a little different perhaps in height, weight, and extension, but as human beings we are all alike, all the same color in one country, all the same shape in any country, so that as mere bodies of flesh they are united, they are the same. We know every man and woman has exuding from him or her what is called perspiration. The doctors will tell you there is a finer perspiration you cannot see, the invisible perspiration which goes out a short distance around about us; we know it comes out from every person, and the emanations of each person are affecting every other person, being interchanged always. All those in this room are being affected by these emanations and also by the ideas of each other, and the ideas of the speakers speaking to you. So it is in every direction; wherever you go, wherever you look, we are united; in whatever plane, the plane of mind as well as the plane of the body; the plane of the emotions, of the spirit, what not, we are all united, and it is a fact from which we cannot escape. Now, then, further: science is beginning to admit what the old Theosophists have always said, that there is going on every minute in every person a death, a dissolution, a disappearance. It used to be taught and thought in the West that we could see matter, that this table is made of matter. It is admitted to-day by your best scientific men in every part of Western civilization that you do not see matter at all ; it is only the phenomena of matter we see ; and it is my senses which enables me to perceive these phenomena. It is not matter at all, and so we do not see matter. Now admitting that, they go further and say there is a constant change in matter so-called ; that is, this table is in motion. This is not a purely Theosophical theory. Go to any doctor of Physics and he will admit to you as I have stated it. This table is in motion ; every molecule is separate from every other, and there is space between them, and they are moving. So it is with every man, he is made of atoms and they are in motion. Then how is it we remain the same size and weight nearly always from the moment of maturity until death ? We eat tons of meat and vegetables but remain the same. It is not because of the things you have eaten. In addition to that the atoms are alive, constantly moving, coming and going from one person to another; and this is the modern doctrine to-day as well as it was the doctrine of ancient India. They call it the momentary dissolution of atoms ; that is to say, to put it in another way, I am losing, all of you in this room are losing, a certain number of atoms, but they are being replaced by other atoms. Now, where do these other atoms come from ? Do they not come from the people in this room ? These atoms help to rebuild your body as well as does the food you eat. And we are exuding atoms from our minds, and we are receiving into ourselves the atoms other men have used. For, remember, science teaches you, and Theosophy has always insisted, that matter is invisible before it is turned into this combination of the life cycle, which makes it visible, makes it tangible to us. So these atoms leave us in a stream and rush into other people. And therefore the atoms of good men go into bad men, the atoms impressed by bad men go into good men, and *vice versâ*. In that way as well as others we are affecting everybody in this world ; and the people in Chicago who are living mean, selfish lives are impressing these invisible atoms with mean and selfish characters, and these mean and selfish atoms will be distributed by other men, and by you again to your and their detriment. That is another phase of Universal Brotherhood. It teaches us to be careful to see that we use and keep the atoms in our charge in such a condition that they shall benefit others to whom they shall go. (Applause.)

There is another view of Universal Brotherhood, and I don't pretend to exhaust the argument on this point, for I have not the time nor force to state all that is put forward in the Theosophical books and literature and thought. That is, that there is in this world in actual Universal Brotherhood of men and women, of souls, a brotherhood of beings who practice Universal Brotherhood by always trying to influence the souls of men for their good. I bring to you the message of these men ; I bring to you the words of that brotherhood. Why will you longer call yourselves miserable men and women who are willing to go to a Heaven where you will do nothing ? Do you not like to be gods ? Do you not want to be gods ? I hear some men say, "What, a god ! Impossible !" Perhaps they do not like the responsibility. Why, when you get to that position you will understand the responsibility. This actual Brotherhood of living men says, Why, men of the West, why will you so long refuse to believe you are gods? We are your brothers and we are gods with you. Be then as gods! Believe that you are gods, and then, after experience and attainment, you will have a place consciously in the great Brotherhood which governs the entire world, but cannot go against the law. This great Brotherhood of living men, living souls, would, if they could, alter the face of civilization; they would, if they could, come down and make saints of every one of you; but evolution is the law and they cannot violate it; they must wait for you. And why will you so long be satisfied to believe that you are born in original sin and cannot escape? I do not believe in any such doctrine as that. I do not believe I was born in original sin. I believe that I am pretty bad, but that potentially I am a god, and I propose to take the inheritance if it is possible. For what purpose? So that I may help all the rest to do the same thing, for that is the law of Universal Brotherhood; and the Theosophical Society wishes to enforce it on the West, to make it see this great truth, that we are as gods, and are only prevented from being so in fact by our own insanity, ignorance, and fear to take the position.

So, then, we insist that Universal Brotherhood is a fact in nature. It is a fact for the lowest part of nature; for the animal kingdom, for the vegetable kingdom, and the mineral kingdom. We are all atoms, obeying the law together. Our denying it does not disprove it. It simply puts off the day of reward and keeps us miserable, poor, and selfish. Why, just think of it! if all in Chicago, in the United States, would act as Jesus has said, as Buddha has said, as Confucius said, as all the great ethical teachers of the world have said, " Do unto others as you would have them do unto you," would there be any necessity for legal measures and policemen with clubs in this park as you had them the other day? (Applause.) No, I think there would be no necessity, and that is what one of this great Brotherhood has said. He said all the troubles of the world would disappear in a moment if men would only do one-quarter of what they could and what they ought. It is not God who is to damn you to death, to misery. It is yourself. And the Theosophical Society desires above all things, not that you should understand spiritualism, not that wonderful occult works should be performed, but to understand the constitution of matter and of Life as they are, which we can never understand but by practicing right ethics. Live with each other as brothers; for the misery and the trouble of the world are of more importance than all the scientific progress that may be imagined. I conclude by calling upon you by all that humanity holds dear to remember what I say, and whether Christians, Atheists, Jews, Pagans, Heathen, or Theosophists, try to practice Universal Brotherhood, which is the universal duty of all men.

KARMA THE LAW OF CAUSATION, OF JUSTICE AND THE ADJUSTMENT OF EFFECTS.

ANNIE BESANT.

In arranging the programme for this Congress of the Theosophical Society, a very definite view of the presentment of the subject was in the mind of those who drew it up. To-day we have been striving to lay clearly and definitely before you, first, the origin of the movement in that great spiritual life to which your attention was drawn this morning; then to justify the claim of Theosophy to be the ancient wisdom religion, by an historical review of the past, showing you how under every creed the same truths were found. From that we have passed onward to the great fundamental teachings, philosophical and psychological, which form the very basis of our thought. And then to-morrow, having dealt to-day with this theoretical side, we are going to try to work the theory out in its practical relations of life, so that we may catch at least some outline of the way in which we are trying to work in and affect the world.

It is my duty, in closing this first great section of our work, to place before you one of the most difficult, but at the same time one of the most fundamental, of our doctrines. That doctrine of Karma; the law of causes, as it is called, the law of justice, the law of adjustment of effects; difficult because so complicated, difficult because so far-reaching; and in the attempt that I must make to lay it before you, I do not for one moment pretend that I shall answer every question that may arise in your minds, nor give you full and perfect explanation of the teaching. Full explanation does not come by listening to the speech of another. It comes by patient and resolute study carried on by the individual for himself. Only a superficial knowledge can be gained from the lips of another; real knowledge comes by personal effort and personal thought, and there is a danger that in this time of hurry, in this time of continual change and constant excitement, there is a danger that men shall grow intellectually lazy, that their minds shall lose their own grip of a subject, that they shall rely on the thinkings of others instead of upon their own thought, and so lose man's most precious heritage, the power to study and to understand the truth, and the duty and responsibility of judgment and discrimination for one's self.

Now *Karma* is simply a Sanscrit word meaning action, and it is used in our philosophy to cover all action of every description in the Kosmos and in Man; action as cause, action as effect, so that it becomes the general expression of a sequence in Nature. The word is one which expresses continual and inviolable sequence, the unbroken chain of cause and of effect, each cause giving rise to an effect, which effect in turn becomes the cause of new effects, so that all thought, all life, all action, all these things, form a single chain in which every link depends on the link that precedes it, out of which no link can drop, for law is inviolable, subject neither to breach nor change. And the reason why this is so is easy enough to grasp. What is the Universe in the widest extent of the phrase? The Universe is but the form in which the divine thought expresses itself. It is but the manifested thought of the divine, but the necessary outcome of the divine nature; and inasmuch as the divine thought is primary and the form in which it expresses itself is secondary, therefore form must follow thought, and be the inevitable expression of the creative thought that originates divine ideation, which is the first manifestation of deity. The universe and everything in it is but the gradual expression in form of the ideation that has preceded. Here is the sphere of causes. Here every thing has its root. Out of the divine thought grow all possibilities of action, and so thought becomes the primary study, and *Karma* is but thought worked out in a manifested universe. You have the concrete expression of this idea, as, in truth, of all great philosophical ideas, in those Eastern scriptures to which so many references have been made to-day. Turn to the *Vishnu Purana*. You will find there one of the simplest and most sublime expositions of that which is the very essence of created activity. Over and over again the phrase comes, preceding each different form of manifested activity, "Brahma meditated, and Creation came forth."

It is from the meditation of the divine that all form proceeds, and so in its measure from human thought, from human meditation, all action springs, and every manifested thought is precipitated as action. It is in the realm of thought that, as Dante phrased it, "In that realm where power and will are one," it is there, whether in the divine, in the Kosmos, or the divine in Man, that we must look for the root of action and the cause of all effect. Where the will has operated, the action is inevitable. That is *Karma* in a phrase. The will is the energizing force, the action is the mere crystallization of the will; and so, when this will has operated, there come forth into the world of manifestation acts which we perform, social systems amid which we live, physical environment that limits our energy, the very mould in which our life is cast.

When one of the great teachers of wisdom desired to make concrete and practical for the Western world the somewhat metaphysical and subtle teaching that you may find on this subject in Eastern books, he took as an example the way in which men, throwing their will and their thought out of themselves, create images that become potent for good or for evil in the world of effects. He taught how the motive in man conditioned the result of the mental activity of man in his willing, impressed, as it were, the nature of the causation on that which he thought and desired; so that, as the man thinks—to use the very phrase of the Masters—he is peopling his current in space with the offspring of his own thoughts, desires, and emotions. Every man is thus employed day by day, year by year, and this peopling of the current in space—once more to take up the phrases I am quoting—"This," he says, "is what the Hindu calls *Karma*." Knowing what the phrase means, it remains to see how it will affect our view of life.

We have been making for ourselves by the creative force of our will, certain causes sent out from the realm of mind into the realm of matter; and it is in the realm of matter that are to be found the acts which from day to day we commit. Thought has made the action inevitable. The thought-form must work out in the material world, so that day by day we are living in the results that we have crêated, and are surrounded from the cradle to the grave by these forms that are the offspring of our own mind. Hence we are born into the world time after time with the general mold, as it were, of our life cast in the preceding incarnations. We, and no one else, are responsible for the tendencies that we bring in. We, and no one else, are responsible for the environment which surrounds us, to work out year after year the lessons of our previous thinking, fettered by the fetters that our own hands have forged, hindered by obstacles that our own hands have piled. But then, it may be said, if that be so, are you not teaching a fatalism that will be destructive of human effort? Are you not proclaiming a destiny that will make all energy impossible, all spontaneous action removed from the possibility of Man? No, for the will that created yesterday those causes which to-day are worked out in the very midst of the environment it has created and must enter, is the same creative potency making new causes for the morrow that shall work out in changed environment, in altered conditions, improving or retrograding as life proceeds. It is true that we have to live in that which we have made for our dwelling, but it is also true that, working from within those limitations we have created, we can break one by one the fetters we have forged, and step out again free men into the world which we have made for ourselves.

For the will, which is the causer, remains ever with us, and just as we deal with the dead act into which we are compelled to enter, so shall be the living outcome of that action. The husk shall fall away and the life step forth. Let me take as a very simple illustration the way in which *Karma*, working, places us in an environment inevitably, but enables us then by dealing with that environment with knowledge to change that which shall grow out from it in the future. Let us say that by past folly, past ignorance, past selfishness, we have made for ourselves to-day an environment of sorrow from which we cannot escape. Some crushing blow from the hand of fate we call it in our ignorance, unknowing that the hand of fate to-day is our own hand of yesterday which has forged the weapon by which we are pierced. The blow falls, we feel the agony, shrinking from that anguish, how shall we face it, how shall we bear it? What shall be its outcome in the life that lies in front? The outcome may be one of two. When the blow falls we may rise against it with a sense of angry injustice. "I have not deserved this agony; I have done nothing that I should suffer this pain. I am crushed under the wheels of a remorseless destiny, and I heartily rebel against the injustice that has struck me." Such may be the aspect of the thinker blinded in matter, unknowing his own past on this plane, not able, as it were, to communicate to the waking consciousness that which is the explanation of the pain. What is the result? That out of this evil seed of the Past, met in an ignorant and rebellious spirit, fresh cause for sorrow is sown for the days to come. Fresh harvest of pain must be reaped with the sickle of experience. Pain, ever-renewing pain, sorrow, ever-renewing sorrow, an iron circle, as it were, surrounding us; a circle of fire from which we cannot escape.

But word has come to Man enlightening the darkness that surrounded him. He is given to understand he has a power that he has wielded in the past and possesses to-day. Wisdom has come as a light on his path, and in the midst of the agony wrought by the past evil he understands himself, he understands the environment he has made. Bravely, patiently, sternly, he faces the result of his own fall, with no cry of anger against destiny, with no thought of rebellion against the pain which is to teach him wisdom, recognizing in the harvest the seed of his own sowing. Too strong to cry beneath the pain—a pain which his own folly has made, he walks out to meet it, takes his burden on his own shoulder —nay, welcomes the agony which means knowledge and the pain by which alone wisdom can be garnered.

"I have sinned," he says; "rightly do I suffer. I have blundered; justly does the penalty of the disregard of law fall on my own head. Shall I complain that the laws of a universe are not altered for my escaping? Shall I ask that the divine nature may be changed; that I who have tried to violate may escape the swing of the law against which I have flung myself? Rather let me bear my pain. Rather let the evil that I have done work itself out to the uttermost expiation. It will teach me the reality of life. It will tell me something of the divine nature. I have sinned; I am willing to suffer, and I ask not to escape the harvest the seed of which I sow with my own hands."

And so out of knowledge grows strength, so out of understanding grows peace; for all the pain, the real pain of life, grows not out of that which comes to us from without, but from the inner rebellion that is not able to accept, to understand what *Karma* means; to understand it as the expression of the divine nature, to realize that all that is worthy in life is to become one with the divine law, united with the divine will, and you will welcome pain which offers the possibility of union, and you will rejoice in the very fires of your agony, for they shall purify you and give you gold and melt away the dross.

Thus is *Karma* the law of readjustment. I have spoken of the law of the Kosmos as the expression of the divine will. But we have human wills differentiated from the divine. One with it in essence, opposed to it for the while in practice. Why this possibility of conflict in a universe of law? Why should it be that in a Kosmos which is to be the expression of the divine thought there should be the possibility of any will in conflict with the one will, any volition of Man that can hold its own against the Supreme volition? It is because in the evolution of soul there is to be something higher than mere automatic obedience to a law compulsorily impressed upon matter; because, the universe existing for the evolution of the soul, that soul is to become in very truth divine, self-consciously divine, at the close of its experience, as it is unconsciously divine at its beginning. But if there is to be human will at all, that must include the possibility of rebellion. If the will can say, "I will obey," it must be able also to say, "I will not obey, I will go my own way, carry out my own desire." And in order that the universe may be not a monotone but a harmonious chord, not the one note ringing ever, but one key-note with countless undertones giving richness and melody and all possibility of infinite harmony and beauty; so that while the key-note is divine the harmonies of the human wills which gradually are trained into unity, and the work of the universe, are the evolution of the harmony, the conscious and willing harmony with this supreme will.

Therefore it is that as the great will sweeps on, the lesser wills that set themselves against it cause friction. Therefore pain and misery. And therefore it is that *Karma*, the expression of that law, works itself out so long as there is evil, by suffering, for only as friction disappears does harmony become possible, and it is the great law of readjustment that exhausts the friction that the human will has made.

And this *Karma* lying behind us in our immemorial past cannot express itself properly in the limits of one brief human life; and so, going deeper into the subject, you will find divisions and subdivisions whereby we express the *Karma* that can be worked out in the one life for which the apparatus, so to speak, is here ready, while there is other *Karma* reserved, as it were, lying behind us, which in due time will come to the ripening and work itself out also in the act. Not only is this complication one of the difficulties of the understanding of the detailed workings, but also we have to recognize the working of *Karma*, not only individual but also national, but also racial, but also human, for all humanity is one. All these threads of *Karma* work in the one mighty strand, and those who would understand it in its detail, those who would understand its full bearing on human life, must take into consideration all these different states and the fashion of their intertwining; and there comes in the abstruseness that I spoke of, which seems to make the subject less intelligible as one really is beginning to understand; and we learn, as we thus study, that the *Karma* of one cannot be separated from the *Karma* of others; that you and I, one nation and another, one race and another, that we are all fundamentally one and have a common *Karma* that must work itself out in our common life; so that here, at the close of the evening as at the beginning of the morning, we come back to the fundamental unity that makes all separation between us impossible, and then you begin to understand what is meant when it is said of the guardians of our race, of those who have achieved, that it is their strong hands that hold back the *Karma* of the world, as the *Karma* is one and indivisible. Just in proportion as we destroy separateness, do we begin to bear the one *Karma* and share that one *Karma* of humanity. It is the reward of self-abnegation that we become the common bearers for the race, not by a vicarious offering but by the unity of our life within, for here there is no difference recognized, no "mine" and "thine" to the expression. That has passed away in the merging into the common life, and if you and I, as we tread the path of life together, however obscure, however trivial, however petty it may seem to be day by day, if in the living of that life we learn to trample on the lower self, if in the living of that life we learn to think not of self but first of others, and then of all as one with ourselves, if our daily life is made a daily offering to mankind, if every opportunity be seized upon which may make us feel our union and make us unconscious of our separateness, then we have put our feet on the path which makes us one with humanity and gives us the glory of bearing the common burden and using our strength for the common good of Man. Nothing can separate us from Man but our own will. Nothing can make us separate from our brethren save our own desire, our own longing for the lesser self, and the final lesson of *Karma* is, there is no such thing as separateness to the human soul. There is no such thing as Thee and as Me to those who are one in the supreme life; and the only reward that Theosophy offers to its followers, the only prize that Theosophy holds out to those who accept it, is that by struggle they shall become one with Man by following self-sacrifice, that perfect sacrifice at last shall be their reward, that their fate shall be one with the fate of the world, their future one with the future of humanity, none outcast that is not one with them, none degraded that is not in their heart, whose pain they do not answer to, whose agony they cannot feel. The vilest and the lowest, the most degraded and the foulest, they are ours by right of our common divinity, and none shall come between us and them. That is the final triumph, that is the extreme goal. As was said in an ancient Chinese scripture, "Never will I accept individual salvation, never will I enter into final peace alone." As one, not as many, we will cross the threshold of the spiritual life; as one, and not as separate, we will open that door and go in together. For it is not worth while to be saved unless everything that breathes is saved along with us; and the one vow that is worth the taking, the one vow that every Saviour of Man perfects, age after age, is the vow which makes him the lowest in order that he may raise all, and makes him willing to be but as the very ground men walk on, in order that, by the force of the spirit within him, he may raise them to the highest and make them one with the divine.

Adjourned until Saturday morning, at 10 a. m.

SESSION OF SATURDAY MORNING, SEPTEMBER 16TH, 10 A. M.

MR. JUDGE—One or two persons have said since our sessions began that they noticed that other Congresses began either with the Lord's Prayer or with some religious Christian hymn, and ended with the doxology or some other religious function, and they wondered why the Theosophical Congresses were opened in a business manner and closed in the same way. What is the reason for this? The reason is not very far to seek; it is found in the words of Jesus; and if we were in India we could give reasons from their scriptures, but here the words of Jesus are quite enough. Jesus told the Pharisees, who existed in that time as they do now in ours, that they should not make prayers in the streets nor shout prayers, but to retire to their closets and pray to the Father who seeth in secret, and he would reward them openly. So we do not begin with prayer, nor end with the doxology. Every individual can pray himself or herself to the God who seeth in secret, and we prefer to follow the words of Jesus and not to make long prayers in the streets nor to be seen of men at our secret devotions, but go at once to our business, which is to endeavor to give men and women a philosophy of life so they will be able to pray sincerely to the Father who seeth in secret.

Brother Claude F. Wright will now address you.

THE THEOSOPHICAL SOCIETY IN ITS ORGANIZED LIFE. ORGANIZATION, METHODS OF WORK, PROPAGANDA.

CLAUDE F. WRIGHT.

The special object of this paper is to lay before you a brief statement of the methods by which the Theosophical Society endeavors to carry into effect its programme of labor for the melioration of the world; and to give some idea of the structure of the association,—of the movement in its organized life.

In order that what is to follow may be perfectly comprehended, it will be well in opening to roughly outline the programme referred to and which you have heard more fully elaborated by other speakers; by so doing at the outset I shall avoid the necessity in the course of my remarks for constant reference to what properly lies outside the province of this essay.

You are all aware that the first Object of the Society is the formation of a nucleus of a Universal Brotherhood of Humanity, without distinction of race, creed, sex, caste, or color. But it should be understood that the binding element in an ideal fraternity such as is here betokened must of necessity have its source in the spiritual side of things. No true student of man's nature would even dream of the possibility of permanently uniting individuals or nations with the tendrils of fellowship and good-will, save through the medium of a common philosophy sprung from belief in the divine possibilities of man, and having for its principal elements the ideal of human perfection and the sacrifice of the self to the good of others. It is Religion in its purity, released from priest-craft, dogma, or sect, that alone can produce in the heart of man desire for harmony and progression. The first Object of the Society was never intended to give birth to a socialistic or communistic sodality based upon laws of finance or necessity, or the visionary and unnatural concept of the equality of man : it essayed the breaking down of the walls of estrangement between sects, religions, and nations, being an endeavor to free the world from the degrading philosophy of self-interest and advance, and to help man to the practical realization of the god within him. The recognition of a spiritual philosophy as the root-nature of true Brotherhood and a desire to spread this idea in the world at large, certainly underlay the formulation of the Objects of the Society. This is evinced by the nature of its second and third objects : (a), the study of Aryan and other Eastern literatures, religions, and sciences—which treat almost entirely of the spiritual nature of things ; and (b), the investigation of the psychical side of nature and of man. The name of the Society also—the Society of Theosophy, Divine Wisdom, or Knowledge concerning God, abundantly proves it.

So that our programme of labor is to all intents and purposes the awakening in man of a desire for spiritual knowledge, and through that the uniting of all peoples by the holy bonds of divine love. To expedite this work, the true Founders—the Arahats dwelling beyond the Himalayas—have given to the Society information for the service of mankind, a spiritual philosophy and knowledge of things hidden from the world for ages, including an explanation of the origin of the world's religions. This has been called Theosophy The majority of the members of the Society are students and exponents of it, for in their belief it is the only system of knowledge that can afford a reasonable basis for Brotherhood. It unites all sciences, religions, and philosophies, is without dogmatic or sectarian possibility, and in particular is a common ground on which all the religions of the world can find standing room. And as the spreading of this philosophy has been proven by extended experiments to be the best method of interesting man in his long-neglected soul-nature and so help to the founding of a true Fraternity, so the very great majority of the members labor to let the world know of it. It is, however, offered only as an explanation of life ; no one is compelled to accept it, for the unsectarian character of the Society must never be tampered with ; yet as for the aforesaid reasons its dissemination in the world is the work of almost the entire body of the Fellows, it cannot be omitted in the consideration of our programme of labor.

So much, then, for the mission of the Society. We may now enquire into the methods by which it is endeavoring to carry out its work.

Primarily, the object is of course not so much to increase the ranks of the movement as to spread these ideas of Brotherhood and the inherent divinity of man upon which that is based. This is accomplished largely by the spread of literature. Numerous magazines, books, brochures, pamphlets, tracts of all kinds are yearly issued by our members in every country on the globe and in almost every language ; written by the members of the Society, they are without exception of a kind calculated to spur men on to a study of religious philosophy. In the main they set forth the science of Theosophy or the arcane wisdom of the Orient, but a very large number are translations from the older Aryan literatures and the writings of the ancient Hindus and other Eastern peoples under the second Object of the Society, of which many a rare gem has through the efforts of our members been allowed to shed its rays among European and American nations. But before presenting a sketch of the general field of Theosophical literature let us pass to an examination of the actual mechanism of the Society itself.

Second in importance to the spread of literature in flooding the world with the ideas and truths we have so much at heart, stands the enlarging of the Society, the establishment of Branches, and through them the sending of lecturers to districts so far unenlightened by Theosophy. This leads us to a consideration of the reason why a Society was formed. Some might say, even have said, that if all that was desired was a promulgation of Theosophy, a dissemination of spiritual ideas based upon scientific research, then a society was unnecessary; all that was needed was the spread of literature of a kind sufficient to awaken interest in psychic and spiritual matters. That might have answered all purposes in a more enlightened age, but in this era of mental, physical, and spiritual warfare the wisdom of the Founders perceived the value of organized work. And events have proved that wisdom. Notwithstanding the fact that the literature brought out by the members of the Society has done most toward permanently altering the minds of the people and turning them in the desired direction, yet it may fairly be said that nine-tenths of the work of advancement has been done through the personal labor of the members; for it is they who have excited an interest in the literature and spread a desire for its study by philosophical discourse and by lives of purity, devotion, and high endeavor. But without the organization they could have done but comparatively little; the laborers in the field would have been scattered and unknown to one another, each working on his own lines and without assistance. With a properly constituted Society such as is ours, the workers accept the advice of the older members, drawn from their experience, as to the most approved methods of labor; missionaries and lecturers are sent where they are most needed, and according to their ability; pecuniary aid by individual donation is rendered possible; members in any given city or centre are drawn together, and by mutual aid quadruple the effects of their efforts; the distribution of literature becomes a comparatively easy task.

Yet the Society is intended as a Brotherhood rather than merely an institution. Each member is strongly imbued with the desire to aid his fellow and to work for the furtherance of the Cause, and this it is which maintains it far more than its councils, fees, and dues. So also the association is as unfettered as possible. It is constructed on the lines of the Constitution of the United States, and every one in it is free to his own opinion on all matters, only restricted in this to the extent of his being expected to exercise the same tolerance toward the views of others on religious and like questions as he asks for his own. The actual framework of the Society is light, and can be examined without difficulty. It consists, in the first place, of what may be called the Society-at-large, with its President, Vice-President, Secretaries, and Treasurers; this is international. It is then divided into Sections, perfectly autonomous, each having its own officers elected as the Branch determines. Each Branch is, therefore, a miniature copy of the General Society, and by the perfect system of self-government maintained throughout every division of the body, together with the principle of freedom of thought and speech existing among the members and habitually promulgated by them and by the officers, there is neither the possibility of nor tendency to dogmatism or sectarianism. And as the endeavor of each individual in the Society is, or should be, as far as possible to make the ideal of Universal Brotherhood a reality in his life and thus establish a perfect unity in the Branch to which he is attached; and as, also, the Branches coöperate in establishing concord in the Section to which they belong, the Sections again working harmoniously and for the good of all; so the whole Society is cemented with the bonds of sympathy, fraternity, and unity, working as one body through the unanimous desire of its members for progress, and inspired to a peaceful existence by the common labor of all, the aiding of mankind.

In an age such as the present the growth of a Society organized on the lines just indicated is from every point of view astonishing. More marvellous yet is it when that growth has shown itself a rapid one. Yet the Society has increased almost at an accelerated rate from the date of its establishment until the present time. While the number of its members has not been published, yet an examination of the increase in the chartered Branches issued from year to year will give a fair idea of its development. The following figures are taken from the last account published by the Headquarters of the Society, January, 1893.

Year	1876	1877	1878	1879	1880	1881	1882	1883	1884	1885	1886	1887	1888	1889	1890	1891	1892
Branches	1	2	2	4	11	27	51	93	104	121	136	158	179	206	241	279	310
New Branches	1	1	0	2	7	16	34	42	11	17	15	22	21	27	35	38	31

Deducting thirty charters extinguished, the Branches existing on 27th December, 1892, numbered 280, geographically distributed in the following manner:

In Europe: England 19; Scotland 1; Ireland 1; France 2; Austria 2; Sweden 1; Greece 1; Holland 1; Belgium 1; Russia 1.

In America: United States 67; West Indies 2.

In Asia: Bengal 36; Kattyawar 2; Madras 58; Ceylon 22; Behar 8, N. W. P., Panjaub, and Oudh 26; Central Provinces 4; Bombay 9; Burmah 3; Japan 1; Philippine Islands 1.

In Australasia 10.

During the present year, however, many new charters have been issued in addition to these in the different Sections, and it is estimated that there are at present about 330 Branches on the Society's roll.

The Society was founded at New York in November, 1875; its phenomenal growth can only be explained by accepting as true the statements of its true Founders—the Mahatmas—through their mouthpiece, H. P. Blavatsky, so far back as 1874, that "the world was ready." But as was said in the opening remarks of this address, a consideration of the size of the Society gives really but a very imperfect idea of the extent of its work. Persons constantly say that they are in sympathy with it and even laboring for it, but refrain from joining it on account of the prejudice of relatives or friends, or because their principle is not to connect themselves with any body or association whatever. It may without exaggeration be said that if all those who are in sympathy with the movement were to enter its ranks, the numbers of the Society would be trebled. An examination of the development of its literature will therefore perhaps give us a better idea—albeit a more abstract one—of its general effect upon the world of thought.

During the first two years of its existence the literature of the Society may be said to have been *nil;* outside a few newspaper articles and pamphlets setting forth the objects and intent of the Society there was nothing published. In 1877 Madame Blavatsky's *Isis Unveiled* was brought out in New York. From the issue of this extraordinary work, pronounced by all to have been the most remarkable production of its time, may fairly be said to date the rise of the copious stream of Theosophical literature that has since flowed through the world. The work, in two volumes embracing about 1,300 octavo pages in all, created a sensation at the time of its issue that can scarcely be said to have died out yet. It has run through no less than six editions at the present date. After 1877 and until the visit of Madame Blavatsky to India in 1879, scarcely anything was added of importance in the way of published matter; in the latter year was founded at Bombay the *Theosophist*, the first magazine issued in connection with the Society and now its official organ. The growing interest in the Society in India from this date induced many Hindus to bring out translations into English from their own arcane literature, and not a few books and pamphlets of this nature thus found their way into Europe and America. The establishment of a Lodge of the Society in London in the previous year formed a centre there and a vehicle for the transmission of any works that might later be brought out. The address, "How Best to Become a Theosophist," appears to have been the first pamphlet issued in England of a Theosophical character. This was published in 1880. In 1881 Colonel Olcott brought out a *Buddhist Catechism*, which, approved by Sumangala, the High Priest of Ceylon, has since been translated into nearly every language on the globe. In the same year Mr. A. P. Sinnett's *Occult World* was published, while 1882 saw the first issue of *The Perfect Way*. In 1883 two new magazines were started by the Hindus themselves, one of them the *Mahrathi Theosophist*, consisting almost exclusively of articles translated from the journal in the English language. In that year no less than half a dozen new books, beside the issue of numerous pamphlets, marked the Society's advance in the interest of the public mind. Among these publications was *Esoteric Buddhism*, now rightly famous. In 1884 no less than twelve new books were published, while in 1885 twenty were issued, including translations into Tamil, German, and French. In 1886 four new magazines were started, *The Path* in America, *L'Aurore* in France, *Revue des Hautes Etudes*, France, and *The Sphinx* of Germany; twenty-four new books were published that year, including translations into German and Urdu. In 1887 a new magazine was founded by Madame Blavatsky in London called *Lucifer*, and in the same year *The Lotus* was founded in Paris; while the next year saw the issue of the first number of the *Buddhist*. In these two years no less than seventy-eight works were brought out, including numerous translations into German, French, Sanskrit, Urdu, Bengali, Canarese, Telugu, Japanese, Swedish, and other languages. 1888 also witnessed the publication of the *Secret Doctrine*, Madame Blavatsky's great work. About seventy-seven works were issued in 1889–1890, many of them being translations by the Hindus from their ancient literature; a new English sectional magazine *The Vahan* was first issued in the latter year. In 1891 fifty-six works were published, including Madame Blavatsky's *Glossary* and translations into French, Telugu, Spanish, Dutch, Swedish, German, and other languages. Five new magazines were brought out that year: *Prasnottara* and *Pauses* in India; *Teosofisk Tidskrift* in Sweden ; *The New Californian* and *The Pacific Theosophist* in America. In 1892 thirty-seven works were published, including the usual translations into the various languages of the globe; and six new magazines—one European, one Dutch, one German, one Indian, one Irish, and one Australian. A great number of works have been issued in the present year also.

These statistics, it must be borne in mind, deal only with the larger works and magazines, and do not, save in the most threadbare manner, give any idea of the extent of the Society's labor in the field of literature. They are drawn chiefly from the reports of the President of the Society at the annual convention of Theosophists held at the headquarters in Adyar, Madras, India. In these but scanty mention is made of the numberless tracts and pamphlets published year by year, and none whatever of the numbers distributed gratuitously by the members. This would in the nature of things be entirely impossible in any report, but it is estimated that about 2,000,000 brochures and circulars are annually disseminated by our fellows among the peoples of every nation.

The demand for our literature yearly grows. No one can have failed to have noticed the creeping into our novels and popular works of Theosophical thought. Already several Occult and Theosophical book stores are to be found in the larger towns of every country, all of which shows a demand on the part of the public for publications of this kind. It would be obviously not possible to give any idea of the amount thus issued to the public, but we may rest assured that it is immense if we make ourselves acquainted with the knowledge of the intense craving for the study of the spiritual sciences that has lately developed in the world, which, it may in strictest accuracy be said, has come about almost entirely through the labors of the members of the Theosophical Society. A single instance will suffice as illustration of this development : the *Secret Doctrine*, a work of the most profound research, and which has drawn expressions of astonishment from the most scholarly men of our time on account of the depth of its philosophy, has yet, since the date of its issue, 1889, passed through three editions.

A great feature in the work of spreading literature of this kind over the world has been the translating of Sanskrit and other Oriental works into English, and thus flooding the Western world with the wisdom of the East. If not so much as could be desired has been accomplished in this direction owing to lack of funds, the Society has yet accomplished more than any other body in the world in gathering together the more valuable of these works, thereby affording an opportunity to the Europeans for studying the origin of their own beliefs. The library at the Headquarters of the Society is now one of the most important, if not the most important, in India; and it has become so because the Hindus, trusting the Theosophists, have given freely of their ancient literature before withheld from the eye of the mlecchha. The report issued in December last showed the library to contain nearly 3,500 Oriental works and manuscripts, some of the latter extremely rare.

But you must not for a moment imagine that the work of the Theosophical Society is entirely a propagandizing of philosophy. To the extent of its ability it engages in practical work of all kinds for the alleviation of suffering and the upholding of justice. Of the latter may be mentioned the founding of Buddhist schools in Ceylon, the registration of which is as far as possible prevented by the government. This persecution forces the children to attend the Christian schools and become Christians; thus they are estranged from their parents and friends or else have to grow up in ignorance. Theosophists have done much to alleviate this distress. A number of schools have been established by their energy, and it is hoped that in that country, as in all the countries of the globe, all oppression—of open or underhand character—will eventually be non-existent, and that every man will be at liberty to worship as he himself desires, and to attach himself to that religion wherein he finds the most comfort for his soul.

Again we have leagues and unions in the ranks of the Society established with the especial intent of performing charitable work. The "League of Theosophical Workers," an organization lately founded, is an attempt among other things to organize this work. It is an axiom of the Theosophist that he will never allow his brother to be in distress. Indeed, at several of the Branches of the Society the Presiding officer, before the opening of the meetings, reads a notice calling on all those members who know of any distress in the ranks or outside to inform the members of the Branch, that they may have opportunity to carry out practically by the alleviation of suffering the first object of the Society—Brotherhood.

It would be wholly impossible to fully detail all the labors of the members of the Society in their endeavor to forward the movement and to inculcate those ideals of charity, good-will, tolerance, and religious and self-sacrificing life which they, by actively realizing in their own lives, have found to carry peace ; and which they are individually assured would, if striven after by the whole world, achieve the salvation of Humanity. The acts of the members too have been labors of love, and many of them must therefore remain forever unknown to few but the doer.

The growth of the Society has not come about through clever

and diplomatic management ; through patronage by the great ; through large resources. It has grown and increased in strength through the devotion of the members to the highest ideals ; to their reliance on the Great Law, the representative of the divine source of all things ; through their active work for the world ; and through their belief in and trust in that true Brotherhood of Humanity, of which the Mahatmas inspiring and directing our Society are the types. It is to form such a Brotherhood among the peoples of all nations that they labor ; to unite together Religions, Sciences, and Philosophies, breaking down the barriers of superstition, conceit, and envy. Our Society whose organization we have just examined must, like all other movements, run its time. It is but a bridge to greater and greater achievements by mankind in the future ; and to the eye of eternity it must be but a short-lived structure. But it will last for many ages, for it teaches the religion of the future —the religion without priest-craft or oppression. Its rest will only be known on the day when it has inspired all men to a reverence for its message—active altruism and spiritual discernment.

Mr. Wright then as Secretary to the Chairman read the following statistics sent by President H. S. Olcott :

BOOKS PUBLISHED IN INDIA UNDER THE AUSPICES OF THE THEOSOPHICAL SOCIETY FROM 1883.

Pamphlet	1.	Sanskrit Primer, by Pandit Nityanunda Misra.
"	2.	An Elementary Primer for Sanskrit, Telugu, and Tamil, by Dewan Bahadur R. Raghunatha Row.
"	3.	An Advanced Primer for Sanskrit, Telugu, and Tamil, by Dewan Bahadur R. Raghunatha Row.
"	4.	Hints on Esoteric Theosophy No. 1.
"	5.	Hints on Esoteric Theosophy No. 2, by A. O. Hume, Esq.
"	6.	Thoughts on the Metaphysics of Theosophy, by Sundaram Iyer.
"	7.	Paradoxes of the Highest Science.
Book	8.	A Collection of Lectures, by Col. Olcott, P. T. S., Madras Edition.
Pamphlet	9.	A Buddhist Catechism in English, by Col. Olcott.
Book	10.	Theosophy, by Dewan Bahadur P. Sreenivasa Row.
Pamphlet	11.	A Tamil translation of the 1st Upanishad, by Mr. T. Iyer.
Journal	12.	A Marathi Edition of the Theosophist at Poona.
Book	13.	Translation of Arnold's Light of Asia into Bengali Verse.
Pamphlet	14.	Telugu translation of articles in the Theosophist relative to Mahatmas, etc., by Purnayza.
"	15.	Urdu translation of Hints on Esoteric Theosophy.
"	16.	Translation into Urdu of the Rules of the T. S.
"	17.	Catechism of Hinduism (in Bengali) by N. K. Banergi.
"	18.	English translation of Isavasyopanishad.
"	19.	Madame Fox's Lectures in Madura, by Madura Branch.
Book	20.	Translation of Varahamiheras Samhita. by N. C. Iyer.
Pamphlet	21.	Translation of Sankracharyas Tatuabodha into Urdu.
Pamphlet	22.	Urdu translation of Col. Olcott's Lectures on the Civilization that India needs.
"	23.	Light on the Path, by M. C. (English Madras Edition.)
"	24	Telugu Catechism on Theosophy, by Guntur, T. S.
"	25.	Translation into Telugu of Panchakosavivada.
"	26.	Translation into Telugu of Patanjali's Yoga Aphorisms.
"	27.	Urdu translation of the Elixir of Life and the Occult World.
"	28.	Hindi translation of Atmanatmaviveka and T S. Rules.
"	29.	Publication of Lecture by Dorasami Pillai on Theosophy.
"	30.	Translation of Kena Upanishad.

Pamphlet	31.	Guzrati translation of Hints on Esoteric Theosophy No. 1.
"	32.	Major-General Morgan's Reply to Gribble's Pamphlet.
"	33.	Lecture on Duties of Man, by P. C. Mukerji.
"	34.	Lecture on the Logic of Common Sense, by Prof. M. N. Dvivedi.
"	35.	Translation of Vakysutha.
"	36.	Translation of Aparokshanubhuti.
Book	37.	Paul's Yoga Philosophy edited by Mr. Tukaram Tatya.
"	38.	English translation of Bhagavadgita, by Wilkins.
Pamphlet	39.	A Handbook of Theosophy in Urdu
"	40.	Urdu translation of the Elixir of Life, by Rai Kishen Lall.
"	41.	A Short Treatise on Homœpathic, by Rai Kishen Lall.
"	42.	A Lecture in English on Yoga, by Mr. V. Krishna Iyer.
"	43.	English translation of Sankaracharya's Atomabodh.
"	44.	English translation of a Portion of the Unpublished Writings of Eliphas Levi.
"	45.	Hinduism : A Retrospect and Prospect
Book	46.	Bengali translation of Colebrooke's English edition of Sankhya Karika.
Pamphlet	47.	Tamil translation of Col. Olcott's Lecture on the Past, Present, and Future of India.
"	48.	A Tamil Translation of Light on the Path.
"	49.	A cheap Edition of that work (English), specially prepared for India.
Book	50.	The Purpose of Theosophy, by Mrs. Sinnett (reprint).
Pamphlet	51.	Magic White and Black, by Dr. F. Hartmann.
"	52.	The Atomabodh translated into English, by B. P. N.
Journal	53.	The Jamai Ul-Uloon, a Monthly Urdu Journal, by Moradabad, T. S.
Book	54.	A Second Edition of Patanjali's Yoga Philosophy, edited by Tukaram Tatya.
Pamphlet	55.	Hindi translation of Tatwabodh.
"	56.	Bengali translation of Prasnottaramala, by Bholanath Chatterji.
Book	57	Prabodhachandrodaya.
Pamphlet	58.	Psychometry and Thought-Transference. by N. C.
"	59.	A New Indian Edition of the Buddhist Catechism.
"	60.	A Madhva Catechism by P. Sreenivasa Row.
Book	61.	A Compendium of Rajayoga, by M. N. Dvivedi.
Pamphlet	62.	Sayings of Grecian Sages.
"	63.	Perils of Indian Youth ; a Lecture by Col. Olcott.
"	64.	The Aim of Life by Siddheshwar Ghose.
"	65.	A translation in Urdu of the Lecture entitled, The Civilization that India needs.
Book	66	The Zoroastrian and other Religions. by Dhunjibhoy Jamsetji.
"	67.	The Phaedo of Plato. reprint. by Dhunjibhoy Jamsetji.
"	68.	Bhagavatgita in Sanskrit, with Commentary in Telugu Character, by C. Ramiah.
"	69.	Vicharasagara in Hindustani. edited by S. S Mahomed.
"	70.	Rigveda Samhita (text only), by Bombay T. S. P. Fund.
"	71.	Bhagavadgita, 2d Edition.
"	72.	Sankhya Karika. by Bombay T. S. P. Fund.
Pamphlet	73.	Epitome of Aryan Morals. 11.000 copies.
"	74.	Psychometry and Thought Transference. 2d Edition.
"	75.	Golden Rules of Buddhism, by Col. Olcott.
"	76.	Visishtadwaita Catechism, by Pandit Bhashyacharya.
Pamphlet	77.	Canarese Edition of Aryan Morals.
Book	78.	Siva Sanhita (trans.) by S. C. Basu.
"	79.	Mumukshamargopadesini in Telugu.
"	80.	Brihat Jataka (trans.) by N. C. Iyer.
"	81.	Shatpanchasika (trans) by N. C. Iyer.
"	82.	Jinendramala with Notes (trans.) by N. C. Iyer.
"	83.	Discourses on Bhagavatgita by Mr. T. Subba Row.
Pamphlet	84.	Light on the Path (trans.) in Sanskrit by Bhashya Charya.
Book	85.	The 1st Ashtak of the Rigveda Samhita with Bhashya.
Pamphlet	86.	A New Edition of Bhagavatgita in Sanskrit.

Book	87.	Krishna Yajurneda. in Sanskrit Devanagari Type.
"	88.	Krishna Yajurneda, in Telugu Type.
"	89.	Divya Suri charitram by A. Govindacharlu.
Pamphlet	90.	Sadhana chathustaya, by R Jagannathiah.
"	91.	The Morals of Bharatam, by R S. Pandiah.
Book	92.	The Desatir, by Dhunjibhoy J. Mehta.
Pamphlet	93.	Raja yoga by Manilal N Dvivedi.
"	94.	Sayings Grecian Sages, Part II.
"	95.	Urdu translation of Paul's Yoga Philosophy.
"	96.	Sinshu catechism.
"	97.	Improved Edition of Visishtadwaita catechism.
"	98	Tamil translation of Elementary B. catechism.
"	99.	Selections from White & Black Magic translated into Urdu.
"	100.	New Edition of Raja yoga.
"	101.	Monism. or Adwaitism.
Book	102.	New Edition of Patanjali's Yoga Philosophy.
Pamphlet	103.	Tamil translation of Probadh Chandrodaya.
Book	104.	Complete Edition of Rigveda Samhita with Commentary.
Pamphlet	105.	Introduction to the Kabalah.
"	106.	Sabdakalpadruma.
Book	107.	Rigveda Brahmana in Telugu character.
Pamphlet	108.	The Gnyana and Karma Meanings of first four Anwakams.
"	109.	Mantrapushpam, with meanings.
"	110.	Sathathapa Dhurma Sastram.
"	111.	Sathathapa Samhita.
"	112.	Sathathapa Likhita Samhita.
"	113.	Sathathapa Likhita Somhita.
"	114.	Senkha Dhurma Sastram.
"	115.	Senkha Likhita Sastram.
"	116.	Budha Dhurma Sastram.
"	117.	Yagmya Valkiya Smriti.
"	118.	Brahaspati Dharmasastram.
"	119.	Pulasthiya Dharmasastram.
"	120.	Hareetha Dharmasastram.
"	121.	Vrudha Parasara Smriti.
"	122.	Devala Smriti.
"	123.	Buddhism, translated into Urdu.
"	124.	The Aitareya Brahmana
Book	125.	Principal Twelve Select Upanishads.
"	126.	Poetical Works of Tukaram Bava.
"	127.	Poetical Works of the followers of Tukaram Bava.
"	128.	Complete Poetical Works of Dadupath.
Book	129.	Srimat Bhagavata
Pamphlet	130.	Atmabodh, translated into Guzrati.
"	131.	Zoroastrianism in the Light of Occult Phil.
"	132.	Raja yoga, by M. N. Dvivedi (2d Edition).
"	133.	Telugu translation of Mahabarata.
"	134.	Telugu translation of Light on the Path.
"	135.	"The Sandhyavandana" or "the Daily prayers of Brahmins."
"	136.	Urdu translation of Key to Theosophy.
"	137.	Bhagavat gita (Pocket Edition in Sanskrit Text in Devanagari) Cheap Edition.
"	138.	Peril of Indian youth. New Edition Col. Olcott's Lectures.
"	139.	The Place of Peace. by Mrs. Annie Besant (Madras reprint).
"	140.	Prasnottara, Vols. I. and II.
"	141.	Rough outline of Theosophy (Madras reprint)
"	142.	The Stanzas of Dzyan. by H. P. B. (Madras reprint.)
"	143.	The Uttaragita, by Tukaram Tatya.
"	144.	Vedanta vartikam by B. P. Narasimiah.
"	145.	Yoga the Science of Soul, by Mr. Mead (Madras reprint).
"	146.	Asceticism, by Col. Olcott.
"	147.	Why I became a Theosophist (reprint).
"	148.	Absolute Monism, by Sundram Iyer.
"	149.	Annie Besant on Theosophy (reprint).

Pamphlet 150. Theosophical Gleanings, No. 1.
" 151. Theosophy for School boys, by O. L. Sarma.
" 151. Kinship between Hinduism & Buddhism, by Col. Olcott.
" 152. Guide to Theosophy, by Tukaram Tatya.
" 153. Ramayana, by Tulasi Dass. Edited by Kundan Lal.
" 154. Kanarese translation of Dwaita Catechism.
Journal 155. Theosophic Thinker, by R. Jagannathiah.

The above list certified as correct this 2d day of August, 1893, at Adyar, Madras.

H. S. OLCOTT,
Prest. Theosophical Society.

LIST OF SCHOOLS IN INDIA AND CEYLON UNDER THE AUSPICES OF THE THEOSOPHICAL SOCIETY.

	Girl's Vernacular Schools.		Boys' Vernacular Schools.		English Schools. Registered.	Mixed Schools.	Industrial Schools.
	Registered.	Unregistered.	Registered.	Unregistered.			
CEYLON ..	4	1	4	9	5	7	2
						Total,	32

	Sanskrit Schools.	Anglo Sanskrit.	Anglo Vernacular.	Sunday Moral Schools.	Elementary Vernacular Schools.	Girls' Schools.	TOTAL.
INDIA	15	4	4	5	6	4	38

Certified as correct this 2d day of August, 1893, Adyar, Madras.

H. S. OLCOTT,
Pres't Theosophical Society.

THE MISSION OF THE THEOSOPHICAL SOCIETY.

PROF. CHAKRAVARTI.

LADIES AND GENTLEMEN—I come from a land hoary with antiquity. I belong to a race bent with age. I profess a religion the dawn of which is, according to our mythology, simultaneous with the dawn of creation, and the greatest research has not been able to prove to the contrary. The religion I belong to was once gigantic in its strength. It was like the mighty oak round whose trunk crept the various ivies, with all the moral, political, and social institutions and organizations of my mother country. But even an Indian sky is not without its cloud. Time came when this oak round which all the institutions were twined, lost its sap. It seemed that all the institutions would wither away with the passing away of the life of the oak round which all of them clustered. It seemed that the mighty edifice with all its grand architecture was tottering, and once we were about to exclaim, " Shrine of the Mighty, is this all that remains of thee?" Yet this shrine of the Mighty Religion seemed once to be gasping for breath. It seemed that every moment might be its last, and that in spite of the inherent strength which it had in its constitution, it must die at last. What better proof can I give you of its native inherent vigor and its essential truth than the fact that it has for ages and ages been able to resist the buffets and blows of the outside world? Centuries after centuries have rolled over its hoary head. Empires after empires have risen and fallen upon its mighty breast. Foreign invasion and destructive revolutions have battered it with mighty armies ; waves and surges of foreign ideas have permeated through its bosom ; and yet it stands to-day, moss-covered, it may be, but yet a monument of what truth can be, and of what the mighty Rishis, the great ancestors and progenitors of the Hindus, the depositaries of the sacred truths, can accomplish. And yet that very religion of whose strength I am now talking to you, seemed to be going into the bottomless abyss of oblivion.

At such a moment as this, at such a juncture, which was only about fifteen years ago, when all those who knew what the religion was felt an anxiety about its future, when they saw that the frail moral bark of the Hindu youth had left the shore, was receding from its haven of rest and peace, and that slowly but surely and steadily it was proceeding on to be shattered against the rock of materialism, which in India had swept in from the West, their hearts were sad with the most dismal forebodings. The materialism of Europe had reached India through the influence of our Governors. Schools were established in which, according to the policy of a religious neutrality, nothing but secular education is given. The minds of the Indian youths who resorted to these schools in preference to the Sanscrit schools where a religious education was given, became imbued with materialism. They would not go to their old schools, and why? Because in India there is also a struggle for life, as everywhere else, although to very much less extent. All the prized positions of life, all the appointments of government, were reserved for those who had obtained the advantage and the so-called blessings of the so-called liberal education of the English Schools and Colleges. The rooms became filled, and in them they learned a lot of intellectual culture, a great deal of science, and a great deal, I regret to say, of material philosophy. Their minds originally pure, originally spiritual, originally imbued with the spirit of their religion, lost their color, and became covered over with a thick crust of ideas which came from the West. They began to think that, after all, their mighty Rishis, after all, the religion that had nestled them in its lap, might be a delusion, might be false; that all the light of the modern sun which had shone resplendent in the West showed no such illusion, does not show to the sight those grand truths that they had taken with their mothers' milk; and, dazed with the false electric light of modern philosophy, with the light of modern civilization, they proved false and became traitors to their traditions, to their associations, to their mothers' milk and their mothers' bosom. They thought that truth could be found only in the pages of Huxley and Spencer, and they ran after those theories of material existence, material thought, and material consciousness with which you are only too familiar.

At the moment of this crisis, help was bound to come, because India's death-note had not yet struck. It had yet its mission to perform in the history of the world. It had yet to help the coming tide of evolution, it had yet to send its ideas across oceans, to lift the million souls; and therefore help came. But not from its mighty Shastras, not from its learned priests and Brahmins, who were the traditional teachers of mankind. But strange and inscrutable are the ways of Heaven. Help came from a quarter from which it was least expected—least looked for. It came from the West. Across oceans and continents reached forth the helping hand which was to save that frail bark which was proceeding towards death. Yes, from the land in which you were born and imbibed doctrines of materialism, to that land belongs the honor, the credit, the satisfaction of having saved India from that terrible destiny.

From this land went out two persons in the form of Madame Blavatsky and Colonel Olcott, with all their inspirations derived from that great storehouse of the East, from that tremendous accumulated spiritual energy of the East, but unknown through the West. There came this Society, with the wonders and successes that have followed in its train. They went about the country and sounded trumpet calls to the Hindus, saying, "Oh, sons of India, how long is the slumber to last? Will you never wake to the consciousness that you are the spiritual progenitors of mankind? From you, as from the sun, have radiated the different religions which are now the centre of light to so many races of the world. Will you never awaken to the consciousness that in your own books, within your own bosoms, may be found that fount of truth from which have proceeded streams of immortal, spiritual verity?" We heard, first with suspicion, then with doubt. It cannot be true. Can this be true? It is too good to be true; but yet we searched, we examined, we looked, we criticised, and to our surprise, what a pleasant disappointment it was! We knew we were wrong. We examined our books, and below the superficial crust we found that amid the ores of our Shastras there were real and magnificent specimens of brilliant diamonds. We awoke to the consciousness that our religion was not, after all, the contemptible and despicable monster which the Christian ministers had taught us to regard it. The truths and the propositions which in our own Shastras lay buried with the dust of ages, began once more to reveal their bright surface to our eyes. Why? Because they were presented, not in the old traditional forms, but in the modern form of the West. To that woman, H. P. Blavatsky, was given the proud privilege of putting truths into the East and into the bosom of the Hindus, in a form which was to draw them again to their own religion. Thus Hinduism was presented again to the Hindus, decked up again with all the trappings of modern science and enriched with the metaphysical notions of modern German philosophical thought, and young India, which had ere long revelled in the intoxicating drink of modern science and modern philosophy, saw that its religion stood even the test of what it considered the climax of human intellection. It returned, therefore, to the study of its own Shastras, to appreciate its own religion, and to-day we are very much nearer our old home than we were fifteen years ago.

It has been asked how it was possible that the East in which there are so many spiritual beings, in the East which has the satisfaction of having the largest store of spiritual knowledge, could have required any aid from the West. The answer is, that the ways of working in the East and the West are entirely different. In the East the ways are very often on the spiritual plane. The man of knowledge in the East waits until he can develop in himself capacities to work on a plane which is higher and nobler than any of which you have any conception. The work done on the spiritual plane produces an element which bears no comparison to any that can be produced on the physical or on the intellectual plane. But in India, as everywhere else in the world, there is a large mass of humanity which is not spiritual enough to be taken into the sanctum of that spiritual training. There is a large class of mankind which can only be reached on the plane of intellect, and this class cannot be neglected. All different parts of human society are different; part of mankind which has not advanced so far as to be directly touched on the plane of spirit requires to be reached on the intellectual plane, and this work was supplied by the Theosophical Society.

In the work of propaganda, in the work of spreading the truths which were really in the Shastras, but which were neglected, unseen, misunderstood, in the work of supplying the mind of young India, gorged with the food of materialism, some real pabulum of truth, in order to maintain its spiritual vigor, the Theosophical

Society has been an inestimable boon, and the people of India realize this, and, as has been already read to you by Brother Wright, they are now opening up their own treasures for the benefit of the West. The great books of occultism are now being translated into the language of the West, for the benefit of the brothers who have been of such opportune help to them.

Here in the West I have been struck with the amount of real advance that you have made, but that advance, I am sorry to say, represents but one phase of the human constitution. It represents but a partial development of the entity which we call Man. It has been explained to you already in the course of these sessions that Man is a composite being, and that the physical part of man, although great, is by no means the all-important one. The all-important part of man is of a spiritual nature, which, indeed, requires cultivation, and without which all material advance is but as dross. You therefore want here what the East can give you—the light of spiritual truths, and when you have that, it will prove to be like the philosopher's stone, which, whatever it touches, it turns into gold. All your luxuries, all your material advancement, will not then be the poor material things which they are now. In the light of the spirit they will all shine bright. They will all have their proper place, and by the influence of the Theosophical Society may be brought about that day when with all your material advancement you may be able to walk in the light of the spirit with dreams of that eternal home, with that sweet, balmy breath which alone can make the things of flesh really pleasant. India feels to-day the debt which it owes to the West, and therefore I believe that the Theosophical Society in the future has a very grand mission to perform. It has for its project the grand unification of the East and the West, the organizing effort of the West and the spiritual energy of the East,—the head of the West and the heart of the East.

And it is only from this unity, it is only from a compact between spirit and matter, it is only by mutual help, each supplying what the other needs, that we can bring about that Universal Brotherhood which all of us are striving for. And even now, I say that it has been my practical experience that the idea has been more or less realized.

Why, I am of the Brahmin community, a community which has been aristocratic enough to show itself unwilling to have intercourse with the modern world, and I have left that community, I have left my home,—and why? To see, to meet, to talk to, to stand on a common platform with my brothers in the West who are fighting for the same idea, living for the same truth, drinking from the brink of the same fountain ; and I shall not surprise you when I say that in this strange land, in this land where I cannot see even one face which belongs to my own race and my own clan, I have met the very kindest treatment,—nay, strong and warm brotherly affection. Wherever I have been, my heart has been touched to the quick by the immense love which has been accorded to me. I have been treated everywhere I have been as a member of their own family, as one who has been dear to them for ages and ages, and one between whom and them there did exist no wall whatsoever. This has touched my heart, and I shall go back and tell my people the welcome you have accorded me, the heartiness with which you have greeted me, the brotherly warm hand you have extended to me. And India is not ungrateful, in spite of the slanders and miserable representations which have been cast upon its poor face. India, I say, is not ungrateful. It will remember your love, and will try its best, whatever its poor mite can, to repay the heavy debt which you have laid it under. And yet—yes, even now—I can see the withered and gaunt hands of the spirit of my mother land, land of mysteries, land of occultism, land of sanctity, stretching out across oceans and continents, and from its fingers flowing out plentiful currents of its sentient spirituality over the heads of the people of America, shedding its blessings of peace and of love.

THE SOCIETY ABSOLUTELY UNSECTARIAN, WITHOUT A CREED, AND OPEN TO PERSONS OF ALL FAITHS ACCEPTANCE OF DOCTRINES LARGELY TAUGHT IN THEOSOPHICAL LITERATURE NOT INCUMBENT. ITS RELATION TO CIVIC AFFAIRS AND EDUCATION.

WILLIAM Q. JUDGE.

BROTHERS AND SISTERS—It is now my duty to attempt to deal further with the subject of the Organized Life of the Theosophical Society. Brother Wright has taken up some points which I would have taken up in other circumstances; Brother Chakravarti has outlined to you as a Brahman, as a member of the Indian Section, what he thinks is the mission of the Theosophical Society and what its mission there so far has resulted in. You have had from Brother Wright a great deal of fact. He must have conveyed to you the impression that the Theosophical Society has accomplished a good deal of work, or else that we have been telling a lie, one or the other. I think that you will believe him, that we have accomplished an enormous amount of work in eighteen years against most strenuous and bitter opposition. And it is the custom in America, and especially in the West, and most especially in Chicago, to measure results by money. How could we have accomplished all this, how could we have printed all those books without printing presses, without paper, without salaries, without people to do the work, and that you think takes money? Perhaps you think we have a secret fund from which we have drawn some millions, laid away amongst the buried treasures of India, which one or two of us can draw from now and then, so as to enable us to do work which other bodies can accomplish only by the use of money. But it is not so. We have little money and never had much. We do not want it, do not expect it, and the day when we shall have a large fund and be able to collect $5,000,000 in imitation of Western missionary bodies will be the day when the

Theosophical Society will die. It is not money that has done this. It is the energy of the human heart. These people who are here with me are only representatives of many, many persons all over the world who are willing to give their life, their energy, their time to a movement which they think will benefit man. They get nothing for it; they get no preference. What is it of honor to preside at a meeting like this? What is it for any person to be a member of a Branch? What is it to be the President of the Theosophical Society? Nothing at all. There is no honor in it whatever. There are no places, no salaries, nothing at all but work.

Brother Chakravarti gave you an idea of our future. It has been said against us that this movement of ours was an invention of the East, but he must have made you suspect that perhaps this movement is unique, that it came neither from the East nor the West. The East has solidified, crystallized, stood still; it would never have commenced such a movement. The West did not know about such things; it did not want them. We are wrapped up in material progress; it never would have started such a movement. Where, then, was the movement really started? It was started in the spiritual world above, both East and West, by living men. Not by spirits of dead men, but by living spirits, living spirits like yourselves, who have risen above creeds and nations and castes and peoples, and are simply human beings. They started this movement by giving the impulse and the message; that is why we who have been in it so long have the confidence born of knowledge, knowledge that it will succeed. And as Claude Wright told you, we began at the time under direction, when we knew that materialism was spreading, not only over the West, but was spreading insidiously all over the East. As Brother Chakravarti told you, it was turning the mind of the East, not to Christianity—never could that be done—but into the grossest forms of materialism. That is to say, that the West itself with its missionaries was corrupting a vast mass of men and turning them into men who believed in nothing but annihilation after this life. If you could have succeeded in converting them to Christianity, it would have been well enough, for then they could rise up higher out of that into another spiritual life. But instead of succeeding with them in that, as I know from facts, from having been there, you were simply flinging them from their own beliefs into materialism, and the Theosophic Society was started to prevent that, and to prevent it in the West also. It has done something towards it. It has not been the one cause, but it has been the little lever, the little point in the centre, around which we are all working with all effectual means for the good of humanity. It is trying to offer the key to all these Congresses and to show all men where the truth is.

Now, when the Theosophical Society was founded in 1875, if you could have heard what I did, you would have heard a huge laugh pass over the country by means of the newspapers. There was nothing else but laughter and jokes. The Society was an immense joke, they said; a new kind of spiritualism; something of that sort to tickle men's fancies, and we have had that to contend with all the time. But we have succeeded always in remaining at the post and saying just what we meant to say all the time for all the laughter. We took no salaries, but we had belief in the human heart.

The objects of the Theosophical Society having been explained to you by Brother Wright, you know the Society has but one doctrine, that of Universal Brotherhood. You cannot belong to it unless you believe in that ; you won't want to belong to it unless you believe in that. But you are not required to believe anything else. You are not required to believe in Brother Chakravarti ; you are not required to believe what, as the newspapers say, are the doctrines of "that woman Besant ;" you are not required to believe in Madame Blavatsky, who was a woman, a human being, just the same as the rest of us ; you are not required to believe in those great beings of whom Brother Chakravarti has been speaking. It has been supposed by some that in order to be a Theosophist you must believe in Mahatmas, that you must believe in H. P. Blavatsky, in re-incarnation, in Karma ; but you do not have to believe in any of those things at all. But, I take it, you must believe in Universal Brotherhood. And the reason why people have been a little confused is this : they have seen the Theosophical Society absolutely without a creed, absolutely without any dogma, and as inside of it they know of a large number of people who believe in those ideas and doctrines, they think that is what the Theosophist must believe. But it is not. For, don't you see, if we started a Universal Brotherhood, and started a Society to find out the truth, and then fixed a dogma, that moment we would be telling a lie and forfeiting the whole object we started to accomplish. We can never have a creed. We do not know what the truth is. It may be that we are wrong ; it may be we will find out more. It is true we will never go back to those old dogmas and creeds, although there are still many members on the books of the powerful churches. We can never go back there, but we may go further on, and we are quite willing to. We are promulgating our philosophies which we talk about as individuals and on our own account. As Vice-President of the Society I have no right to say that any particular thing is true, and I never do say so. But I have the right to say, as I myself emphatically do, that I as an individual believe certain things are true, and I would be a poor sort of man if, believing certain things to be true, I did not try to show that they are. But at the same time I have no right to say, as man or official, you must believe it because I do. I simply present it to you for your consideration, and it is for you to decide, not for me. I am not going to stop saying that I believe so and so because a few other persons cannot believe it. They can go on with me and we will agree to disagree, and we will only forward the cause of Universal Brotherhood. Because beliefs in particular creeds have nothing to do with how you treat another man. What creed is there in the statement republished by Jesus, promulgated by him, to do to others as you would have them do unto you? No creed about that ; no paving of hell with the skulls of infants about that ; no belief in a particular sort of transmission of the spiritual life from St. Peter or Paul in that; nothing at all to abridge the treatment of man and woman by man and woman in the way they should treat them. We have no creed, then, and we should have none.

But the question is often asked: What have you as an organization to do with labor, with legal questions, labor-saving forces, with education, with society? We have nothing to do with them. Is it not true that man, if he has a knowledge as to how he ought to live, needs no law whatever? Was not St. Paul right when he spoke of that and said: you would become your own law; knowing the truth, you need no law? What, then, has the Theosophical Society to do with law? If there are to be laws, let them be passed and execute them, but the Theosophical Society has nothing to do with it as such. But every brother in the Theosophical Society must obey the law of the land in which he lives, for he would be a poor Theosophist if he did not. And the Theosophical Society has nothing to do with education. But its members may have as much to do with it as they please. But they have no right to say what is the Theosophical Society's idea of education. They can only say "That is my idea of it." And always they must and shall preserve these distinctions. We have been asked, what about this labor struggle? We have been asked why we do not join the Bellamyites and other co-operative societies? If you want to go in, go in. The Theosophical Society, as such, has nothing to do with it. I am perfectly satisfied to live where I am and do my duty where I stand, without any new law of property, or with it, whichever you please. And the religion of the West which logically ought to support all the various socialists and anarchists and nihilists is the Christian religion, because in the beginning it was a community. Jesus' system was a community in which everything was common property, and the early Christians threw all their money and property into one common box. Why, then, should not the Christian religion logically carry out all the plans of the socialists, anarchists, nihilists, and all the other ists who want to change the face of the earth by legislation? But the Theosophist knows that legislation changes nothing whatever. There are laws now on every statute book in every State in the United States, laws enough if men would only execute them and live up to them. But a law that socialists shall share in this, or that there shall be no Trust in that, is passed; and then there are the lawyers to get around the law, as they always can. So what is the use of passing the law at all? There is no use whatever. Hence the Theosophical Society, as such, has nothing to do with such trumpery and democratic things as legislation. Let the men engaged in legislation go on legislating. If a Theosophist and he is born to be a legislator, or is born to be a judge, let him legislate as a citizen and not as a Theosophist, or let him be a judge and skilled lawyer. If they will know that philosophy which shows them what human life is, they will have begun to follow the law without knowing what the law is. America is the only land of all countries where the law is followed without the people knowing much of it. In America the people are orderly; they understand life a little better than other people in the world, but they don't know so much about the masses of laws they have on their books. I believe personally that the day is coming when America is to be the country where the new race will be born that will know all about the true laws and what is right, and will be able to perform it. So, then, the Theosophical Society is not prepared to give out promulgations as to this or that particular item of legislation or education or civic affairs that people would have taught.

They ask also about marriage. Why, you understand about marriage. You know how it is accomplished. We have nothing to do with it as a Society. We know there are many kinds of marriage, sometimes merely by tying a string, sometimes by walking around the fire. As a body we have nothing to do with these forms nor interfere in them. And as to prayer, if you want to pray, pray. But if you pray, and if you say you have a certain belief, live up to it. If you do not do so you are no Theosophist, nor a man, nor a proper living person. You are only a hypocrite. (Applause.)

Now, the Theosophical Society is an unsectarian body. It does not have a creed. It never will have one if those persons in it now can possibly prevent it. It does not need a creed. It is open to everybody, of all sects and faiths, and for that reason it has been possible to bring into it men of all religions, men from India, China, Japan, Brahmins, as you have seen and as you have already before your eyes, which could not have been accomplished by any sect, Christian, or Buddhist, or Brahman. If the Buddhists started in India a Buddhist society, the Brahmins would not accept it. And if the Brahmins started a Brahmin propagandist society, the Buddhists would say they did not want it. So it is with the various Christian denominations : the Baptists, the Catholics, the Methodists, the Presbyterians. If any one of them, as a society, asked others to come in, none of the other different stripes or classes of Christians would come in. Each says it teaches the truth ; still the others do not come in. But Theosophy comes forward boldly and says : " All religions have underneath one single truth. None of the religions are perfectly true. It is impossible that they should be, because man is prone to err. Come into the Society in which as brothers helping each other we will examine all these faiths so that we may find out the truth under all. For we believe that in the beginning of human evolution great teachers gave the truth out, one single truth before the mingling of tongues on the tower of Babel, to man." That single truth was variously accepted and variously perceived, and out of these different perceptions they built up different creeds, and so they made a great many different sorts of faiths. But suppose you look into all of them. You find the Christians teaching for many years that man has a soul. Do you think that the Christians are the only ones who taught about the soul? The Hindus have been teaching about the soul for ages. They have said always that man has a soul. The Japanese do the same thing. So do other races and religions. So in that one point they have always together been teaching the same thing. The Christians have been teaching about heaven and hell; about a sort of heaven which is very material, I admit, with pearly gates and golden streets and angels with robes such as no one ever saw and crowns upon their heads; and hell full of fire and brimstone, with devils throwing people around with forks into the fire. The Buddhists have been teaching the same thing for ages. I can read to you out of their books about a copper vessel full of boiling oil into which they say fate puts a man. In this he goes down and down for thousands and thousands of years until he gets to the bottom; then he begins to rise again to the top, rising for ages again, and when he gets to the top and thinks he is going to be let out, he begins to sink again, and that goes on for ages more. Is not that as bad and as material as the Christian hell? And then the Eastern teaching of heaven, of an inimitable and incomprehensible place, yet just as material but better than the Christian heaven. The Abbé Huc went to Tartary many years ago. He was a Catholic priest. There he found ministers, monks, nuns, similar ceremonies to the Romish, the ministers using the different vestments and draperies of the Catholics, the taper, bell, candle, the book, the rosary, what not, everything. He brought back the tale to Europe and he published it. The explanation of the priests—of course they would not say so now—was that it was the invention of the Devil, who, knowing that Christianity was going to be abroad, went ahead of it and founded that imitation in the East so that Christian people would be confused. Well now, that is not the way to explain it. The proper way is, that man has these things as a universal property and always makes some mistakes. And so it is in Buddhism and every other religion. In Tibet they have a pope who is the great successor of the original founder of the thing, just the same as the Catholic pope. I don't care what sort of Western religion you bring forward; the religions in the East are the older religions and the fountain, but there is a single stream of truth underneath all, and that single stream is what the Theosophical Society digs for and implores these religious men to find out. We ask them not to go before each other and say their own religion is the true one. But they ask if we can give mercy to a man's soul, wash away the blood from his hand, and take away his sin? We say, Come, we will wash away your sin. How? By giving men reasons to make them do differently. The history of the past shows that belief does not make men better. We think there is a philosophy which will compel them from within to do right, and that is what this search will reveal. It will reveal underneath all these religions this one diamond which shows its light through them all; then all men can perceive it, then there will no longer be any necessity for the Theosophical Society, or for either creed or church; it will simply be truth and the people will know. Look fairly and squarely at Christianity. I am simply asking you to consider facts. Here we have Jesus saying: Worship in secret. The Christians do not do it. Then there are all the different and contradictory statements made by the same religion. How can churches have the enormous cathedrals, the immense wealth, the cannons and soldiers in their possession, if they are the representatives of Christ? How can that be possible unless men are running after creeds and not truth? Even in the words of Jesus is to be found everything we want. I simply repeat to you that old truth taught by him long ago, for to find out the truth in respect to ethics is the chief object of the Theosophical Society, and to establish by Universal Brotherhood a basis from which that ethic may be preached, practiced, and followed without any mistake. Therefore, then, we ask you this: You have seen us here and you have seen our heathen; some of them are now on the platform. We would like to know what you think of our heathen (applause), and what you think of this heathen Society that has been so much abused? Is it a Society for spiritualism, for wonders, or for folly? It is here to talk common sense and not merely to talk about H. P. Blavatsky, a woman who is dead, but who was the grandest woman or man that I ever knew. It is not for that. It is to bring back the truth about the soul, which truth these heathens represent as well as we, and they themselves are just as much in error as we. They do not know much more about it than we do. But these poor heathen have in their philosophy a little better statement of the truth than we have been able to invent. (Applause.) So I would ask you to wipe out of your mind that hymn which has done so much harm to Christian men and women, which reads:

> "What though the spicy breezes
> Blow soft o'er Ceylon's isle,
> Where every prospect pleases,
> And only man is vile."

Wipe that idea completely out with a sponge, and then you will see that we are all brothers and that by tolerating each other, by looking into each other's beliefs, not setting up creeds and dogmas, we shall at last realize that great ideal germ of perfection, human brotherhood, which object has equally engaged the attention of the great Initiates of all the human race.

I am requested to announce that the World's Congress officers, in recognition of splendid success, have placed the Hall of Washington at our disposal for an extra public meeting on Sunday evening. (Applause.)

Adjourned until 3 p. m.

REINCARNATION OF THE SOUL A LAW OF NATURE.

JEROME A. ANDERSON, M. D.

By Reincarnation is understood the return of the human soul as a distinct, individualized ego or entity to earth, through repeated rebirths in physical bodies ; by a law of nature, that this process of reclothing in matter, or re-expressing in form, of the inner, ideating consciousness, is a universal law and obtains in every kingdom and upon every plane of the manifested Universe. The term Reincarnation is, of course, limited to those forms which are reclothed in flesh ; re-embodiment expresses the general law of which Reincarnation is a special instance.

A demonstration of the truth that Reincarnation of the human soul takes place under a general law of nature may be arrived at by phenomenal exegesis or by philosophical inquiry. As, however, mere phenomena, no matter how scientifically observed and classified, prove nothing except as they are philosophically explained, so phenomenal examination and philosophical explanation must, of necessity, proceed hand in hand, which will be the method of this paper.

As a kind of basis by means of which to study and classify all lower phenomena, three all-embracing aspects in nature of that which philosophers speak of as the Absolute must be considered. These are Matter, Force, and Consciousness. Differing schools of thought have given differing degrees of importance to each of these ; some going so far as to claim one or more as mere " properties " of the others. Theosophy is the sole philosophy in the West which recognizes all of the three as eternally co-existing hypostases of the One Absolute Existence, the Unknowable CAUSELESS CAUSE.

It is an axiomatic truth that the sum total within the Kosmos of both Force and Matter can neither be added to nor taken from. A very little consideration makes it evident that Consciousness is also an immutable Whole. It is equally apparent that neither Force, Matter, nor Consciousness has ever been nor ever can be dissociated upon finite or manifested planes ; that the presence of one always implies the presence of all three, in some degree. That this is a fact in regard to matter and force is now recognized and expressed in the scientific generalizations of the Conservation of Force and the Indestructibility of Matter. If incapable of dissociation, then, from its co-hypostases, Consciousness must also be conserved ; so that in these two generalizations of science are to be found the most conclusive evidence of the conservation of the consciousness of man, or of human intelligence. For Theosophy declares that, although composed of substance almost infinitely finer—and also infinitely more stable—than the coarse matter of our bodies, the human soul has a material basis whose associated force is displayed as ideation. Under the law of force-conservation and indestructibility of matter, this ideative or psychic force must be conserved, for it cannot be dissociated from its indestructible material base. The conception, even, of pure Consciousness without attributes, of pure Force without a material vehicle, or of Matter not held in form by some mode of energy, is unthinkable. That consciousness is conserved throughout one life is so universally present and palpable a fact that few recognize it because of its familiarity; yet the constant widening of our mental horizon, from the cradle to the grave, through conscious experiences, shows that psychic energy, thus called into activity by the play of our senses, is conserved, and enters largely as a factor into the formation of our personal character. At birth, mentality is almost a blank; in the ordinary life, it is the lower mental or sense-consciousness which has built up the greater portion of the man. So evident is this that materialism has fallen into the error of thinking that it has built up *all* the man—a thing which will be shown to be impossible farther on. It suffices for our present purpose to prove, by the indisputable evidence of the conservation of consciousness in one life, as shown in and through that constant widening of our conscious area because of continuous sense-experiences, in that ceaseless modification of character through this widening, that consciousness *is* conserved; and this not in any general or diffused way within the molecules of the brain, but as a real growth of personal character. One might, indeed, fill his brain-mind with an almost infinite amount of heterogenous sense-impressions—a veritable mental chamber for all kinds of past experiences—but of what avail would all the rubbish be if there were not the Inner Experiencer, in whom and by whom is experienced and expressed the modification of character thus brought about by this true conscious conservation? The rubbish in an old garret would be of just as great service in that conservation of consciousness shown in the creation of a personal character, as mental rubbish stored in the physical molecules of the brain, if there were not this permanent centre of consciousness, this Soul, as the conserving centre and basis, by whom all these sense-impressions are experienced, and in whom all their varied effects, in no wise resembling their original physical causes—the molecular sense-impacts—are conserved. We must admit, therefore, that consciousness is conserved; that the addition of consciousness through sense-experiences, or in any other manner, is as veritable an addition in magnitude as is that of molecule to molecule, or, mathematically, that two plus two equals four. A law which we find universal upon one plane of nature—even though this be the material or molecular one—must of necessity have an identical or analogous action upon all planes, for two utterly opposing forces or modes of motion in nature cannot exist. For they must be equal or unequal. If unequal, then in the abysses of past eternities the greater must have annulled or destroyed the action—and even the existence—of the lesser; if equal, then would all motion or change be impossible, and nature rest throughout eternity locked in the embrace of an infinite "dead center," and all the pulsings of Infinite Life cease. Therefore, if scientists are right—and who dares dispute this?—in assuming matter to be indestructible, the material base of the human soul is also indestructible ; if Force be eternally conserved, this includes psychic or mental force or energy ; and, unless we postulate the unthinkable proposition of the creation within space of something previously outside it, Consciousness is also conserved, and, of necessity, that which accompanies and controls both the other factors in human evolution, or the human soul.

But if, under the law, consciousness be conserved, how are we to be assured that this applies to the human soul as a *self*-conscious centre of permanent consciousness ? For a conservation of consciousness which does not carry forward to the new account the same Ego as a self-conscious experiencer and basis of this conservation is valueless as far as any practical elucidation of the mysteries of human existence is concerned. Again questioning nature, our unerring teacher—if we but possess the power to compel her to surrender her secrets—we observe, in harmony with preceding generalizations, an entire absence of any general or diffuse matter, force, or consciousness in any of her kingdoms. Every manifestation of force has its material vehicle, as also its directing intelligence, and—although this may sometimes be indiscoverable by our imperfect senses and clumsy instruments—its expression in form, in terms of true three-dimensional matter. In the Unknowable and Unmanifested, we may, perhaps, speculate about the "formless." In all the manifested Universe, "formless" is but a relative term—the measure of our finite capacities. Therefore, in the Manifested Universe there can be no consciousness except as expressed in conscious entities of some degree ; no force which is not modified and directed by the will of some grade of conscious beings ; no matter which is not ensouled by and the expression in form of some single entity or hierarchal host of associated entities in the awe-inspiring Universe of Life—aye, a Universe in which all is Life, and in which there is not, never was, and never can be such a thing as real death !

The Universe, then, is embodied consciousness ; is composed of infinite hosts of entities in equally infinite states of consciousness and manifestations of form. Upon our earth, scientists declare that all organic life is in a process of evolution ; that the threshold of consciousness in man and throughout nature is being continuously displaced by this process. This is too often looked upon as an evolution of form only. It is an evolution of form, indeed, but a form whose sole object is to afford higher and more perfect vehicles for the expression of the inner consciousness. Thus evolution, which Theosophy carries into every kingdom and upon every plane of nature, shows that the conservation of intelligence, as gathered from conscious experiences in matter, is at the very foundation of nature's methods ; the logical and philosophical *raison d'être* for material existence. Yet as matter, force, and consciousness are eternally associated, as the entire Universe is composed of hierarchal hosts of conscious entities, Reincarnation, or re-embodiment, is the only process by which this conservation of intelligence becomes possible. How can the wisdom resulting from material experiences—the joys, the agonies, the intellectual achievements, the incessant modifications of character through this widening of the conscious area—be conserved, unless the experiencer of them all remains untouched by the change called death? How has the water-breathing vertebrate passed the fathomless chasms which interrupt physical evolution, until we now behold it a flying denizen of the heavens, if there has not been an inner abiding entity, which *was* the fish and which *is* the bird? Into what impossible region of nothingness has the widening consciousness been preserved at each of the innumerable deaths of the outer form which have interposed between the idea present and potent in the fish and its conscious consummation in the soaring eagle? "By being stamped upon matter," perhaps the shallow theorist babbles—not far enough advanced in his own evolution to have become a really rational thinker—"by having been transmitted from parent to offspring through physical heredity." In all the boundless domains of nature, where can there be found one single instance of the transmitting of the results of the self-conscious experiences of one life to its offspring? The son of the wisest parents gets naught from them but his physical form,—a material strait-jacket which but cramps and limits the powers of his soul, and which transmits nothing but such limitations. He profits not from the wide experiences which the parent has undergone; he is isolated from the knowledge and wisdom resulting from those experiences by a gulf which nothing material nor physical can possibly bridge over. Out of his own experiences must he really learn that fire will burn him on the physical plane; that vice will taint him, and pure thoughts elevate him, on the moral plane. So, from his own centre of consciousness, out of his own experiences, must he reconstruct his old-new character. And he who thinks the process of character constructing is begun anew with each birth, is but a myopic observer. Nature is not mocked; consciousness is ever conserved; and the mighty sweep of evolution on all her planes proceeds with as irresistible a power as that with which the avalanche descends to the valley beneath. The conservation of energies arising out of conscious experiences must be by the same entity, or it is no true conservation, and nature but a chapter of chaotic accidents.

"Every entity in the Universe," says the *Secret Doctrine*, "either is, was, or prepares to become a man;" thus throwing the light of the East upon the half-understood and but half-accepted evolutionary hypotheses of Western science. Every atom, every elemental ensouling the humblest lichen, every hierarchal host embodied in the lowest mineral form of which we can conceive,—each and all are on their way to manhood, and thence to godhood, in a Universe which is but an infinite becoming. Science recognizes the fact that each separate cell of the human, or of any other organic body, is a life, with its own life-history on its own plane of conscious experiences. Eastern wisdom concurs, and further declares that every atom is a life, and that atomic choice, as seen in so-called chemical "affinities," is a display of consciousness which evolution and conscious conservation will some day lift to the plane of self-consciousness—and a man will have become! In all the stupendous process, no other entity has ever trespassed upon the sacred, indestructible area of a centre of consciousness thus differentiated within the Whole; and, in all the unthinkable æons of conscious experiences yet to come, never can so trespass. That which has entered the domain of manifested life, the great Cycle of Necessity, can only disappear when all manifested being becomes again Non-Being—returns to enter those eternally subjective realms in which it had its origin.

But enough of philosophical generalizations. Let us now seek for specific proof that Reincarnation is the general law of nature and the very process of evolution, as has been asserted. At the beginnings of organic life, evidence is at once available; for, whether in the vegetable or animal kingdom, there can be no rational cause for ova, almost identical in form and absolutely so in molecular construction—so far as microscope or molecular physics can determine—diverging, the one into the form of a delicate fern, the other into that of the giant Sequoia; for this developing into the canine, that, into the human form. The general forces of nature brought to bear upon each ovum are the same; the matter of which the form is constructed is absolutely identical. And the cells, even, of which each body is built up, when their consciousness is analyzed, are found to be almost infinitely below that of the entity of which materialism fancies they are the creator. The thinking, reasoning, willing, philosophising human soul, being assumed to be the product or sum of the consciousness of cells so far beneath it, is a case of the effect being assumed to be greater than the cause—of the stream rising higher than its source —with a vengeance! No; there has been an inner energy guiding and controlling the form-building; or, under the general, impersonal forces of nature, divergence would have been impossible. This inner entity is, therefore, no more dependent upon the body for its existence than is the swallow upon the nest which it likewise constructs for the purpose of temporary habitation. There is no possible reason for the origin and subsequent repetition of form, except the return to material existence of an entity which has rebuilt the old form, and now proceeds to its evolutionary task of imperceptibly modifying that form to afford expression for its slowly widening conscious area. There is also no possible explanation for any subsequent evolutionary modification, except as the result of the energy of an inner entity thus seeking a vehicle for the more perfect expression of its conserved consciousness.

Hearken to the overwhelming testimony of nature! In the vegetable kingdom, every rebuilding of the same form, flowering, and leafage of the plant from root, rhizome, bulb, or seed, is absolutely unimpeachable evidence that the same entity has returned, as cycle or season has afforded opportunity. And these can only afford opportunity; they have no more to do with the actual repetition of form, with the wonderful divergence which follows the fructification of the germ cell, than has the ocean with the intelligence which directs the ships from port to port across its wastes of water.

The seeds or bulbs are identical in the material elements entering into their construction; the same soil receives them; the same sun warms them; identical showers moisten them; they breathe a common atmosphere,—all the external forces of nature which play upon them are absolutely identical. If there were no inner force, no centre of modifying energy within, then would all form not only be identical, but form itself be inconceivable. It is upon the stable, unvarying action of the forces of nature composing our external environment that all physical sciences depend; that enables man to forecast his future, to sow in its season the grain, and to construct all that marvelous domain which we contra-distinguish from nature when we term it Art. Then how absurdly illogical, how utterly unreasonable, it is to attribute to these outer common forces of nature, upon whose stable, unvarying action our very material existence depends, the source of that higher, conscious energy which compels such infinite variation in the very face of and in opposition to these lower forces of nature. In the variation thus in opposition to the material forces of this plane, we are shown the superiority of the inner force; in the repetition of the same form and foliage, we are taught that the forces of this inner one are also stable and unvarying action, and which renders thus additionally sure the conservation of consciousness stored upon these planes. All existence proceeds under the law of alternating objective and subjective cycles—of day and night, of sleeping and waking, of action and re-action—and to this law, men, atoms, and gods alike bow. And the plant, that gave no evidence in the withered root or bulb that the beautiful foliage and coloring of last year lay hidden in the ugly shriveled mass, has but again reached the objective arc of its existence—has passed through its arc of apparent non-existence, without losing one iota of those distinguishing characteristics which made it a denizen of a definite genus, family, and species.

Passing to the animal kingdom, we find the evidence of an inner, controlling, reincarnating entity still more pronounced. In the metamorphosis of insects, in that wonderful transformation of the form and functions by which the repulsive caterpillar emerges as the beautiful butterfly, without even having abandoned the old material vestment, is to be found the most positive evidence that an inner, independent entity has rebuilt the old molecules into the new form. Every such transformation is the law of reincarnation or re-embodiment exemplified before our very eyes, as though nature were determined we should not misinterpret her design nor mistake her methods. The metempsychosis of larvæ into pupæ and perfect insects is just as wonderful, just as incomprehensible, as is the metempsychosis or transmigration of the old butterfly entity through its subjective arc of seeming annihilation. That accomplished before our vision is just as subjective as that which has escaped our ken; the metamorphosis of pupæ into insect being accomplished in an entire absence of that food supply which is so necessary to the scientific conception of the creation of the energy necessary for molecular change. We are as entirely unable to explain the one as the other, and the real entity about which the form is builded is just as hidden from us in its objective transformation as in its subjective metempsychosis.

It is only by the continuous widening of consciousness by repeated—almost endless—re-embodiments of consciousness-conserving entities that evolution becomes possible. It is only thus that the human kingdom is slowly attained, and self-consciousness, the apparent object of all evolutionary effort, conquered. The method of nature seems to be, briefly, this:

An automatic centre of consciousness differentiates within the Absolute; passes by involution, or the reverse facet of evolution, through the elemental into the very depths of the mineral kingdom; adds to its primal, atomic consciousness that of molecular association; rises to the vegetable kingdom, widens its conscious area by expression in all the wilderness of forms in this kingdom; becomes too great by virtue of this widening to longer find a fitting vehicle here, and is compelled by the great evolutionary wave to seek the animal kingdom; widens or adds to its consciousness again, until it at last reaches the human-animal plane, that of the beginnings of self-consciousness, and thus becomes a fitting vehicle to afford expression for the human soul. Every step in this ascent of the ladder of being, though so easily pointed out, has occupied æons of time, and not one instant during the unthinkable periods of this becoming has it lost the identity stamped upon it at the dawn of differentiation by that unknowable, incomprehensible Wisdom and Power, of which we grope for a conception when we name it, in words which have for finite minds no real meaning, the CAUSELESS CAUSE! There has been a steady progress from atom to man, and will be from man to god. Reincarnation, *plus* re-embodiment, is the key, and the only rational key, to the whole awe-inspiring process.

Thus has man come upon this stage of life; in this grand law may we read the history of his wonderful past and the prophecy of his glorious future. In his every relation to his environment, whether mental, physical, or spiritual, may be seen the workings of the law by which he has attained to his present state, and at a few of these evidences, especially along philosophical and ethical lines, we must now briefly glance.

We have seen that the conservation of force includes that of consciousness, and therefore the conservation of our sense consciousness,—of the thoughts, emotions, feelings, volitions, and sensations of our daily existence. All of these, as science truly teaches, are manifestations of energy, requiring the transferring of the products of that energy to some stable centre or plane, if they are really conserved and the universal law not violated. That the law is not violated, that the energies of a human life are not dissipated at death, the differences in human character amply testify. There is nothing in the environment of one brief life to cause or account for the infinite diversity in character which is manifested in the world to-day. Each such character is the product of an almost infinite past; and it *is* this past, and not the impersonal environment which acts and reacts upon all beings alike, which has caused this difference. The product of sense-consciousness, thus stored unconsciously, constitutes character; and is carried forward life after life as a basis upon which and to which the energies generated anew by the sense-consciousness and other experiences of each life are to be added. But, in order to avoid any appearance of begging the question, the present examination will be confined first and chiefly to the evidences of reincarnation which attend birth; leaving, for briefer consideration, all the vast array of proofs provided by a survey of the entire human life.

At the entrance upon this sphere of existence by a human soul, if that soul be a new creation as taught by Christianity, or the mere bundle of "properties" of matter, capable of experiencing agony or joy, as Materialism claims, we are confronted with the gravest and most grievous questions of justice and injustice which surround this entrance, and of which the new-born soul is either the perfectly innocent victim or the unmeriting recipient. This, too, upon both the mental and physical planes. Upon the latter, we have one child born heir to the British throne; another to Hottentot or Bushmen parentage; one soul comes to gentle, pure, refined parents; another to brutal, diseased, drunken, or criminal ones—inoculated with both vice and disease by its very mother's milk! One emerges from the womb crippled or deformed; another inherits all the graces of both form and feature.

Mentally, the injustice is even more appalling. One child is born a genius; another an idiot; one inherits the most lovable disposition; another wears the gallow's brand stamped upon his brow from birth. Justice demands that each soul should have equal opportunities, equal mental and physical capacities at birth, if it be a new soul, whatever inequalities may attend a future in which it does have some choice. If, in choosing these natal and ante-natal conditions, it has had absolutely no voice—as must be the case if it has never been on earth before—then is the law of cause and effect an idle fancy arising in the mind of the scientist, and justice an idea to be dreamed of by man, the creature, but denied to Nature, the Creator! another illustration of the folly of attributing to the effect qualities which are not equally present in the cause. The very conception of justice, faint and perverted as it too often is, which arises in men's minds, is due—cannot but be due—to that perfect and inviolable justice which holds the entire Universe in its perfect control, and under which man's being, in common with every manifestation of life or energy, proceeds. The one-birth theorist, whatever his belief or disbelief in other directions, assigns all these cases of monstrous injustice to the "accident of birth." He who believes in a god, omniscient and omnipotent, must attribute to that god, if all-wise and all-powerful, an indifference and cruelty against which his own mind would revolt if not benumbed by an abject fear of this god whom he thus unconsciously blasphemes. He who bases his faith upon the "properties-of-matter" theory of the soul, must admit that in that case nature is devilish and cruel, while both, as has been pointed out, with the strangest inconsistency make the created greater than the Creator—the effect greater than the cause—a thing we might forgive the theologian, but hardly the scientist or philosopher! For, if man be the product of material evolution alone, of "blind force taking the direction of the least resistance," if there be no consciousness hidden within the subjective realms of nature greater than that which is thus apparently the result of physical evolution, if man indeed represents the highest consciousness in the scale of life on this planet, then does his mind, as having arisen out of the play of "blind, unconscious force thus taking the direction of least resistance," make the effect—the created, self-conscious man—infinitely greater than the cause, the unconscious, blind force which has called him into existence! And if a creator be assumed, yet Reincarnation denied, then is that omniscient, omnipotent creator, the cause, far below the effect, man, in his conceptions of justice, to say nothing of those of mercy or compassion! The fact that man can recognize the injustice of these birth inequalities shows that the idea of justice is an attribute of the divinity in nature, and that any seeming injustice must be explained by a deeper inquiry of nature as to her methods.

This deeper, more philosophical conception required to explain the seemingly unjust inequalities which thus accompany the soul in its passage through the gates of life to the material, objective, or sensuous arc of its cycle of existence, is fully met by the recognition of the all-embracing law of re-embodiment. There is no problem, either in physical, moral, or mental environment or limitations, which does not yield to the touch of this universal solvent. By its means we perceive that such inequalities are but each soul's coming to its own heritage, under the action of the law of cause and effect. The energies of its past lives on earth *have* been conserved, and now irresistibly draw it where these can best be displayed in the new life. Whether these have been virtuous or vicious, noble or ignoble, through all the infinite variations in character or motive, the law acts unerringly—is incapable of erring. It is but mental or psychic force, taking the direction of the least resistance, under the action of the same law which science has recognized as controlling molecular physics on the plane below. Each soul comes to its own, so far, at least, as physical parents can afford a fitting vehicle. For, being the product of many lives, the whole of its conscious area cannot be expressed in any one body, nor in any one life on earth. Therefore, following the line of least resistance—which is but that of greatest attraction—it comes to those parents presenting the greatest sum of attractive energy. It may rise far above, or fall equally far below, every conceivable possibility of merely physical heredity in those potencies which it inherits from its own past alone. Thus, in the case of mathematical, poetical, musical, or other forms of so-called genius, we perceive but a soul which, having cultivated these faculties through, perhaps, many lives, brings them over from its own conscious past. Physical heredity utterly fails to account for these cases of genius—for a Shakespeare, "rising out of the muddy stream of an illiterate tenant-farming and petty-trading Warwickshire family"; for a musical prodigy—a "Blind Tom," born of ignorant slave parentage; for a mathematical wonder—a Zerah Colburn, springing from Missouri clod-hoppers; for a Napoleon, bred from a humble camp follower; and so on, almost infinitely. Indeed, physical heredity fails to rationally account for any difference in that mental or moral capacity which separates man from man, not only at birth, but throughout his subsequent life. And the reverse of genius—the stupid sons of wise parents—also completely violates the law of conservation of force as displayed in merely physical heredity. There is no hypothesis, no court of appeal from these perplexing, heart-rending injustices and inequalities which even precede actual physical birth, and follow like an avenging Nemesis the soul throughout all its subsequent life, unless we admit the fact of reincarnation and recognize that each soul comes to its own; that all the infinite modifications of character exhibited by mankind to-day are the result of an equally infinite modification by conscious experiences in past lives.

To briefly sum up: It has been shown that matter, force, and consciousness are equally indestructible and eternally associated; that the presence of one proves that of all; and the conservation of one necessitates the conservation of all. We have seen that the human soul, because of the impossibility of dissociating these hypostases of the Absolute, is a centre of substance, force, and consciousness, individualized within and proceeding from these Aspects of the Absolute. Without any attempt to explain Why or How this occurred in the first instance—for the finite can never hope to measure or contain the Infinite—its subsequent evolutionary modifications have been shown to be perfectly intelligible by the law of re-embodiment or reincarnation; that human or any other existence can be rationally explained in no other way; that here in the clamor and chaos of seeming injustice, where the heart fails and the intellect draws back with dread, this LAW becomes a magician's wand to conjure away the dreadful night-mare of sorrow and despair—becomes the very voice of Nature itself, calling across the abysses of intellectual chaos "Let there be LIGHT!" and there IS light.

We have seen the law foreshadowed in the mineral kingdom, exemplified in the vegetable and animal kingdoms, demonstrated in the human kingdom! We have seen that the scientific generalizations of force-conservation and the indestructibility of matter contain it; that justice absolutely requires it; that immortality demands it; that in it is the only sure and scientific basis for human ethics. It is the great Revealer of the Past; the glorious Prophet of the Future. Nothing but soul-blindness can prevent its instant recognition. We find ourselves here now; we know that we exist. Are we so vain, so stupid, as to suppose that that which Nature has done she cannot repeat; that, having been powerful enough to bring us upon this plane of existence once, she is unable to do so again? Nay; let us bow down in the recesses of our inmost hearts before the great compassionate Mother, accepting the grand truth which she so patiently endeavors to teach us, that through the illusory gates of life and death we have come from an infinite, conscious past; that by means of these same portals, now so dreaded, we may pass on to an infinitely glorious, happy, and *self*-conscious future. So shall our hearts thrill and fill with sympathy for our fellow-men; so shall the petty cares, ambitions, and selfishness of this life disappear in the warmth of the light of the higher knowledge; so shall we work tranquilly, patiently on, unterrified by death, and O! far surpassing this, undismayed by Life!

THEOSOPHY AND MODERN SOCIAL PROBLEMS.

Its Claim that Social Evils have their Roots in Mental Faults, and that in Addition to Legislative, Educational, and Social Improvements, the Truths and Laws of Being must be Taught for the Fundamental Regeneration of Society, and the Recognition of Karma and Reincarnation must be Made the Basis of Concerted Public as well as Private Efforts.

BY ANNIE BESANT.

I have to speak to you on Theosophy and modern social problems. It is claimed that social evils have their roots in mental faults, and that in addition to legislative, educational, and social improvements, the truths and laws of being must be taught for the fundamental regeneration of society, and the recognition of Karma and Re-incarnation must be made the basis of concerted public as well as of private efforts.

The subject is one which seems to take us on to a different level of thought from those with which we have been occupied yesterday and to-day. We are now coming down, as it were, to the employment of more material forms of energy, coming down to deal with the transitory, with the impermanent, with the facts rather than with the cause. Distinctly lower work; distinctly less productive of results; distinctly to be dealt with in other fashion than those higher themes to which our thoughts have been turned. And I who have spent so many years of life in dealing with these problems on the material plane, I who have given so much of time and of thought to the effort to bring some remedy to the social ills of man, I take it to be my duty at the outset of this brief statement to bear witness founded upon knowledge that the employment of one hour in spiritual energy for the good of man works a hundred-fold more good than years of labor employed on the material plane. Spiritual energy, in truth, does not find its expression on the platform. Spiritual energy can scarcely translate itself by the slow process of intellectual thought and speech. And yet it seems to me that even by the vehicle of intellect and of language you must have got from our Indian brother some impulse from those higher planes, some recognition of higher force, than those we are wont to deal with in our modern and civilized life. Yet inasmuch as we live in matter as well as in spirit, inasmuch as our work, at least for the less developed of us, lies here and not over there, it is fitting that in this Congress some word should be said of the lower plane of life, and, even while we recognize its inferior position, we have no right to leave it until the spirit within us has grown to know its energy and to give itself in nobler fashion for the good of Man.

Turning, then, to this aspect of our work, we shall strive to apply to it the philosophy that we have learned—strive to apply that philosophy in order that we may waste as little effort as may be wasted by applying mere palliatives instead of cures, by dealing entirely with effects instead of causes. For there is a necessary sequence of effects, a sequence which includes all on the material plane, and that sequence is, first, thought; and then from the thought, generation of the image on the astral; then from the astral, the precipitation of the image into action. No material effort to act takes place without those preceding stages, and it is only because our eyes are blinded that we lay so much stress on the act and neglect the causes that have preceded. And the value of Theosophy in dealing with social problems is that this sequence is understood and recognized, so that however much we may energize on the material plane, however much we may strive to bring palliatives to the wounded and the maimed in life's struggles, still the Theosophist can never forget that these are but palliatives, they are not cures; and that the cure must rise upward to the mental generating cause and not confine itself merely to the final crystallization of the effect.

That that is so, we very easily understand when we cast our glance over the history of the past. If to-day amongst ourselves the social conscience is beginning to awaken, if to-day among some civilized people social compunction is beginning to show itself, if instead of the old reply of Cain, falling from the lips of modern civilization, "Am I my brother's keeper?" there is beginning to fall from the lips of some men and women at least the cry "Let me help wherever I am strong and serve wherever there is need," if such words are beginning to ring through modern society, if men and women are beginning to give themselves for humanity, it is because the other stages have gone before. It is because the great Thinker has sketched the mighty ideal; it is because the seer has seen a vision, has dreamed a dream and spoken out his dream to men, and though in his own generation denounced as visionary, though in his own generation branded as Utopian, the Utopias of to-day are the realities of the future, and without the dream and the ideal, what we falsely call the real could never be.

Now, legislation deals with acts. Our brother Judge has truly said that as Theosophists we have nought to do with legislation. Dealing with it, however, as finding ourselves karmically placed in special countries and in special social environments, we realize that these legislative changes that are proposed can only be the outcome of previous mental changes in the minds of those who have lived a life in society. The law ought to be the final expression of convinced intellectual opinion. It ought to be the expression of the wisest and best incorporated in legislative shape. That is law, as it were, from the ideal standpoint, different enough from too many of the laws of to-day, but, as Brother Judge also truly said, we have plenty of laws on our statute books. Both you in your land and I in mine know of laws which, if put into practice, would change the very face of society, especially perhaps in our ancient English legislation. You have a mass of enactment which, fairly carried out, justly administered, righteously executed, would make our terrible poverty impossible and the misery of our great cities only a memory of the Past.

Unhappily, the law has only come into being as the outcome of a few enlightened consciences, and the minds of the majority of men have not yet passed through the stages which those minds have passed through in which first the thought of the new laws took form. In those minds the thought first took form; then on the astral, the image appeared; and this began to influence all the minds around it, and finally, out of that, took birth and action.

Let me take as an illustration a kind of law familiar enough to me, of which I know at once the theoretical value and the practical uselessness. I mean the law that we have on our statute books across the sea, against various forms of sweating. If those laws were carried out, the sweating which is now carried on in London —and I speak of London rather than of New York, although I have seen in your tenement houses in New York sweating as disgraceful and as scandalous as any I have seen in my own land—I know that there in London we have laws which, if rightly administered, would make the worst of this sweating impossible. What is the fact? That the law is evaded; that the sweating goes on despite the law, just as though the law had no existence; that the very persons who are sweated by the pressure around them are co-operators and accomplices in the evasion of the law. We denounce the sweater, we hold him up to public reprobation, we brand him as outcast, we draw away our garments lest they should be soiled by the touching. That on the plane of illusion. And what on the plane of causes? Every man and every woman who in their daily life and daily thought are willing to take more than they give, desire to grasp more than they yield to their fellows, count every service rendered as great and see every service given to them as small, who live upon their neighbors without compunction, who use their strength of brain or position in order that they may profit while the weaker are trampled under foot, who buy clothing that they know is sold at a price only rendered possible by the payment of wages to the women wage-earners which have to be increased by the sale of those women in the streets—every such man and woman is sweater at heart, every such man and woman is a cause which prevents the operation of the law, for the law is a dead thing while your thoughts are living potencies, and it is idle to denounce the one who does for you what in your hearts you desire, and to make the sweater outcast in a society while he only exists because your thoughts and mine have incarnated in form so foul.

And so with education. Education can do more than legislation, for legislation is only dealing with the plane of action, whereas education goes farther inward and deals with the plane of mind. But what mind? The lower mind alone. And even then, not the lower mind at its best, but the lower mind as it may be most easily turned into an instrument for struggle and the gaining of advantage over one's neighbor. For the whole of the educational system is founded on the idea that the child is to be trained into a successful man, and success on our modern lips does not mean success in service. It means success in self-aggrandizement, so that if you take one of the favorite books given as a prize in our English schools, you will find it a book called "Self-Help," and if you read the book "Self-Help," you will find that it is full of the stories of self-made men, so that the rather caustic remark arises in the mind when looking at the self-made man—proud and pompous and self-opinionated—well, at least it is some consolation to find that he has made himself, because he would not be a credit to any one else.

If education is to be real, you must change your system; you must put a stop to competition in the school; you must no longer set child against child in the struggle; you must give up the system of making the prize the symbol of victory over others, and the pride of the successful student that so many of his comrades are behind him and not in front. The whole thing is false, fitted only for a society which takes the law of the survival of the fittest which belongs to the beasts in the jungle instead of that law of self-abnegation by which only the soul of man can rise. So, when the child comes into your hands with its outer envelope ductile, with its nervous system plastic, the soul of the child has scarce yet got grip on its outer envelopment, and the contact is not yet complete between the thinker and its vehicle, what do you do with your modern education? You distort the outer vehicle that the soul is to use. You plant upon that fertile soil the evil seeds of competition, of desire for triumph, of wish to succeed at the cost of others; so that every child in your class is glad when the pupil above him stumbles, because it brings him nearer to the top of the class and to stand as the successful child when the examiner shall come round. Rather teach your children that the child who learns most quickly should be the helper of the child who learns most slowly. That every power of brain and body is to be given for the helping of others, and not for dominance. That is the duty to the souls that come into the hands of the teachers, and they ill perform their sublime mission who try to dwarf and stunt the habitation that the soul has to dwell in.

Socially also when we come to deal with social improvements, we are coming to a question in which our philosophy applied to modern life has in truth some words to say.

We cannot deny from the scientific standpoint the importance of the re-action of the environment on the individual. It is enormously exaggerated, preposterously exaggerated; for where a soul is strong and experienced, no environment can keep it back and no disadvantage can check its course, but on weaker souls, on the developing mind, in man, the higher mind, what is the result of the conditions that in our previous thinkings we have brought out in society? Those of you who followed the philosophy of the Secret Doctrine, will be aware that in the long evolution of humanity different races come to birth and succeed each other on the surface of our globe, that with the evolution of each race there is also the evolution of a certain aspect of consciousness in Man, so that as the races are reckoned upward in their climbing fresh aspects of consciousness become manifested in the course of this evolution.

To-day, according to Theosophical doctrine, we stand in the fifth race that has occupied the globe, and, comparing the race with the aspect of consciousness which should be developing, we find the corresponding principle of consciousness is that of Manas, or the thinker, that is to say, that in the fifth race the powers of the Thinker find greater expression than in the race that went before, and that as a corresponding point is reached in the evolution of the fifth race, the development of the mind will reach a higher point than that which it touched in the corresponding period of the fourth. Manas, the mind, thus beginning to manifest itself, lies at the root of the enormous intellectual development of the day, but that development should be general not partial, not confined to the few but spread over the many; so that humanity, passing upward collectively in this fifth race, should develop collectively the higher intellectual faculty, and so lay the foundation upon which the next stage may be built, from which the next rung of the ladder may be mounted.

Our civilization is one-sided in its development. Over-culture and over-refinement, for it is only superficial; under-education and under-refinement, on the other. The refined class, so proud of itself that it hedges itself round with a wall of exclusiveness as though the refinement, if it were real, could be scratched off by a little friction with the outer world. In truth, if it is only a veneer put over the surface of base material, then it is well to avoid the scratching, for the scratching may show the poor material that lies behind it.

But if, as it ought to be, the outer man is to be the expression of the inner; if the graces of manner and the beauty of phrase are but the expression of the soul veiling itself in the form of language or the form of gesture, such refinement cannot be done away with; such refinement cannot be rendered commonplace by use; and it exists not that the refined person may stand aside, but that he may go out and spread the grace of his presence in the world, so that others may see in him the reflection of the soul, and be stirred by the beauty of the reflection to seek that light which lies beyond.

Therefore it is that when we are dealing with the subject from this standpoint, we begin to understand what, if I may use a word drawn from our poor language, may be called the "policy" of the great teachers of men in dealing with the present phase of development in the world. That great man whom I quoted yesterday, many of whose letters were published by Mr. Sinnett in the *Occult World*, dealing with problems of Western science and sending a message to those who expected help for that science from them, answered, " Your science has no claim on us till it allies itself with philanthropy," and he went on to explain that scientific knowledge as such was to them a matter of indifference where it did not contribute to the helping of man, to the raising, to the purifying, to the bettering of society; and so it is that brotherhood must be gained before further knowledge will be given ; that the will to use for service must precede any assistance in the gaining of the intellectual knowledge. For you might as well remain ignorant, nay, almost better, than to remain unloving, for a civilized cruelty is worse than the cruelty of the savage, and the brutality of those who know better is more cruel than that of the brute, which shows its nature and has not the stimulus of mind to refine its malice.

We have in our midst slums, fearful places where men and women starve, putrify, and perish. What is the result of a slum upon the nation? Not only on the individual souls whose Karma leads them to that foul surrounding, but what shall we find our philosophy teaches us when we come to deal with the slum regarded from the standpoint of the nation?

For, in these legislative and educational and social environments, we now into the midst of them thus roughly described bring the lesson of our philosophy, and we have seen that, as regards legislation, the will to be just must precede the law which is only the formulation of the maxim. That in education the child should be dealt with as an evolving soul, with its faculties to be drawn out and assisted in the conquest of the matter that veils it, so that everything should work for this evolution of the soul. What shall we learn as regards the social environment? What bearing have Karma and Re-incarnation on this pressing question of modern times?

To regenerate needs wisdom ; to regenerate needs a sound philosophy. You may change everything to-morrow by a sudden act, but the day after will find you facing the same difficulties if the root of the evil has not been touched. So that when we are dealing with legislative change, with educational change, with change in the direction of greater justice, that which H. P. Blavatsky once called the Socialism of Love, and not of hatred, the socialism that gives instead of the socialism that takes, when we begin to deal with that, what bearing has Karma on the subject, what teaching has Re-incarnation as to the methods we should use? Karma makes you understand that that which exists in the slum is the materialization of past selfishness, past greed, past desire for dominance, past denial of the brotherhood of man. That that slum is the inevitable result of the Past. If the Past was, the Present must be ; and it's no use throwing the blame on one and another living here to-day. No good can come of abusing this class or that class, because in this wretchedness and social wrong we are all guilty of our brother's blood ; we all share in the common fault. The slum-dweller and the prince, the middle-class man and the nobleman, they have all coöperated in the Past to make the slum. It is the outcome of their own ignorance, their own folly, and their own crime. Let them, then, not waste time in abusing each other; let them not throw away the chance of reparation by perpetuating the hatred out of which the slum has grown. Said the Buddha, "Hatred ceases not by hatred at any time; hatred ceases by love." And no amount of attack, no amount of denunciation, no wild words of passion or of anger, will heal our social ills.

Better join hands on either side with rich and poor, prince and pauper. Let us say, "Brothers, we have sinned together in the past, we will atone together in the present." We do not want to separate the responsibility; it is ours, for we are all the sons of men.

And Re-incarnation will tell us something more. It will explain to us why, as I said just now, the slum is a national concern. Souls that are seeking Re-incarnation are drawn to the environment for which they are fitted. Souls carrying with them vicious and idle and malicious tendencies will be born to fathers and mothers who manifest vices of similar character, and who have poisoned the material of their own bodies, and so render them fit for the vibrations of evil that come from the degraded soul. If you cast into the slums those who are already miserable and degraded, and because they are miserable need most help, and because they are degraded need most your brotherly love, you are perpetuating conditions for the incarnations of the future the worst of the souls that are seeking a fleshly habitation. You are erecting already houses for the tenants who are seeking such dwellings, and who will move in—crowd in—and take possession of that which suits them for the manifestation of the evil tendencies, the evil passions they have fostered in their own past, and so your nation will become a focus for contracting all evils and faults. Your nation will become a centre of attraction for those souls whose citizenship will be mischievous, and who will be forces for disintegration and not for good.

Do you think that the state of a people matters not? Every nation builds up characters and impresses them on the bodies, as it were, of its people, suitable for different classes of re-incarnating souls; by physical and astral heredity, bodies are builded which are suitable for the manifestation of certain types of intellectual and spiritual energy. You may have a nation whose very bodies are, as it were, tabernacles in which the most advanced Egos seeking incarnation will find their way, because there is the physical instrument which will respond most delicately to the most subtle vibration; and so in this fashion a nation builds its future by attracting either the nobler or the baser from the crowds of souls that seek this fleshly dwelling. What, then, may a nation be? We may perhaps give some form to our ideal if we think what a nation has been in the past.

In these discussions in our Theosophical Congress, we have heard much of India, much of Indian wisdom, much of Indian spirituality, much of praise for Indian thought and admiration of Indian past. Do you know, do you ever dream, when you think of the India of to-day, what the India of the Past has been and what the India of the future I hope may be again—India not as you know her to-day, trampled under the foot of the Indian government, a materialistic nation to the heart, with her foot on the neck of the spiritual mother of the nations. Not from that can you judge of India. Not from her degradation, but her ancient glory.

She is conquered because she allowed herself to be conquered from within, and when from within the conquest has been made, the outer view may well come in and give it shape. For out of spiritual pride and spiritual selfishness grew the degradation of India, until she who once led the world was no longer able to stand in the front But the India of the past—Ah, that was different! When her Gods came down as Avatars, and her Rishis made the grandest literature that has grown up in the past or present, so that our nations have been inspired by it—that literature written in the language of the Gods. They who trained their people and led them step by step along the path of knowledge, when the Brahmins were those whose bodies were fit dwelling for the most highly evolved souls, and even the name of Brahmin meant spiritual teacher, and therefore the rightful guide and instructor of men. That is what a nation may be when a spiritual ideal is supreme, and the working out of this by the nation makes bodies that are able to answer to the most delicate vibrations of the highest of souls.

Shall that be the ideal of your American nation, or will you turn aside to your Western thought? Will you have your material wealth, will you take gold instead of wisdom, and mere material triumph instead of the knowledge of the soul? You may do it as you will, for every nation's fate is in its own hands. Yours the choice, and none other can choose for you what the future of the American nation shall be. Shall it be material? Is it the material that you need? Rather lessen your material wants and give more thought to the evolution of your material energies. Spend less time in the body, more time in the soul. Give less thought to the acquirement of position and of wealth, more thought to the growth of the Spirit and the evolution of the purely human within you, and then even greater than the nations of the past the nations of the future may be,—nobler even than the realities of the past the realities of the future shall become; and if you would have the treasure you must pay the price, and the price is the recognition of the supremacy of the spirit, and the utterly inferior and transitory nature of that body of which we make so much.

Adjourned until afternoon at three.

FIFTH SESSION, SATURDAY AFTERNOON AT 3 O'CLOCK.

Mr. Judge—The session of the Congress this evening will be in the Hall of Washington at 8 o'clock to present Theosophy to the Parliament of Religions; but, as announced this morning, the officers of the Parliament in recognition of the great success of our meetings having assigned us to the same Hall of Washington for an extra meeting, we will there on Sunday night have further discussions. That will in fact close all the meetings of the Theosophical Society in the Parliament of Religions. Dr. Buck will now address you.

THEOSOPHY AND SCIENCE.

THEOSOPHY HOSTILE TO SCIENCE ONLY WHEN MATERIALISTIC, WHEN IT REPUDIATES ALL SPHERES AND PROCESSES OTHER THAN PHYSICAL, OR DENIES THE REALITY OF SOUL AND SPIRIT AND THE UNSEEN UNIVERSE.

DR. J. D. BUCK.

The word Science, like the word Religion and the word Philosophy, necessarily conveys to different minds different meanings. There has grown up in what we call the Western world a superstructure without form, though not altogether void, that it would be as difficult to define as the generic term religion. This superstructure claims to exercise as much authority over the current thought of the age as does religion, if not more. It will therefore be pertinent to our line of thought this afternoon to inquire in what sense the Western world uses and applies the word science, and in what sense those who advocate what we call Theosophy use this word "science."

A very great misapprehension rests upon the minds of the Western world, including the scientists, and that is, that what we call science is a thing of very recent date ; that the olden times had superstition, that men had what is known as religion, that men speculated a great deal into the nature of things and had some philosophy ; but science—O, science is a thing of the present times, a new thing. It would be impossible for me to convince you of the misapprehension that lies in any such suggestion this afternoon, in the brief time that is allotted to me to speak upon this subject. But nothing would be easier than to convince any candid individual, any reasoning mind, that no greater mistake could possibly be made than to suppose that what in the strictest sense is called science is not a thing of the distant past, and that the distant ages, as we call them, did not possess a science just as demonstrable as that which we call science to-day.

There was a difference in the application of this science in the olden time from that method by which it is applied to-day, and that difference was well represented to you this morning by Prof. Chakravarti and Annie Besant.

Now, in order to be perfectly just and fair, I will take two or three of the later utterances—comparatively late utterances—of one of the leaders of modern science, in order to show what he defines as the basis and the method of what we call science in the West. I recite from an essay published quite a number of years ago by Prof. Huxley, entitled "A half century of science." In this he says :

"The object of science is the discovery of the rational order that pervades the universe." It would be very easy to convince

Prof. Huxley, if he would listen to evidence, if he had desire enough to follow along the lines which could be investigated, that this rational order was known thousands and thousands of years ago. Otherwise these grand philosophies could never have had any existence. Another point which could easily be shown is that the method pursued by Prof. Huxley himself, that the direction in which he looks in order to find this rational order that pervades the universe, has never revealed to man that rational order, and never will. That rational order that pervades the universe cannot be found by the methods of modern science. It cannot be found by investigating phenomena, it cannot be found alone by the inductive method of reasoning. It must be looked for in other directions and derived by other means. The method of science, as defined by Prof. Huxley, is that science proceeds by exact observation and correct reasoning. Here no intelligent Theosophist will take any exception as far as it goes, but the definition of the method remains incomplete. One thing more must be added to it, and that is experience. In other words, you will have to bring in the problem of consciousness, and go deeper than mere observation through the physical senses. You must go to the mind, and even beyond the reasoning faculty, in order to discern the rational order that pervades the universe.

Prof. Huxley also says that all physical science starts from certain postulates. Now, what is a postulate? It is an assumption, it is an hypothesis and nothing more or less. They are called postulates when they are involved with other postulates, and when particularly the effort is made to weave them into what is called a system of postulates or a system of philosophy. Well, physical science starts from certain postulates. One of them is the objective existence of a material world, and I shall expect to show that this is not only one of them but that it is the crowning one in modern science. The validity of these postulates is a problem of metaphysics. They are neither self-evident nor are they, strictly speaking, demonstrable. Now, when we look to modern science as being exact, when we look to its decrees as being final, let us bear in mind this confession of one of the foremost if not the very foremost advocate of modern science—a man who cannot be used in support of materialism, however. It is only by the lesser lights, it is only when Prof. Huxley is misquoted or misunderstood, I think, that he can be declared to be a materialist.

These problems or postulates, he says, are neither self-evident nor are they, strictly speaking, demonstrable, and this is the basis of modern science. Here comes now a confession from Prof. Huxley which seems to me very strange. It startled me as I read it. I don't know where he got it. He says, "Perhaps it may occur to the reader that the boasted progress of physical science does not come to much if our present conceptions of the fundamental nature of matter are expressible in terms employed more than two thousand years ago by the old Masters, of those who know."

To whom could Prof. Huxley have referred in—"the old Masters, of those who know"?

Quoting still from Prof. Huxley, a fallacy. "In antiquity, these postulates meant little more than vague speculations." He very much mistakes. At the present day they indicate definite physical conceptions susceptible of mathematical treatment and giving rise to innumerable deductions the value of which may be experimentally tested.

In the first paper which I had the honor to read to the Congress, I referred to the historical evidence showing that what we call Theosophy may be traced back to the Middle Ages, to the beginning of the Christian era, to Plato and Zoroaster; and what was the key-note of the philosophy of Pythagoras, the science of numbers, of mathematics; and looking at the schools of mathematics as they existed in those days, and looking at the way they experimented in regard to Man by numbers and harmonies, do you think they can be accused of not knowing mathematics, or that they could not apply the principles of mathematics to the postulates of their philosophy?

"In the meanwhile," he says, "the primitive atomic theory which has served as the scaffolding for the edifice of modern physics and chemistry, has been quietly dismissed," that is, in the form in which it was received in the Western world. But the form in which it was taught in the Secret Doctrine can never be refuted. The difficulty is in the concept of matter. "In the meanwhile," he says, "the primitive atomic theory which has served as the scaffolding for the edifice of modern physics and chemistry, has been quietly dismissed. I cannot discover," he says, "that any contemporary physicist or chemist believes in the real indivisibility of atoms or in an interatomic matterless vacuum." That was the old theory which seems to have served as a "scaffolding for modern science."

Now, he comes to the important point, the question of genesis, or abiogenesis. Whether matter has ever passed into living matter without the agency of pre-existing living matter, necessarily remains an open question. "All that can be said is that it does not make this metamorphosis under any known conditions. They who take a monistic view of the physical world," (that is, regarding matter and spirit as being essentially one) "may fairly hold abiogenesis" (or spontaneous generation) "as a pious opinion." And here is the only little fling that I find in this magnificent lecture. He says it may be "held as a pious opinion supported by analogy and defended by our ignorance." "As matters stand," he says, "it is as equally justifiable to regard the physical world as a sort of dual monarchy." I think this is a proper and fair claim for us. The theory has only an equal justification with that other theory which he simply terms an $à\ priori$ opinion. "The kingdoms of living matter and of non living matter are under one system of laws," and the fact of their profound mystery is consistent with the Theosophical philosophy, "and there is a perfect freedom of exchange and transit from one to the other." This implies by fair reasoning all that the Theosophical philosophy claims for that universal ether, or that universal spirit or consciousness, or that universal life, call it by whatsoever name you will—it furnishes the basis of the Theosophical philosophy. "But no claim," he says in conclusion, "to biological nationality is valid except birth."

Now, this is as fair an outline as I can procure of the points presented by Prof. Huxley that bear on the points claimed by the advocates of Theosophy to-day.

The fact is, that just so long as science makes its formulations with regard to matter, with regard to force, with law and mathematics, we have no quarrel whatever with the scientists. It is only when they come to deny with regard to intelligence, with regard to soul, with regard to spirit, that we take issue with them.

You find in what is called science in modern times, that it represents simply one department in human knowledge. And we hear even yet, although it is only, perhaps, the echo that is dying away, a good deal about the conflict between religion and science. The unity, the sequence, the co-ordination of the knowledge of Man as an individual, as a knower, is a matter of great importance. And the result of modern methods of investigation is to divide what we call knowledge into three departments, Religion, Philosophy, and Science, and to establish or to permit very little association or recognition between these departments. This seems to have served for the cultivation of each department in its own way, in its own realm, but it does not minister, it never has nor ever can, it seems to me, minister to the intelligent enlightenment of Man to have his knowledge divided in any way without any recognition of the fact that knowledge in one department is not different to the individual knower than knowledge in any other department of his being.

Now, the element that the Theosophical Society brings into modern thought is the basis upon which Philosophy, Science, and Religion all find a resting place. There is here no disagreement whatever; here religion never contradicts Philosophy, here Science never disagrees from either Religion or Philosophy. This basis upon which the knowledge of Man rests is a revelation from the elder brothers of the race. This has never yet, so far as History records, been discovered by investigation of natural phenomena alone. Men who deal simply with phenomena, no matter how carefully they may observe the phenomena, no matter how logically they may reason upon the phenomena, until they push their investigations farther than this, they can never come to what justly may be termed actual knowledge. Now, there is one term with which we are all very familiar, " Self-Consciousness!" We are familiar with this. Now, what is, in a general way, Self-Consciousness? Man is conscious. Every atom of matter in the universe, according to our philosophy, in its own degree, in its own way, under its own limitations, possesses the germs or the element of consciousness. The animals are conscious, but their consciousness differs from that of Man. It is only when you come to the human consciousness that we use the term self-consciousness, and what is that self-consciousness? Self-consciousness is that manifestation or that evolution of the universal consciousness of nature, when the individual himself is conscious of his consciousness, when he can investigate and analyze his own mind, when the thinker, the real man, can retire within the citadel of his soul and take cognizance of his own methods of knowing.

Now, the point where modern scientists again divide is upon this problem of consciousness. They have not the advantage of the Eastern philosophy, which regards matter, life, intelligence, force, consciousness as one all-pervading, universal principle, and it is only from the Theosophical view of the subject that the value of this primary postulate becomes clear, where it can be truly appreciated. Under this method of reasoning we deal with consciousness, and what is consciousness in this connection? It is simply the use by Man of his intellectual faculties, of his reasoning faculties, of his sensory faculties, to investigate by process of observation and of sensation the phenomena of a material world. And Prof. Huxley himself says that Science investigates, or, at least, that its method is the observation of phenomena and correct reasoning upon the nature of these phenomena. What, now, is the method of philosophy? Science proceeds by what we call the analytical method. The scientist, like the little boy, takes the thing apart, separates it into its constituent elements, in order to find out what makes the wheels go round, but he does not find out by any method of sensation alone. Prof. Huxley says we experiment by applying the process of correct reasoning to what we have observed. But then when you come to reason upon things, we find that different individuals will reason in a different way, and that the basis of the reasoning of every individual will be the evolution of his faculty to reason. And, therefore, the results at which individual investigators arrive must necessarily differ in every individual case; and who shall determine the result, and therefore the criterion of truth, inasmuch as every different individual must come to a different conclusion from every other? You have here what I conceive to be a logical definition and a very fair statement of science, when science is regarded merely as one of the three departments of knowledge in the mind of Man. Now, Philosophy, as I understand it, is the supplement of science. Just as by the analytical method of science you take things apart and observe phenomena, so in all true philosophy you put things together and ascertain how they came, and try to discover what Prof. Huxley calls the rational order of the universe.

But I do not think that either of these two methods alone while pursued separately will lead Man to truth by any means.

Now, there is Religion, divorced in modern times, set apart from Science, and not recognizing Philosophy; and furthermore, there is recognized unfortunately a conflict between Religion and Science, and this degradation of Philosophy into what is called mere idle speculation, tolerated neither by the religionists nor by the scientists. As to Religion itself, we have made it a superstition. It has been walled about and separated from other kinds of knowledge till it has lost its energy. Now, there is a duty to Science and Philosophy, and another duty to Religion; and that is, devotion to truth, devotion to the highest ideal.

The purpose of investigation is to define by religion—and it is the core of the great religions of the world—to point out not only the method, not only the means, of acquiring it, but also the use that shall be made of the true religion, which is one with that trinity which we may call Science, Philosophy, and Religion. Therefore I say that we have no warfare with science so far as it deals with matter, force, and phenomena, so far as it affirms the existence of material phenomena, but when it denies in regard to spirit, when it simply puts the problem one side and refuses to investigate it, then we take issue with the school. Now, the whole of modern science may be said to proceed on one line or one basis, and that is, it undertakes to reduce all problems in nature and in life to questions of mass and motion. Physical Science is necessarily materialistic, and so far we have not a particle of fault to find with it. But when it undertakes to represent mental phenomena, vital force, consciousness, and all the higher attributes of Man and all of the higher aspects of nature, in terms of mass and motion, it becomes perniciously materialistic, and we have a perfect right to call a halt at that point.

Now, the problem that I referred to a few moments ago, the problem of consciousness or self-consciousness, is a great stumbling block to modern science. Prof. Tyndall, one of the foremost advocates of modern science, a great many years ago made the declaration that between the molecular structure of the brain and consciousness there was a gap—he did not say "over which we could not pass," but he says that it was one that was inconceivable, a gap over which there were no bridges—there could be no connection established whatever. In other words, modern science has not determined whether matter can think, or how, or why.

You may take all the philosophies of the world, and very fairly and justly classify them into two categories One is the assumption that matter alone exists, and that everything is an attribute, or property, or potency, or outgrowth of matter ; the other class will take the opposite view exactly, namely, that spirit alone exists, and that everything else is spirit precipitated or differentiated. Now, in the Theosophical philosophy we postulate a single substance that lies back of both matter and spirit, of force and intelligence, that one inscrutable, eternal, unknowable principle which is neither matter nor force, neither matter nor spirit, but the root from which all of these come, and its consciousness is universal in nature, as it is manifested in individual man.

Therefore we have in what would be called the Science of the Secret Doctrine or the Science of Theosophy, no such missing links. We have no necessity in our scientific investigations to make any such assumptions as are made, or any such admissions of gaps or missing links as are found in science, and we take issue only with the advocates of modern science when they cease to be scientific, when they begin to be dogmatic, and when in the face of the logical conclusions justified by the investigations pursued by the senses, and justified by rational processes pursued in these investigations, they begin to deny, to scoff, to ridicule philosophy or religion or the realm to which the mind of Man is open and which he may investigate as a matter of experience if only he will.

This problem, then, of science is the one that I have already said is the bugbear, the stumbling block, of modern science, and it is the basic proposition in the philosophy and the science of the secret doctrine.

When the true relations between what we call intelligence or reason and consciousness and mind are once determined, when we have the starting point in Man, the thinker, the Eagle, the reasoner, when we have that well fixed in our minds, then everything else flows from them with a logical sequence that leaves no missing link, and that leaves no gaps in our knowledge, so far as we go. Knowledge then, real knowledge, becomes an investigation, and an experience of the soul. Science as it is pursued, I don't think can justly be called a result. It is rather a method. Therefore when the advocates of science undertake to hold up to us something which is indefinite and vague, which they call the authority of science, we call a halt. We claim that it is a method of the human mind, and that there is no such thing as a body of doctrines or a formulated series of results that can have any more authority over the human mind than can the dogmas of religion. One really rests upon the same basis as the other. It is simply a premature conclusion, and so far as the materialistic conclusions that are drawn from the statements of men like Huxley and Darwin and Herbert Spencer and many that are quoted as advocates of materialism, I say, so far as their own statements are concerned, you will very seldom find them materialistic. The larger the mind the broader his intelligence, the deeper his consciousness, the stronger his conscientiousness. In other words, the larger the man in every sense, the more careful and guarded and charitable will be his statement. It is only when the lesser lights come to hasty deductions and draw illogical conclusions from the statements of these scientists that materialism grows up; and therefore we have no hesitancy in making the declaration as publicly as we can, that there is nothing that has been demonstrated in modern science that is inconsistent with the Secret Doctrine, that there is no proposition laid down by them which is reasonable and which agrees with one's common sense which is not also advocated by the Secret Doctrine and which cannot be found in the Secret Doctrine. The prediction has been made by the authors of the *Secret Doctrine* that although in the present age science is perhaps too proud, too conceited, to examine these doctrines in order to ascertain candidly and dispassionately just what they contain, still the prediction is made that in the twentieth century they will be investigated and receive a recognition of their true worth and true value; and it seems to me that the twentieth century is very close upon us to-day, when we have been able to gather here so many interested individuals to hear about these doctrines, and I don't think we need fear in any sense whatever as to what the result must finally be.

Of course there are two organizations which will yield last to the modifying influences which Theosophy undertakes to introduce into human thought; and they are the religious organization and the scientific organization. And so far as I can observe in all fairness, the more dogmatic of the two to-day is science. Altogether more so than religion itself.

These problems, of course, are of such a character that to take them up in detail, as I said in the beginning, would be impossible in a brief argument such as I am trying to pursue. The number of points at which, however, modern science is becoming harmonious with ancient philosophy is very surprising, and the reference of Prof. Huxley which I read to you in regard to the atomic theory proves it. For instance, where he says it is not demonstrable in the ordinary sense through the agency of the senses that the constitution of matter is a metaphysical problem and that the atomic theory is now an exploded one though it was a very good scaffolding. When you come to the experiments by Prof. Crookes, his metaphysical investigations into the constitution of matter, when you read the writings of Prof. B. W. Richardson, when you read the address of Prof. Lodge, one of the foremost chemists in England—the paper he read to the advanced men of modern science, where he told these men that they might as well drop all expectation of realizing the ultimatum of science by the aid of reason and experimentation alone—you see plainly that they are trenching upon the ground of ancient philosophy, and in these later utterances you will find the dying wail of materialistic science, you will find at last the note, the morning song, of the new science of the new philosophy which has come into the world, which is born of metaphysics, which is born by pushing the intellect of man out into space, and reasoning upon the foundations of matter and force, and supplementing all that has been derived by an analytical investigation, by correct reasonings as to the basis of life, as to the basis of matter, and as to the basis of force, and of all these things; and therefore, I say, that in presenting this subject to the attention of the Western world we have no hesitation whatever in saying that the basis—the scientific basis—of the Theosophical philosophy stands in no fear whatever of modern science, that it can maintain itself against all comers, that the gaps or the missing links of science are filled without a single exception in these ancient philosophies, and furthermore that in the problems of mind, of thought, of reason, of consciousness, in all the higher problems in the life of Man, there is given here a basis which cannot be found at all outside of the ancient Wisdom Religion.

ALTRUISM INCUMBENT BECAUSE OF COMMON ORIGIN, COMMON TRAINING, COMMON INTERESTS, COMMON DESTINY, AND INDIVISIBLE UNITY. THEOSOPHY AND ETHICS.

PROF. G. N. CHAKRAVARTI.

One of the greatest fallacies that are committed in the spiritual life, both in the East and West, is that because the spiritual teaching advocates the subjugation of the flesh and the giving up of the gratification of the senses, the way can be attained by falling away from the duties that one has to perform, and by retiring into the forests and jungles to meditate upon something, heaven knows what. Not so, however, can the animal tendencies and the overpowering attractions created throughout a series of incarnations be conquered, not so can one pass out of the wheel of births and rebirths. If he runs away, a chain a thousand times stronger brings him back on the arm of the wheel of birth, to be broken, pounded, maimed, and injured until he regains his position again. The fallacy arises from the fact of putting forward the physical body and the energies of the physical plane above everything else in the universe. Think you that merely by taking the physical body out of the centre of activity you kill the activity of the mind? A prison with its iron bars is not more stringent in confining you within its bounds than the thought, the passions, the desires, the grand attractions that you have every moment of your life created on the plane of the mind. Every moment of your life you are thinking of matter, and, according to the esoteric teaching, every thought that comes out of your brain has a potency for good or evil, it has a kinetic energy, a momentum which goes on rolling from time into time eternal. All these bands which you have been forging from incarnation to incarnation cannot be so easily broken. The body alone is not the whole of man. When I entered that most beautiful and magnificent of the harbors of the world, your own harbor of New York, I was delighted, I was edified by looking at that grand statue of Liberty with the torch of knowledge, equality, and fraternity in its hand. But it was not without a shadow of regret that I looked upon it; my sensation was not altogether free from cloud. Thought I, Is liberty really possible thus? Is liberty to be attained merely by the intellectual appreciation of the thing? Is liberty really possible when the mind of man is enslaved with the thousand passions that work in his bosom? Is liberty possible when the heart of humanity is rent into a thousand pieces by the darts of selfishness? (Applause.) So long as the root of the poison, the root of selfishness, flourishes luxuriantly in the heart of the people, why, liberty, why, unselfishness, why, fraternity must forever remain a mere term, an illusion never to be realized. Instead of fraternizing with each other, what have you got in the

West? A struggle for life; the higher trampling upon the lower; and still you talk of liberty! Where is liberty to be found? Not until your soul has been liberated from the turmoils and the various passions that are now storming in your nature, can you realize that ideal which you want to set up in that glorious monument in the harbor of New York.

One of the great reasons for this delusion that mere retirement from the scene of the world leads to spiritual progress, is probably due to the fact that in India it is regarded as the ideal of spiritual life; you have so many persons there roaming about the country without any ostensible end in view. Some of them are working for the good of humanity, although they don't work in the same way as you do. I confess, and I confess plainly before you, that there are hundred and thousands of sham yogees who sham and wear the garb of holiness so as to satisfy the cravings of the flesh and to gorge their stomach upon the charity of the people. I do not mean to say that there do not exist ideals of simple unselfishness, the ideals of spiritual purity, even among those who spend every moment of their life in the contemplation of the divine and in serving humanity with all their heart, and that their soul is pure, which really is the necessary consequence of the realization of the higher life. But what I do mean is this: that this imitation of things only proves the existence of the genuine article, and there are quite enough to deceive the world by leading it to believe that in India, the land of spirituality, a life of laziness, a life of elimination of one's duties, is sufficient. Not so. In the Shastras, Krishna very pointedly says: What is the use of your retiring, because even your body will not go on without acting; and why can you be so selfish, why can you be so degraded, that your hands and feet may work only for the few feet of flesh that is in you, and not for the world into which you are placed, not for humanity of which you are a factor? What is the use of retiring into the jungles and considering yourself to be a pure saint, when your minds revel simply in the infection of the tremendously vicious and the foul moral atmosphere of your own mind? It is pure hypocrisy. And it is said in the Bhagavat Gita (reciting Sanscrit) that the man is a hypocrite who does retire in this way. Not only our teachings in the sacred rolls go to show what is this ideal life; and it is not to retire from the world. Even the popular traditions and mythological fables lead you to the same conclusion, to the rigid and the strict performance of one's duties. On this point I am going to relate to you one of the finest stories that can be found in our sacred literature, showing you what ideal of duty has been held before India, in spite of the degeneration of our present days.

There once reigned a king renowned for piety, renowned for devotion, and who never refused to grant any favor asked of him. There was also a sage who at that time was one of the spiritual gods of the country, and once upon a time this sage took it into his head to try the piety of this virtuous king. He came to him and asked him if he would grant him a favor. Out of the generosity of his heart the king at once said, "Why, yes; anything you want." The sage said, "I want your kingdom, I want nothing short of that." Realizing the ephemeral nature of all possessions, considering as trash the most glorious throne on which a human being can sit, without a moment's hesitation the king gave away his kingdom. That was not all. The custom is in India that if you make a present to Brahma, here represented by the sage, you must give some gold along with it. The sage reminded him of that custom. He was confused ; he knew not what to do ; he had parted with all that he had, and whence was the gold to come? Yet he was not to be balked, he was not to be taken out of the sphere of his duty. He said, "Yes, I shall give you the gold, and let me know, holy sage, what is the proper quantity." He was told that seven kotis of gold were required for such a present as this. Well, the king went with his royal queen to the market, and there he was prepared, for the sake of performing a duty to Brahma, to hold his wife up in the open market to be sold away as a slave. The wife, devoted as the Indian wife is, the ideal of chastity, the ideal of spiritual exaltation and purity, regarded not the lot, although her husband the king was the very sunshine and lotus of her heart, and it was without a pang of regret that she went out and said, "Verily, I shall stand by you in the path of Karma, in the path of virtue ; through me must you perform what is right." She was sold and fetched only four kotis of gold. There were three yet to come. The king himself offered himself to be a slave to somebody, and he was taken out to be a chandala, that is, a person whose duty it is to assess taxes upon bodies who come out to be burned on the bank of the great river. Thus they parted.

The wife had a little son along with her, to whom no extra allowance of meal was given by her master. Out of the portion allotted to her did she support this child. But one fair morning when this child was sent out into the garden to cull certain flowers used in the worship of the master, a black, venomous viper crept out of its shady retreat and put an end to the sunshine of the queen's life. This little child was dead ; and with that child in her arms, with ashes in her breast and with tears in her eyes, she went out to the burning ghat, the place where the dead were burned, to consign the last relics of the dearest one to the flames, as is the custom in India. What is it that she saw there ? Her own husband, the king who never before his wife had refused anything to anybody, was standing there with the rod of his master, demanding tax for every body that was burned. In vain did the wife plead poverty, in vain did she plead her desperate condition, in vain did she plead to his heart as being his own truest one and the child their own. Immovable as the rock stood the king. He had his duty to perform to his master, and no human being, however sacred, was to swerve him from that rigid path of duty. At a moment like this the sage was satisfied, the gods were glorified with such devotion, such a rigid idea of duty, and, says the fable, came down from heaven fiery cars with gods in them to take the husband, wife, and child living, up to the heaven of bliss. This, then, is the ideal which is laid down in the Indian Shastras, to be reached by every human being according to the light that is in him, according to the strength that is in his breast. And, indeed, from the very conception of Indian philosophy, this has already been laid before you as in their view of life possible.

The universe I tell you springs from one source and returns to the same source. In the first half of its evolution there is differentiation, there is parting, but in the latter half of its course there is again involution, reuniting, and each man advances according to his realization of this unity of all beings. The more totally a man realizes the essential unity of all existence, the more advanced is he on the plane of being. This being the case, you cannot cut yourselves away from the mass, you cannot shrink from the world's garments that lie around you. It is for you to realize that you cannot leave your brother behind. Ties unseen, ties unbreakable, ties which are in the nature of things, really bind you to the whole, and therefore with the whole mass you progress. This view of things leads you to perform your duty, to sacrifice yourselves for the good of others, because thus alone you can realize the unity of all being, thus alone you can see the links that bind you to your brother, and thus alone, therefore, can you make spiritual progress. It is nothing but the realization of the unity of all created beings. It is therefore a law which no one can subvert, that it is only upon the cross of sacrifice that you can atone for your sins, it is only from the altar of suffering that you can catch the spiritual fire ; only by burning itself does the candle show light to the world. Even so with the human being. You must burn your personality, you must discard all that you love and all that attracts you before you can reach the realms of the spirit. This is the grand work that we have to perform, and not run away to the jungles like cowards. You have to meet and face bravely and like a hero a thousand trials and troubles that meet you in your dreary journey through this vale of tears, and as you conquer each weakness it becomes a rung in the ladder of progress. Each little act that you do by sacrificing yourself for the benefit of humanity becomes a lovely bloom laid on the altar, made to the spirit that you worship.

In this task, I need hardly say, there are great sufferings, great pains. As soon as you begin to live the life of unselfishness, why all the lower forces of your nature awaken with redoubled activity, and then begins to rage within you a warfare more stormy than any that you can imagine on the physical plane, more bloody than the battle of Thermopylæ, more vigorous than any in the field of life. It is majestically represented in the allegory of the eternal fight between God and Satan. Yes, your heart's blood will have to be shed in this mighty struggle ; but you have no reason to despair, because if your devotion is unflinching, if you really pursue the truth, if you have got a glimpse of the eternal sun, nothing can vanquish you, and out of the dust and storm arising in this fearful struggle the moral hero will come with a crown of unsurpassed resplendence and beauty, decked with the diamonds of eternal peace, eternal life, and eternal bliss.

THEOSOPHY AND ETHICS.
(*Continued.*)

ANNIE BESANT.

In the part of the Syllabus that we are considering this afternoon, we have to conclude the discussion opened by our Indian brother, tracing on from step to step the meaning of Altruism, the growth of morality, the sanction, the motive of ethics, and the identity of moral teaching in every great religion in the world. That we have chosen as a final presentment in this Congress of our philosophy, for all philosophy has its right ending in ethics and in conduct, which is of the most vital importance to men and women in their daily life.

First of all, then, we have the word Altruism, "incumbent," it is said, " because of man's common origin, common training, common destiny," and so on. And it is true that in the earliest stages of moral life, altruism must be the goal that we set before ourselves. The service of others is what we should strive to perfect. But sometimes it has also seemed to me that altruism is itself but a stage of progress rather than the goal. That as long as service is consciously service of others, that is, of others separated from our own self, that there is still incompleteness in the ethics, there is still lack of spirituality in the soul.

Some of you may remember that exquisite Persian poem in which the lover, seeking his beloved, finds closed against him the door of her chamber, and knocks, pleading for admission. From within the closed room sounds a voice asking "Who asks for admission?" And believing that his love was the best claim that could be given for his entry, he answered, "It is thy beloved that knocks." But there was silence within the room and the door remained closed against the suppliant. Out into the world he went and learned deeper lessons of life and of love; and coming back once more to the closed door, he struck thereon and asked for entry. Again the voice came, "Who is it that knocks?" But the answer this time was other than at first. No longer "Thy beloved" came the words, but, "It is thyself that knocks," and then the door unclosed, he passed the threshold. For all true love has its root in unity, and there again it is not twain but one. So it would seem that in the highest ethic this is the true note that we should strike, inasmuch as for our best beloved there is no such thing as service regarded as altruistic, because the deepest joy and the highest pleasure come in serving that which is in very truth the better self of each; so as we grow in spiritual life and understand the true oneness of humanity, we shall find in that humanity the best beloved. We shall serve our higher self in serving it, and thus once more we come back to that from which we started, the Invisible, the One and the All.

And Altruism, glorious as it is in the lower stages of morality —Altruism itself—is lost in the Supreme Oneness of the human soul, in the absolute indivisibility of the Spirit in Man. While, however, we are still consciously separate, Altruism may rightly be regarded as the Law of Life, based on a common origin in the Divine, based in the common training, in the pilgrimage which every soul of man must tread, based also in common experience, in that life after life where we have to learn every lesson, acquire all knowledge, share the various possibilities of human lot, and build out of common material a sublime character. In that life our destiny is one, the perfection of a divine humanity; one in origin, one in training, one in destiny, what shall avail to separate Man from Man and to build up walls of division between brothers?

Thus this Unity is the foundation of our brotherhood, as Brotherhood is the word that includes all our ethics. For it is in the law of Love that all true conduct has its root. As long as external law is needed, that law is the measure of our imperfection; it is only when no law is wanted, when the nature expressing itself spontaneously is one with the divine law, it is only then that humanity is perfected and liberty and law become one forevermore.

Here again is the sanction of right ethics, found in this fact of brotherhood everywhere discoverable in nature. All our European World discussing ethical systems to-day, is asking for some categorical imperative which shall announce duty and right to man. Take what systems you will in our German Schools of Philosophy, the system of Kant in Germany or any of the many schools of ethics being gradually builded by our English-speaking people—everywhere you will find the question propounded, What is the Imperative? What is the Ought? What is the Thou Shall, which is to be the training in human life?

"It is not possible," say some schools, and you may find this expressed very clearly and well in one of the well-known books of Professor Sedgwick in dealing with the question of Ought—we are face to face with a difficulty as to why we ought. Can we get any further than a conditional imperative? Can we go beyond the statement to Men, If you want to reach such a goal, such and such is the path you should pursue?

To take his own illustration, you may say to a pupil, "If you want to paint and be a great artist, you must hold your brush in such fashion; you must train your eye by such and such rules; you must gradually gain the knowledge which underlies form, and by these many steps you shall at last reach your goal."

Is morality the same in this sense as Art or Science? Is it always to depend upon an If, so that if Man refuses the goal he shall reject right conduct and stand lawless in a universe of law? If that be so, it seems to me that progress will be very slow amongst men, for you would have them first to evolve the conscience, and it is the very training of the conscience for which right ethics is needed. You would be walking constantly in a vicious circle having no point of starting. You would be endeavoring to use a lever with an absent fulcrum, and so find no vantage point to which your force could be applied. It is the categorical imperative we need, not the conditional. Not "If Thou wilt be perfect, do this or that," but, "Thou shalt be perfect, and the Law of Life is Thus.".

And is it not true that Nature speaks in such fashion? Is it not true that from the lips of Nature, physical, we will say, there sounds ever the categorical imperative? Man, ignorant and foolish, unknowing the laws that surround him, desires to follow the promptings of his own untrained will, driven perhaps by the desires of the lower nature and hearing in them the voice that allures and compels. From the lips of Nature drop sternly the words, "Thou shalt." Answers the will of Man able to choose, " I will not." And then there falls upon the silence but the two words, "Then suffer."

Such is the way in which physical nature teaches the inviolability of law. Man, following his own untrained will, strives to follow it, be a fence of physical law around him or not. He dashes himself against the iron wall he cannot break, and the pain of the bruising, the anguish of the mutilation, teaches him that law is inviolable and unchangeable, that it must be obeyed or the disobedient will perish in the struggle.

Is Nature different on her different planes? Does she speak clearly, as well in the moral and in the spiritual world as in the physical? Yea, for all Nature is one. The expression of the one divine will is nature, and until you can change the divine will, no law that is the expression of that will can be altered; and, therefore, in morals as much as in physics, this imperative, this categorical imperative, is hers. But unhappily, it has not been undisputed; unhappily, men have thought they could play with morals where they would never dream of playing with physical necessity. They have thought that they could sow one seed and reap another, when they were sowing virtue and vice instead of the mere corn or oats. And they have wondered and they have not understood when each seed is ripened after its own nature, and the moral seed has ripened according to law, and given a corrupt society and degraded humanity and a soul stupefied and drugged by sense.

Does such teaching seem stern and cold? Does it seem as though Man in a remorseless universe, found in the wheels of destiny rolling round him no·place of refuge, no harbor in which he might escape? Does he feel that these wheels moving round him crush him, that law is iron, and destiny cannot be escaped? My brothers, ill do you read the Universe if to you law seems cruel, if to you death may seem soulless. Law is but the will of the divine, and the divine who desires your happiness. Law is but the expression of the perfect, and only in perfection can joy and peace be found. Lose sight of this will for a moment, of those wheels that seem to crush you, for though the wheels roll on unchanging, the very heart of the universe is love. Therefore it is that some of us who have caught glimpses of this unity, who have seen that love and justice are one, and that injustice and cruelty would be identical, therefore it is sometimes that, looking at the universe, we feel that while the law is changeless it lifts us instead of crushing us. And has not your own Emerson taught you the same lesson? Can you remember in one of those marvellous essays of his he taught the great truth that Nature only looks cruel while we oppose her; she is our strongest helper when we join ourselves to her. For every law that crushes you while you oppose it, lifts you when you are united to it. Every force that is against you while you are lawless, is on your side when you make yourself one with law. He tells you to hitch your wagon on to a star, for then the wagon shall move with all the force of the planet above you; and is it not a greater destiny even to suffer until we learn the law, than to escape it and remain in ignorance when the law is that which brings us ultimately to triumph? Nature is conquered by obedience, and the divine is found in a unity of justice and of love.

Brotherhood, then, in its full meaning is a law in nature. Stress has more than once been laid on this in our meetings, but not too much stress has thereon been laid. For it is the very object, the desire, of our work that brotherhood shall become practical in society, and it will never become practical until men understand that it is a law, and not only an aspiration. It is a common experience that when men have discovered a law of nature, they no longer fight against it. They at once accommodate themselves to the new knowledge. They at once adapt themselves to the newly-understood conditions, and in that very way have preached brotherhood. And yet brotherhood is but so little known in our Western World! Is it not possible that men have disobeyed, not because they do not recognize the beauty of the ideal, but because they have not understood its absolute necessity, and the failure of every effort that goes against the universal law in life.

Brothers in our bodies by that interaction of physical molecules of which our Brother Judge has already spoken; brothers in our minds by that interaction of mental images and mental pictures whereby every one of us is constantly affecting his brothers. In our spirits, above all, and on every plane of life, brotherhood exists as fact.

And it must be remembered, in dealing with this brotherhood, that the word is meant to imply everything that it means in what we call the closest relationships of daily life. We are apt to make a distinction between brethren in churches and those outside. We should follow in that which we preach of, if it is that real brotherhood of love that we desire amongst men. Sometimes it is said that by ceasing to love the nearest we shall grow to love impersonal humanity. It is not so. The life of love is a growth upward, an expansion ever widening, growing out from the family to the city, from the city to the state; from the nation to humanity. It does not begin by dwarfing the love of the home. It starts there and it carries on all the passions—the passion and the pity that the mother feels for the child of her own body, and extends that love to embrace every child and son of man—not by cooling down love, but by strengthening and widening it out.

Thus is brotherhood to grow and the race to become practically, as it is essentially, one. For it is these relationships that teach the wider possibility, and so, in the Book of the Golden Precepts, one of the most exquisite gifts that we have received from the East through H. P. Blavatsky, we are told, "Follow the wheel of life below the wheel of duty to the race and kin ; as those duties are properly discharged we become worthy of the wider work." The heart widens out and because it is never closed against any. And at the very beginning of the path, the first step the disciple is bidden to take is to make his heart respond to every cry of nature, so that, as the heart-string quivers under the touch, he, as string, shall quiver to every cry of need that comes from his brother's lips. But if we confine our love to those with whom nature has put us, it is lower love. The lower love is selfish, exclusive, taking from the outside to give to the personally beloved, and careless for the wants of others provided one's own is satisfied. I mean one's own in the family, not one's own personally. That is not true love. It is a form only of selfishness, and when you find in our teaching that such love is to be destroyed, it means that love must be purified of every taint of personality, and so we must grow ever upward, widening as we grow, because the love that we are to give to our brother man is to be measured by his want of it and not by any of the lesser ties of personality. That may bind us to him or may be absent between him and us. The measure of want—that is the measure of giving. The agony that cries for help—that is the claim that we have to answer. And so our teachers train us to discharge the nearest duty so that we may carry on the strength of that to the wider duty, and thus make our love to man as the love of husband to wife, as the love of brother to sister, finding in the pain but joy in the sacrifice, because the happiness of the beloved is deeper than the momentary pain of that which is given to us.

Thus, then we learn, as it were, the sanction, the motive, that which nature tells us as regards this human brotherhood, and from that we step onward to deal with those who are not yet quite touched with that light of reality which makes the appeal to the divine in man the mightiest of impulses.

For, as man develops, he answers to nobler and nobler impulses, and at first, very often, the method of the teacher must be the method of Nature, which allows men to learn by pain the reality that I was speaking of with regard to the law. And so by Karma we scent another sanction for right ethics ; so we teach men that selfishness can but breed sorrow and evil, can have no other offspring than misery. If they will not learn by love they must learn by pain. If they will not learn by longing for God, they must learn by experience of the evil ; and if that real tree of life which is in every human heart does not sufficiently attract them to the eating of its fruit, the tree of Life Eternal whose fruits are but of love and duty, then they must eat of the tree of knowledge of evil as well as of good, so that if, to quote one of the sweetest of our English poets—"if Goodness move him not, then Misery may toss him to my breast." For that is the voice of the Spirit crying in the world, crying to all that has gone out from it to come back. If its voice does not attract, then suffering must be used for a time to drive. Back the wanderer must come ; the exile cannot remain abroad ; his seat is empty in the home, it waits for his return, and if he will not come by love, then by starving on the husks that are fit food for swine he must learn the lesson. And the unrest of the transitory, the dissatisfaction of the temporal — that shall turn his steps once more homeward till he come near enough to be drawn by love and no longer by pain.

Thus, then, we have the foundation which deals with facts as sanction for righteousness, and thus Re-incarnation once more comes in in order to show us that only by right living can progress be made, that if selfishness is to be eradicated unselfish acts must be performed, selfish thoughts must be destroyed, for in re-incarnation it is thought which moulds the character, and none can mould the character towards evil and thus discover tendencies to good. Thus we remove arbitrariness from the moral world by knowledge of self. Knowledge has removed it from the physical. Thus we take away all the doubt and the hope that springs from the doubt, that we may escape the results of our own actions and creep into unearned bliss by some side door of vicarious atonement, where we have not labored and where we have not wrought. We learn that each must walk on his own feet—that each man must grow by his own effort. Though brother souls must help him, he must also help himself. For Truth does not need invertebrate people saved by the goodness of another. Truth needs men and women strong to stand in the strength they have acquired for themselves, strong that by their example the still weaker may be inspired, and gradually each one may show himself divine.

But all this is not new. There is nothing new save the words that clothe it, nothing new save the garment that is woven round it. We have had all this as our priceless heritage for millions of years, and yet we have not recognized our treasure. Every great teacher of Religion has taught what here I feebly repeat to-day. Every great one who has come into the world in order to strike the key-note of morality has spoken the same language, has uttered the same thought.

Turn to the scriptures of the world and see how one moral nutriment is found in all. Will you go to China, Lao-tze will teach you the law of love, and teach you the very doctrine familiar in your own creed; for Lao-tze, speaking six hundred years before Christ was born, laid down that law of curing evil by good. Yes, we have not yet learned the only law of Peace. "The untruthful," he said, "I will meet with Truth, as I meet the truthful also. I will meet the liberal with liberality, I will meet the illiberal with liberality also. The faithful I will meet with faith, the unfaithful I will meet with faith also. I will cure the miser by generosity, I will cure the liar by truth."

So, as from the lips of a Chinese teacher, there drops from those of a great Hindu sage exactly the same thought, when in the tenfold system of duties Mano put forgiveness of injuries as the vital law of the progress of the soul. So, six centuries before Christ, the Buddha repeated the lesson—" To him that causelessly injures me I will return the protection of my ungrudging love. The more evil comes from him, the more good shall flow from me." Exactly the same lesson flows from the lips of the great Jewish teacher, when in the Sermon on the Mount he bids his disciples " Love your enemies, bless them that curse you, do good to them that hate you, that you may be the children of your father in Heaven, who sendeth his sunlight on the evil and on the good, and sendeth rain alike on the just and on the unjust."

The Voice is one, whether from Jew or Buddhist, whether from Hindu or Chinaman, the words are well-nigh one, the spirit is identical. What want we, then, of new morality, while the old remains unfulfilled? Why ask for new teaching when the old is so high above our accomplishment to-day? It may be that amongst far-off generations, when the growth of Man has been perfected, it may be that in some future cycle of evolution, some morality undreamed of to-day, some ethic more noble, more sublime, more pure, may come from the lips of some God to man. We are not ready for such teaching, we are not yet prepared for such instruction. Enough for us the ancient law of love, for until we have fulfilled that, no other horizon can open before our eyes.

And so, at this last of our sessional meetings, we close with that with which we started, the law of a divine life that brings all things with it, the law of a divine love that is the guiding light of man.

Born of the spirit, we go towards the Spirit. Born of the divine love, we live until that love is perfected in us, and when that love is made perfect, what lips of Man may syllable, what brain of Man may conceive, what further heights of beauty, what further depths of joy, what further possibilities of illimitable expansion, lie before those souls whose life is one with the divine. Bound to the feet of divinity, they last as long as it. Boundless as deity itself, no limitations can check the spirit that lives in man. (Applause.)

Adjourned until 8 p. m.

SIXTH SESSION, SATURDAY 16TH, 8 P. M.
IN HALL OF WASHINGTON.

GENERAL PRESENTATION OF THEOSOPHY TO THE PARLIAMENT.

The Hall was crowded, about 3,500 persons being present. In consequence of the strained condition of Bro. William Q. Judge's voice, Dr. J. D. Buck was given the chair.

DR. BUCK—We are here this evening, ladies and gentlemen, to present to the Congress of Religions a general statement of the Theosophical doctrines, of that which the Theosophical Society has undertaken in these latter times. An historical account of the Society was given this morning by Claude F. Wright, in which statistics were furnished, the organization of the Society was presented, and the work which has been accomplished was at least outlined. In the announcement that was made in 1875, three objects were given as the motive for the existence of the Society and for its organization. These were, *first*, to found the nucleus of a Universal Brotherhood of humanity, without relation to race, creed, sex, caste, or color. You will please notice that to found the nucleus of a Universal Brotherhood of man was the object. The early Theosophists, the founders of the Theosophical Society, have been accused of a great many things of which they were in no sense guilty. They were not guilty of the folly of supposing that at the present day a Universal Brotherhood of man could be established and fully realized. Humanity will have to travel a very long way over the road of evolution before it will unite as one mass in forming a Universal Brotherhood of man. It was, however, supposed, and, as the very latest developments have demonstrated, with very good reason, that there might be found among the people of the world enough to form the nucleus of a Universal Brotherhood, and therefore in the establishment of this nucleus, the nucleus would become just what a nucleus always is: the very life and centre and the soul of the Theosophical Society. It is the same in vegetable structures, it is the same in the building of worlds, and the same way we know it will tend in that most complicated of all structures—human society. Around this nucleus, pledged to this one principle of Universal Brotherhood, it was hoped that the peoples of the earth, of nations, of men, might gather by aggregation, just as the process of organization takes place in living tissue, and just as any formation crystallizes around the nucleus, which sets, you may say, the rhythm or possibility of the organization or structure that is being formed around this rhythmic centre, imbued with this one idea, might in time gather others, and others and others again, until the nucleus itself became the structure of the Society. Now, the objection to this proposition is often made, that there is nothing new under the sun. It is new, however, to the Western world in the form in which it is presented by the Theosophical Society. We don't claim merely that brotherhood is a thing that ought to be accepted; we don't claim that it is a thing simply which is greatly to be desired; we claim that it is a fact in nature, a universal fact in the process of the evolution of Suns, and holds no less in the process of the evolution of humanity. Deny it as we will, we can no more change that which is a fact in nature than we can change the law of gravity or than we can subvert materially the law and processes of evolution. Therefore you see that the initiation of this fact of Universal Brotherhood comes to us with a different force from that with which it is presented by the various religions and philosophies of the world; because in the philosophy that unfolds under such a doctrine, it is demonstrated that this is a fact which cannot be controverted. And as was shown in the meeting this morning, he who resists this law simply puts himself as an individual against the whole trend of the current of evolution. Nature issues her commands; under her invariable laws man may follow the lines of least resistance and work with nature if he will, but if he blindly resists, he takes the line of greatest resistance, and therefore the laws of progress, the whole evolutionary scheme of nature, is turned against him, and pain and suffering will result. We have all learned this fact in the processes of our individual life, our individual evolution. We have learned it and see by experience. But it has remained for philosophy, drawing from the immense resources of antiquity, from the philosophy of the far East, it has remained for the Theosophical Society to demonstrate this fact upon a scientific basis, to incorporate it into a system of philosophy that is knowledge and philosophy; one in which there are no missing links; one in which every proposition agrees with every other proposition; one in which the whole scheme of philosophy, man, and the universe agrees with all that modern and ancient science has discovered with regard to the laws of the universe. And then, passing this philosophy and this science, underneath is the background and the supporter of true religion.

We are endeavoring, therefore, to revive that which at the beginning of the Christian era was called the gnosis, knowledge in its true sense, in its highest sense, in its purest sense; knowledge of that great secret which was the burden and the veil of the alchemists, the secret of the human soul. Those who imagine that those Theosophists of the middle centuries and the dark ages, those philosophers who had a home in Europe and were known to the Western world as alchemists, that the true alchemists were not searching literally for the philosopher's stone or the luxury of life, or something to turn baser metals into gold,—those who say so have but read the surface of their writings; they certainly have never read between the lines. For that process of transmutation to which they referred was simply to convert the baser elements of human nature, of human life, into those spiritual and divine essences from which the very life of man proceeds.

The second object that was announced in the formation of the Theosophical Society was the examination and study of the ancient religions and philosophies and sciences, and to demonstrate the importance of that study. Now, why was this stated as one of the objects for the formation of the Theosophical Society? Because all of our Western world, whether you call it philosophical, religious, or scientific, was grossly wanting in the real knowledge of the soul, knowledge of the higher nature of man; and because this study could give rise to but one result. It first so read the first proposition, viz.: the nucleus of a Universal Brotherhood of man, but as it was equally important, it would demonstrate incontrovertibly the brotherhood of all great religions of the world, which had come down in the secret books in glyphics and symbols, the key to which was lost, the key to which was possessed by ancient Initiates in knowledge and preserved by the Rishis and Masters of old India from age to age, corrupted in the doctrines of Pythagoras, Plato, and Zoroaster, and a great many lesser lights since that time; I say the key to this knowledge was to be found in the investigation of those Eastern religions. It was not by any means the purpose of the founders of the Theosophical Society to put any of the other religions that exist in the world to-day above the Christian religion or above any one of the other religions, but they hoped to demonstrate a Universal Brotherhood of religions equally with the Universal Brotherhood of man. The admission, the demonstration, of one of these principles verified the other, and therefore they were like the two hands upon the one body. Men who work for the brotherhood of man must necessarily work for the brotherhood of religions, and he who admits the brotherhood of the great religions of the world is doing the best he can in that way to demonstrate the fact and to bring about the return of the Universal Brotherhood of man.

The third principle that was held out as the object of the Theosophical Society is the investigation of the latent psychical powers in man. Now, here is the point at which knowledge was needed more than at almost any other: the psychical nature of man. With the trend of Western thought, with all that was given out under the name of Western science, with all that came to the West under the name of evolution, men were becoming more and more materialistic, and man was losing the consciousness that he has a human soul. I remember only a very short time ago an individual very interested in these subjects asked me the question: "Do you really believe in the existence of the soul?" The only answer that I could make to him was to reply in his own terms: "Do you really doubt or deny it?" It is the consciousness of the soul that will come to every one who will open his own soul to the higher light of truth, to the light and to the ministrations of his own higher self; it is in this line that will be discovered the existence of the soul. And then when we come to its laws, its processes, its method of evolution, the fashions under which evolution or progress can be most rapidly and most certainly made,—this was the knowledge that was needed by the Western world more than almost anything else. And then there was another reason why it was particularly necessary fifteen years ago, and is necessary still. There came in the process of time a check to this wave of materialism that was rolling over the Western world. I refer to that phenomenal existence or experience known as modern spiritualism. Take it with all of its eccentricities, take it with all of its physical manifestations and all its various phenomena, there are unquestionably a very large number of facts that are incontrovertible as facts ; but without any correct knowledge of the nature and processes and operation of the human soul, knowledge, impractical knowledge, derived along these lines of investigation, pursued ignorantly by spiritualists and their interested aiders, was far more likely to result in evil than good. The time therefore came when modern spiritualism ran into phenomenalism, and so far as furnishing a motive in life, so far as furnishing correct knowledge of the nature of man was concerned, I can say, I think, in all fairness and in all charity, it was rather the conception than the real. When this movement and this philosophy were furnished, a pretty large proportion of those who entered into the investigation of spiritualism were influenced to make further and deeper efforts. They came as simple truth-seekers to investigate the phenomena themselves. When you add that it is admitted by all fair and candid writers upon the subject that a very large proportion of the phenomena are evidently fraudulent, that a strong proportion of what are called professional mediums should pursue their calling for a fee and thus bring many into the investigation of the higher nature of man, are admitted to be frauds, and bring many unfortunate people into temptation, and so on this account there was greater than ever the need of exact, rational, definite, and satisfactory knowledge as to the nature of the human soul or the psychical nature of man ; and it was therefore the third object of study, to investigate the psychical powers latent in man.

Now, because of this statement and because of the widespread ignorance in regard to this subject, the most foolish and inconsistent and contradictory reports have gone out with regard to the Theosophical movement. It is the most common thing in the world for people who know little of themselves and perhaps little more of spiritualism, to identify Theosophy with spiritualism. When asked What is Theosophy, they say, Simply an adjunct of spiritualism. But it is a very different thing indeed. We make an investigation of facts, and, when facts are demonstrated to us as such, why not admit them ? And especially if facts which under a broad and comprehensive philosophy that we have learned to accept as springing from the psychical nature of man. The most bitter opposition that has been accorded to the Theosophical Society has come from the spiritualists, simply because they have misunderstood generally the motive of Theosophy. They believe that it had for its object the destruction of spiritualism. It has been also accused of an intent to destroy Christianity and to set up Brahmanism or Buddhism or some other ism in its stead. But nothing could be wider from the mark. There is one particular fact in regard to this psychical investigation that should be understood once for all ; that is, admitting all the facts, the authenticated and incontrovertible facts of spiritualism, Theosophy claims not only have the spiritualists not got the only logical and rational interpretation when they claim that these phenomena are caused by the disembodied spirits of men and women who have departed from this life and are therefore evidence of the immortality of the soul. We take issue with them just at that point. We claim it is not the only rational interpretation, but we claim that a better knowledge of the psychical nature of man will modify all these views and in a large number of instances change entirely the conclusions. We believe as firmly as any orthodox man, the member of any church, or any spiritualist, in the immortality of the soul, but we do not believe that that immortality can be demonstrated by communications with disembodied spirits. We believe it is the embodied spirit that should have consciousness of its own immortality, and at the same time be able to put in their own places all these psychic phenomena that can be demonstrated as facts that have been given to us by our brothers, the spiritualists. There need be no controversy at this point beyond mere disagreement as to the interpretation. There is not the slightest ground for any bitterness or ill feeling between the Theosophists and any other body of believers or experimenters. That is our view. It is not put forth as orthodox. As to those who still cling to the spiritualistic interpretation of the phenomena, there is no one who has a disposition so far as I know, certainly there is no one who has the authority, to say that they have not a perfect right to interpret the phenomena in their own way; for there is no creed or orthodoxy in regard to Theosophy.

Now, taking these three objects of this Society, the first one of them was made obligatory upon those who sought membership in the Theosophical Society. The first and foremost, the most important object for which the Society was formed, was this nucleus of Universal Brotherhood; and better by far if all else had been forgotten and left out of the question than that this should be covered up or neglected in our duty; because in the dimness of the future and in basing the life of the individual on the fact of Universal Brotherhood we find the surest way for charity among men, for recognizing the brotherhood of all religions; and furthermore, if the development of these very faculties in man which shall reveal to his own soul its own existence, its immortality, its nature, its destiny, its powers, and its possibilities, there is no way by which these investigations can be pursued so certainly as by altruistic or charitable work in the world among our fellow men.

There has been a great deal of misapprehension not only in regard to spiritualism, or the supposed relation existing between Theosophy and spiritualism, but upon certain teachings given out by Theosophy itself. It was not an uncommon thing in the early days of Theosophy for one who had got a little scattering knowledge of Theosophy and the possibility of the evolution of these powers in man, as referred to by Bro. Chakravarti this morning, it was not uncommon, I say, for one to get a little smattering of this philosophy and these ideas, and then begin to inquire where he could find a jungle in the forest so that he might retire from the world and develop these powers. No greater mistake could possibly have been made. Take an individual in our own civilization here, an intelligent individual, a very intelligent individual, charitable and kind as the world goes; what would he do in a cave? What could he do if under a teacher, when he cannot control his fleshly appetites? He was really ready to take this like any other psychic food and make the most of it, and it would have resulted, if he had persisted, in wrecking his life in one way or another. Nothing of the kind was ever admitted or inculcated by the Theosophic Society, nothing by its teachings and its doctrines except the ordinary evolution of the higher nature of man, wherein man must work out his own salvation with fear and trembling; not fear of an angry God, but of his own lower nature; fear of the temptations of the flesh and the appetites weak and depraved of human nature. When a man has along this line conquered himself, then certainly he should be ready to conquer another world than that of the physical senses, than that of the seen and known. So I say, follow along these lines the mission of the Theosophical Society, so well defined and kept steadily before the people, although the Theosophical Society as such, and its leaders, have been held responsible by individuals for their own misapprehensions as to what it was: all this we are trying to get before the world.

It is evident from a consideration of these historical facts and these movements of modern times, it is evident the greatest aim of the world to-day is not for the organization of men simply to help each other. The greatest end is not for the Theosophic amelioration of man, bad as that condition may be. The great end of the world to-day is for correct knowledge upon the higher nature of man; because correct action never can proceed consistently, logically, and persistently except upon the basis of right knowledge. It is not mere faith, blind belief, mere superstition, we need. It is simply a correct knowledge of the nature and possibilities of the human soul.

Now, you can believe as individuals or not as you please, that the Theosophic philosophy is found in the writings of the ancients. In writings put forth by letters on masonry you will find this the lost creed of humanity; it is the knowledge of the human soul, this great 'secret symbolized on masonry by glyphics of secret meaning, that secret imparted under penalty of death by the Essenes, the Gnostics, by the Ecstatics, by thousands and thousands of societies whose names have been forgotten throughout the past. I say this is the great secret, the religion of the nature, destiny, the possibilities of the soul of man. That is what is symbolized in all Masonic lodges by the legend of Hiram Abiff; this sacrifice by the son of the virgin. It is the individual, this man dwelling within man that is the building of the temple concerning which we hear so much in some of our secret organizations. What is the temple? That house not made with hands, the spirit of which is eternal in the heavens. So that in the older philosophies and older mysteries, by symbols, by glyphics, by all manner of methods it was attempted to preserve or to convey to all intuitive enough or spiritually intuitive to understand the doctrines of this knowledge of the human soul. Organizations that once possessed 'it lost it through their own degeneration and by falling into matter. Prof. Huxley was right in his book, *The Ancient Religions of the World.* I quote the idea rather than the exact words. On the next to the last page of *The Ancient Religions of the World* he says that the result of his investigations in these ancient religions is to convince him they all came from one primeval religion, revealed to man from without. That is exactly the claim put forth by the Theosophical Society; and those without the pale of humanity, that also applies to those very Masters, those Mahatmas, those ancient Rishis, those men who have at different times unveiled all the possibilities of human nature, and it was through them that this revelation was made in the first place, by them it is preserved from age to age, and I quote Prof. Huxley as saying himself, where he got the quotation I don't know, "that this philosophy was presented to the world by the Masters of those who know." There are not only those who know by actual experience of the existence and powers of the human soul, but there are those who stand above even those. Who are these Masters? They are the Avatars, the Buddhas, the Christs of history, and no greater mistake was ever made by the Western world on any subject than to suppose that the infinite goodness, that the eternal spirit that pervades the universe, was so poor or deficient either in power or resources that only 2,000 years ago he would send one of these redeemers to man. What was the infinite goodness doing through millions and millions of ages preceding the Christian era?

My friends, we are living to-day perhaps in the oldest country on the globe; the new country is nothing but the old world revived after one of these relapses or sleeps that come in the cyclic history of man; therefore we are living to-day in what we call the new world, and we are taught in the secret doctrine that civilization has spread around and around this globe times almost without number; we are the children, the youngest heirs of all this mighty past, and all the affairs of man, his governments, his civilizations, his religions, his philosophies simply follow the pattern of individual life. They are conceived in the womb of the eternal spirit; they are born in the time of need in the life of the world, they reach their adolescence, their manhood, their old age, and finally they totter and die. That is the history of every civilization the world has ever known; that is the history of every religion that has ever inspired the soul of man and led him to look up to something higher than himself. Can we accept the statement that at this late day our religion, our philosophy, our science is the first and only one that ever gladdened the heart of man, and that we shall escape the universal destiny of old age and decay? Then comes the rejuvenescence of all these civilizations in another form, and they are under the cyclic law which obtains among the heavenly orbs, with the moving of the planets and the suns; and it is thus also concerning all human activities, his civilizations, his sciences, his religions, everything that pertains to his activities.

Now the basis of altruism which is put forth by the Theosophical Society you will see is based upon this Universal Brotherhood, and I hope that no one present here in this audience to-night will ever again make an assertion so inapplicable to the Theosophical movement as, in speaking of the principle of altruism announced by the Theosophical Society of Universal Brotherhood, by saying "That is nothing new." "We had that in other religions." That you see is pointless as directed against the Theosophical Society or our movement. Because the one strong point we make is that it is not new, and not exclusively the possession of any religion, of any philosophy, any civilization the world has ever known. We are told by those who know, there was never a time when it existed not upon the earth, in different quarters at the same time with barbarous nations, the half civilized, the wholly civilized, and finally those who through their altruism imitate the gods in their beneficence towards their fellow men. We don't claim that this is anything new or exclusively Theosophical. And certainly it is not something that belongs exclusively to the religions of the West. The very first sign of progress I think that we should make is to be just; not even charitable; simply just towards the other religions, the brother religions of the world, giving them their just proportion of due, their fair and honorable recognition; and when we do this we shall have found the same truths expressed in different languages to different people at different times, but all with the same great motive; and therefore underlying all those religions of the world, whether past or present, everything that ever deserved the name of religion, you will find this principle of Universal Brotherhood announced by its redeemers, by its teachers, by its Avatars, and you will find altruism, the preferring of another's good to your own selfish enjoyment, the best ethics in all of these.

Now, then, put these things together, it seems to me there need be no misapprehension as to the real motive for the organization of the Theosophical Society. It does not stand apart. It welcomes to its membership men and women, black and white, no matter what their creed may be, provided they have gone far enough in the line of human evolution, far enough above the animal plane and the survival of the fittest and the bare animal struggle for existence, to recognize the principle of Universal Brotherhood and to undertake to carry it out in their daily life in the best possible way they can. That is all that is necessary for the needs of the Theosophical Society, and we therefore invite everyone, no matter what his creed or belief may be, to join us in this movement, whether in the Society or out. The doors of the Society are always wide open, and there is certainly strength in co-operation, and we have kept this so designedly from all other matters whatsoever, so there can be no difficulty with the members of any church, or of any creed, of any religion on earth joining our ranks; and so far as I know there is none of the religions of the world whose representatives are not also known as members of the Theosophical Society, working along these lines, laying aside everything else and endeavoring to bring about the reign of universal altruism and the Universal Brotherhood of man.

I have the honor to announce that Brother Judge will now address you. I may say that while Brother Judge's name may not be familiar to everyone in this hall, his name is inextricably connected with the organization of the Society. He is at present the Vice-President of the entire Society of the world, and General Secretary of the American Section.

WILLIAM Q. JUDGE—Mr. Chairman ; brothers and sisters ; men and women ; members of the Parliament of Religions : The Theosophical Society has been presenting to you but one-half of its work, but one-half of that which it has to present to the world. This is the Parliament of Religions. This is a Parliament of the Religions of the day. Theosophy is not only a religion ; it is also a science ; it is religious science and scientific religion, and at a Parliament of Religions it would not be possible, indeed it would not be proper, to present the science of Theosophy, which relates to so many matters outside of the ordinary domain of the religions of to-day. The time will come when religion will also be a science. To-day it is not. The object of Theosophy is to make of religion also a science, and to make science a religion, so we have been presenting only one-half of the subject which we deal with, and I would like you to remember that. We could not go into the other part ; it would be beyond the scope of this meeting.

Now, we have discovered during the last week, as many have discovered before by reading, by experience, and by travel, that the religions of the world are nearly all alike. We have discovered that Christianity is not alone in claiming a Savior. If you will go over to Japan you will find that the Buddhists of Japan have a doctrine which declares that any one who relies upon and repeats three times a day the name "Amita Buddha," will be saved. That is one Savior of the Buddhists, who had the doctrine before Christianity was started. If you will go among the Buddhists elsewhere you will find that they also have a Savior ; that by reliance upon the Lord Buddha, they claim they will be saved. If you will go to the Brahmins and the other religions of India, you will find they also have a Savior. In some parts of that mysterious land they say : "Repeat the name of Rama"—God—" and he will save you." The Brahmins themselves have in their doctrines a doctrine which is called the "Bridge Doctrine" : that which has God for its aim, has God himself as the means of salvation ; is itself God. And so wherever you go throughout this wide world, examining the various religions, you find they all have this common doctrine. Why should we then say that the latest of these religions is the inventor of the doctrine ? It is not. It is common property of the whole human race, and we find on further inquiry that these religions all teach, and the Christian religion also, that this Savior is within the heart of every man, and is not outside of him.

We have discovered further by examining all these religions and comparing them with the Christian religion, which is the one belonging to the foremost nation of to-day, that in these other religions and in Christianity are found certain doctrines which constitute the key that will unlock this vast lock made up of the different religions. These doctrines are not absent from Christianity any more than they are absent from Buddhism or from Brahminism, and now the time has come when the world must know that these doctrines are common property, when it is too late for any people West or East to claim that they have a special property in any doctrine whatever.

The two principles which unlock this great lock which bars men sometimes from getting on, are called Karma and Reincarnation. The latter doctrine bears a more difficult Sanscrit name.

The doctrine of Karma put into our language is simply and solely Justice. What is justice? Is it something that condemns alone? I say, No. Justice is also mercy. For mercy may not be dissociated from justice, and the word justice itself includes mercy within it. Not the justice of man, which is false and erring, but the justice of Nature. That is also mercy. For if she punishes you, it is in order that she may do a merciful act and show you the truth at last by discipline. That is the doctrine of Karma, and it is also called the ethical law of causation. It means that effect follows cause uniformly; not alone in mere objective nature, where if you put your hand in the fire it will surely be burned, but in your moral nature, throughout your whole spiritual and intellectual evolution. It has been too much the custom to withdraw from use this law of cause and effect the moment we look at man as a spiritual being; and the religions and philosophies of the past and the present have the proof within them that this law of cause and effect obtains on the spiritual, the moral, and the intellectual planes just as much as it does on the physical and objective. It is our object to once more bring back this law of justice to the minds of men and show them that justice belongs to God, and that he is not a God who favors people, but who is just because he is merciful.

The doctrine of reincarnation is the next one. Reincarnation, you say, what is that? Do you mean that I was here before? Yes, undoubtedly so. Do you mean to tell me that this is a Christian, a Buddhist, a Brahminical, a Japanese doctrine, and a Chinese one? Yes, and I can prove it; and if you will examine your own records with an unprejudiced and fearless mind, afraid of no man, you will prove it also. If you go back in the records of Christianity to the first year of it, you will find that for many centuries this doctrine was taught. Surely the men who lived near Jesus knew what the doctrine was. It was admitted by Jesus himself. He said on one occasion that Elias had already come back in the person of John, but had been destroyed by the ruler. How could Elias come back and be born again as John unless the law of nature permitted it? We find on examining the writers, the early Christian fathers who made the theology of the Christian churches admitting, by the greatest of them, Origen, that this doctrine was true. He, the greatest of them all, who wrote so much men could not read all his books, believed in it. It is said in the Christian scripture that Jesus also said so much they could not record it, and if they had, the volumes could not be counted. If these teachings were not recorded, we can imagine from what he spoke and from what his early followers believed, that this doctrine was taught distinctly by him in words. (Applause.)

It is the doctrine of which the Reverend Mr. Beecher, brother of the famous Henry Ward Beecher, in a book called *The Conflict of Religions*, said, "It is an absolute necessity to Christianity; without it Christianity is illogical. With it it is logical." And a great writer, the Rev. William Alger, whose book, *A Critical History of the Doctrine of a Future Life*, is used in the religious educational institutions of all denominations with perhaps one exception, has written twice in two editions and said that after fifteen years' study of the subject he had come to the conclusion that the doctrine was true and necessary.

Furthermore, we find that in these countries where Christianity arose—for Christianity is not a Western product—reincarnation has always been believed. You ask for human evidence. You believe in this city, not only in this city but everywhere, in a court of law, if many witnesses testify to a fact it is proven. Well, millions upon millions of men in the East testify that they not only believe in reincarnation, but that they know it is true, that they remember that they were born before and that they were here before, and hundreds and thousands of men in the West have said the same thing. That they not only believe it, but that they know it. Poets have written of it all through English literature. It is a doctrine that almost everybody believes in their hearts. The little child coming straight from the other shore, coming without any defects straight from the heavenly Father, believes that it has always lived.

If the doctrine of immortality which is taught by every religion is true, how can you split it in halves and say, you began to be immortal when you were born and you were never immortal before? How is it possible you did not live before if there is any justice in this universe? Is it not true that what happens is the result of your conduct? If you live a life of sin and wickedness, will you not suffer? If you steal, and rob, and lie, and put in operation causes for punishment, will you not be punished? Why should not that law be applied to the human being when born, to explain his state and capacity? We find children are born blind, deformed, halt, without capacity; where is the prior conduct which justifies such a thing, if they have just been born for the first time? They must have lived before. The disciples asked Jesus, "Why was this man born blind; was it for some sin he had committed?" When committed? When did he commit it if he had never been born before? Why ask Jesus, their master, this question, unless they believed the doctrine, unless, as we think, it is the true one and one then prevalent?

This doctrine of reincarnation, then, we claim is the lost chord of any religion that does not promulgate it. We say it is found in the Christian religion; it is found in every religion, and it offers to us a means whereby our evolution may be carried on, it offers an explanation to the question, Why are men born with different characters? We find one man born generous, and he will always be generous; we find another born selfish, and selfish he will be to the end of his life. We find one man born with great capacity, a great mind that can cover many subjects at once; or a special mind and capacity like that of Mozart. Why was he born so? Where did he get it if not from the character he had in the past? You may say that heredity explains it all. Then please explain how Blind Tom, born of negro parents who never knew anything about a piano, who never knew anything about music, was able to play upon a mechanically scaled instrument like the piano? It is not a natural thing. Where did he get the capacity? Heredity does not explain that. We explain it by reincarnation. Just so with Mozart, who at four years of age was able to write an orchestral score. Do you know what that means? It means the writing down the parts for the many instruments, and not only that, but writing it in a forced scale, which is a mechanical thing. How will that be explained by heredity? If you say that among his ancestors there must have been musicians, then why not before or after him? See Bach! If Bach could look back from the grave he would have seen his musical genius fading and fading out of his family until at last it disappeared.

Heredity will not explain these great differences in character and genius, but reincarnation will. It is the means of evolution of the human soul; it is the means of evolution for every animate and inanimate thing in this world. It applies to everything. All nature is constantly being reëmbodied, which is reincarnation. Go back with science. It shows you that this world was first a mass of fiery vapor; come down the years and you see this mass reëmbodied in a more solid form; later still it is reëmbodied as the mineral kingdom, a great ball in the sky, without life; later still animal life begins evolving until now it has all that we know of life, which is a reëmbodiment over and over again, or reincarnation. It means, then, that just as you move periodically from house to house in the city, you are limited by every house you move into, so the human being, who never dies, is not subject to death, moves periodically from house to house, and takes up a mortal body life after life, and is simply limited a little more or a little less, just as the case may be, by the particular body he may inhabit.

I could not go through all this subject to answer all the objections, but Theosophy will answer them all. The differences in people are explained by the fact that the character of the individual attracts him to the family that is just like himself, and not to any other family, and through heredity he receives his discipline, punishment, and reward.

The objections to reincarnation are generally based upon the question, why we do not remember. In the West that objection arises from the fact that we have been materialists so long, we have been deceived so long, that we have forgotten; we are not able to remember anything but what makes a violent impression on our senses. In the East and in some places in the West the people remember, and the time will come when the people in the West will remember also. And I warrant you that the children of the West know this, but it is rubbed out of their minds by their fathers and mothers. They say to the child, "Don't bother me with such questions; you are only imagining things." As if a child could imagine that it had been here before if it had not been. They never could imagine a thing which has not some existence in fact or that is not built up from impressions received. As you watch the newborn child you will see it throw its arms out to support itself. Why should the child throw out its arms to support itself? You say, instinct. What is instinct? Instinct is recollection imprinted upon the soul, imprinted upon the character within a child just born, and it knows enough to remember that it must throw out its arms to save itself from being hurt. Any physician will tell you this fact is true. Whether they explain it in the same way as I do or not, I don't know. We cannot remember our past lives simply because the brain which we now have was not concerned with these past lives. You say you cannot remember a past life, and therefore you don't believe it is true. Well if we grant that kind of argument, apply it to the fact that you cannot remember the facts of your present existence here; you cannot remember what dinner you ate three weeks ago; you cannot remember one-quarter of what has happened to you. Do you mean to say that all these things did not happen because you cannot remember? You cannot remember what happens to you now, so how do you expect to remember what happened to you in another life? But the time will come when man not so immersed in materiality will form his soul to such an extent that its qualities will be impressed upon the newborn child body and he will be able to remember and to know all his past, and then he will see himself an evolving being who has come up through all the ages as one of the creators of the world, as one of those who have aided in building this world. Man, we say, is the top, the crown of evolution; not merely as one who has been out there through favor, but as one who worked himself up through nature, unconsciously sometimes to himself, but under law, the very top and key of the whole system, and the time will come when he will remember it.

Now, this being the system of evolution which we gather from all religions, we say it is necessary to show that cause and effect act on man's whole being. We say that this law of cause and effect, or Karma, explains every circumstance in life and will show the poor men in Chicago who are born without means to live, who sometimes are hunted by the upper class and live in misery, why they are born so. It will explain why a man is born rich, with opportunity which he neglects; and another man born rich, with opportunity which he does not neglect. It will explain how Carnegie, the great iron founder in America, was a poor telegraph boy before he was raised to be a great millionaire. It will explain how one is born with small brain power, and another born with great brain power. It is because we have never died; we have always been living, in this world or in some other, and we are always meeting causes and character for the next life as well as for this.

Do you not know that your real life is in your mind, in your thoughts? Do you not know a great deal is due to your own mind, and under every act is a thought, and the thoughts make the man, and those thoughts act upon the forces of nature? Inasmuch as all these beings come back and live together over and over again, they bring back the thoughts, the impressions of those they have met and which others have made upon them there. When you persecute and hurt a man now, you are not punished afterwards because of the act you did to him, but because of the thought under your act and the thought under his feelings when he received your act. Having made these thoughts, they remain forever with you and him, and when you come again you will receive back to yourselves that which you gave to another. And is not that Christianity as well as Brahminism and Buddhism? You say, No. I say, Yes; read it in the words of Jesus, and I would have you to show you are right if you say, No. St. Paul I suppose is authority for you, and St. Paul says "Brethren, be not deceived; God is not mocked; for whatsoever a man soweth, that shall he also reap." I ask you where and when shall he reap that which he has sown? He must reap it where he sowed it, or there is no justice. He must come back here and help to cure that evil which he caused; he must come back here if he did cause any evil and continue to do all the good he can, so he may help to evolve the whole human race, which is waiting for him also. Jesus said : " Judge not, that ye be not judged; for with what measure ye mete, so shall it be measured out to you again." When ? If you go to heaven after this life and escape all you have done, certainly not then, and you make Jesus to have said that which is not true, and make St. Paul say that which is not true.

But I believe that St. Paul and Jesus knew what they were talking about and meant what they said. (Applause.) So, then, we must come again here in order that God shall not be mocked and each man shall reap that which he has sowed.

It is just the absence of this explanation that has made men deny religion ; for they have said : "Why, these men did not get what they sowed. Here are rich, wicked men who die in their beds, happy, with a shrive at the end of it. They have not reaped." But we know, just as Jesus and St. Paul have said, they will reap it surely, and we say according to philosophy, according to logic, according to justice, they will reap it right here where they sowed it, and not somewhere else. It would be unjust to send them anywhere else to reap it but where they did it. That has been taught in every religion ever since the world began, and it is the mission of the Theosophical Society to bring back the key to all the creeds, to show them that they are really at the bottom in these essential doctrines alike, and that men have a soul in a body, a soul that is ever living, immortal and can never die, cannot be withered up, cannot be cut in two, cannot be destroyed, is never annihilated, but lives forever and forever, climbing forever and forever up the ladder of evolution, nearer and nearer, yet never reaching the full stature of the Godhead. That is what Theosophy wishes men to believe; not to believe that any particular creed is true. Jesus had no creed and formulated none. He declared the law to be," Do unto others what you would have them do unto you." That was the law and the prophets. That is enough for any one. Love your neighbor as yourself. No more. Why, then, any creeds whatever ? His words are enough, and his words and our ethical basis are the same. That is why we have no form of religion. We are not advocating religion ; we are simply pointing out to men that the truth is there to pick up and prize it. Religion relates to the conduct of men ; nature will take care of the results ; nature will see what they will come to ; but if we follow these teachings which we find everywhere, and the spirit of the philosophy which we find in all these old books, then men will know why they must do right, not because of the law, not because of fear, not because of favor, but because they must do right for right's own sake. (Applause.)

PROF. CHAKRAVARTI: The Great Eternal, Ineffable One is represented in one of the grandest Vedic slokas [quoting Sanscrit] by which is meant that there exists but one and one only without any duality. This is the key-note of the whole system of Hindu Cosmogony and Cosmology. The great *Parabrahm*, as we call it, is the essence by which the whole Universe is supported, by which the whole universe is permeated, which is co-extensive with the universe and with which the universe is identical. This is the idea of Godhead according to Hindu Philosophy. This is the highest conception of that essence which lives on from eternity to eternity.

At the beginning of each Cosmic Evolution, this Eternal Essence breathes out the whole universe with the complete system of divine hierarchies, with the mighty drama, with the design of the whole universe in his mind, the Demiurgos of the Greeks, down to the minutest atom that there is. And at the end of the *Kalpa*, when the time comes round, there is an inbreathing, an involution, a drawing in of the whole universe back again into the bosom of this *Parabrahman*. This is the highest God according to all systems of religion; this is the great Armitha, the Immeasurable of the Buddhists. This is the great God which cannot be realized by the Body, by the Mind, or by the Spirit, because it is Absolute. All human consciousness is relative, and therefore can have no conception of that which bears to it no relation. It is therefore the Great Unknown, and the Great Unknowable of Herbert Spencer. It is the Great Unattainable, the Great Sun into whose Light you might enter, but into which itself you can never pierce. It is, to express the simile of one of the highest English thinkers, one of the sweeps of the parabola to which the curve of human consciousness constantly approaches but can never touch. It is, therefore, the rootless root, the causeless cause of the whole universe. It sweeps from eternity to eternity. Upon its bosom there springs up universe upon universe, system upon system, planet upon planet, race upon race; and into its bosom merge again all that has been, all that is, and all that will be.

At the time of cosmic evolution there springs up in its bosom the grand centre of a spiritual energy, the Sun from which as from a focus the universe is to proceed. As in the physical universe, light is everywhere diffused but is invisible until it is focused through a physical sun, so is this grand spirit diffused and eternal, and becomes active only when it passes through a certain centre which springs in Parabrahm. This centre is the God of all Religions. This centre is the Logus of the Greeks, and this centre is the one which is spoken of in the Bible—in the Beginning there was the Word and the Word was God and God was the Word.

But the mere postulation of the existence of a centre necessitates the existence of something beyond it, and that other phase which makes the individualization of such a spiritual focus possible is the other pole of existence which is called Prakriti in Sanscrit, or Matter. Then this forms the highest trinity of the Hindu philosophical system, Parabrahman at the head reigning supreme and arising in its bosom two different aspects coming out of its essence, the Purusha and the Prakriti, Spirit and Matter.

From Purusha then emanate rays of light which are to be the basis, the Sun, and the Inspirer of the whole universe. Rays of light emanating from this Purusha fall upon different grades of matter, and, being reflected from these planes as from so many mirrors, give rise to lights of various degrees of intensity, which constitute the four great planes of universal existence according to our philosophy.

The first great plane on which this light shines is called the Spiritual plane, or the plane of Sutratma. Light reflected from this plane is once more reflected on the plane of the Soul. The light after another reflection falls upon the lowest plane, the plane of physical existence called in our Shastras the Vashaiva Nara plane. This light, then, is the real source of all existence. It is reflected from one mirror to another, and according to the number of its reflections it gets distorted, losing its pristine purity and effulgence.

Corresponding to these four planes of existence are also four states or planes of consciousness in the human entity. Four different grades of knowledge which function on these four different planes. On the plane of spirit functions that which is called the Karana Sarira. The spiritual body of Man functions on the soul-plane of man and is called Sukshma Sarira; and last of all, corresponding to the physical plane of course, we have the physical body with which you are familiar and which in our technical language is called Sthula Sarira.

The exposition of this philosophy will render clear to your minds that all these different states of existence, all these different planes of consciousness, are but reflections of one grand light which emanates from the sun which first springs up on the bosom of Parabrahmam. It is therefore the one source of all energy that manifests itself either on the plane of the spirit or on the plane of soul or on the plane of matter. True, its appearance is not the same in all these planes; as a light which has to pass through several concentric glasses loses its brightness as it passes from one to the other, so does this light of Atma or Purusha lose in its brightness, its divine nature, as it has to pass through these various envelopes which form the basis and the strata of the different planes of consciousness.

The great aim, therefore, is to realize the doctrine that there is but one reality of which all these are different modifications, that there is but one source of light, of delight, of pleasure in the universe, and all that we have on any other plane of consciousness, either of life or of knowledge or of joy or of harmony, is nothing but a more or less distorted picture produced by this one light. This is the doctrine which is inculcated at every step to a student of the spiritual knowledge of the East. You are first to discriminate between what is real and what is unreal. The answer to the question what is real and what is unreal is, Why, all is unreal except that light which gives the appearance of reality to everything else. Hence it is that Krishna says in one of his most magnificent slokas, [quoting Sanscrit] "Whatever thou seest of beauty, of brightness, of effulgence in this universe, know that it is due but to one ray of my divine existence and nature."

To find out that this is the source of all delight, never mind in what different aspects this delight may appear, is the essence of all spiritual teachings. A moment's consideration will make it clear to you that all the delight that you run after wildly does not arise from the object which you in your ignorance pursue. Why, even a flower blooming brightly on a stem does not shed into the mind of the poet, into the mind of the philosopher, and into the mind of the brutes that walk the jungle, the same amount of delight. If delight really resided in that portion of matter that your physical senses are capable of cognizing, whence arises this difference in the vibration of mental delight that it is capable of giving rise to in the different organs in the human breast? The source of delight is really different to you from what it is to another; the strength of bliss runs from an inner channel the fountain of which is located in the *sanctum sanctorum* of your heart; and when in your illusion you run after external things, why, you lose the very source of all happiness.

It is from this delusion that comes pain. You think that external things are capable of giving happiness to your lives. You run after them persistently, eagerly, with the result that you dash your heads against the wall. Know you, that the same cup of pleasure cannot be tasted twice. The same object is incapable of giving even to the same individual the same quantity of delight at two different moments of his life. Once if you have a greater degree of spiritual bliss in it, next time there will be another drop of poison mixed with it. Why, then, run after shadows? Why not retire and run after something from which all that you have of delight, all that you have of duty, all that you have of music and of intellect, and all else, proceeds? And if you retire there, think not that you lose anything. No, because you cast off merely the dross. You retire to the centre of the living Waters, and once in touch with that eternal essence of all joy, you have all—much more—a great deal more, than any physical delight that the world can ever bring to you.

A beautiful illustration of this is generally given in the systems of Hindu philosophy. A person, when coming to bathe on the bank of a stream, saw that in the bottom of the stream was lying a beautiful golden bangle. His avarice was aroused, his temptation was aroused, and he thought that he would be so much the richer and the happier for possessing that beautiful bracelet that was lying at the bottom of the stream. He stripped his clothes off; he jumped into the stream, restrained his breath, dived down to the bottom, and fumbled for the thing for hours and hours together. But his desired golden bracelet was nowhere to be seen. After hours of weary struggle, after hours of useless search, he came out fatigued, crestfallen, on the bank of the stream, and with his head bent with its despair and agony, thought of the useless hours he had spent.

In the meantime comes there one who was more observing who knew more about nature, and asked him what was it that had grieved him.

"Why," he said, "there is that bracelet which is now under me, which is even now lying on the bottom of the water, and yet with all my force I have not been able to be in possession of that object I so earnestly desire."

"Fool," said he, "Look there," and putting his hands over his head, made him look upwards, and up in the tree he found the golden bangle the reflection of which he had so long, so vainly, pursued. (Applause.)

The man of wisdom, the man of knowledge, the man of discrimination, who knows whence delight, whence beauty, proceeds, looketh not, therefore, to find it among the various shadowy and misty reflections that delude you and deceive your eyesight. Right on, he marches upward, turns his eyes heavenward, and grasps the eternal verity, the real substance which makes life what it really is.

This life, then, about which I have been talking is the reality which permeates the universe, which pervades all that is, and makes all that we have of beauty, of joy, of energy, and of life. It is present, though not to the same extent, though not with the same beatific expression, in the mineral kingdom. It is present in the vegetable kingdom to an extent greater than in the mineral kingdom, but yet not reaching any differentiation. In the animal it exists in an individualized—but partially individualized—existence, and therefore we regard each animal as one which is progressing toward this goal of evolution, as a candidate for all the grand perfection which divinity and nature are capable of imparting.

And it is this light again which makes the light, the intellect, the spirit, and all that is glorious in every human being. Hence it is that Theosophy has taken for its first maxim the doctrine of Universal Brotherhood, similar to the doctrine of the fatherhood of God and the brotherhood of Man. But we go a step farther. We go even behind the idea of Manifested God. We go beyond the narrow circle of humanity, and declare the fatherhood of Parabrahmam and the brotherhood of the Universe. (Great applause.)

ANNIE BESANT.—In finishing this brief description of some of the leading Theosophical teachings, I have been desired to take up and deal with the Evolution of Man. Man, as you take him in the past, man as we see him in the present, man as he shall be in the future, the very first fruits of that future being men living on the earth to-day.

Evolution in our modern civilization has been a word of power over the minds of men. Those glimpses that the West has got of evolution give us but half the story, draw for us but half its circle, and with a half truth give us an unintelligible, inexplicable mystery of a life that comes from no centre of this evolution, that finds no intelligible goal. For just as we see in our Western evolution that life appears, that a certain interaction of force and of matter has out of death made life, out of unintelligence springs existence, out of the brute springs man; so that evolution springing from the lower stages of life is to pass onward and onward to an end as emotionally, as intellectually unsatisfactory as its beginning is wrapped in that of possibility of explanation. For in the latest presentments of science we are told that in this chain of evolution the latest link shall be as low as the first; the gradual retroaction, the gradual degradation, until worlds evolved only from matter by energy shall evolve back again into uninhabited desolation, either burned by fire or frozen into obliviousness of life, until, disintegrated once more, they will be built up again in the far-off future of existence.

Such an evolution, were it true, would be the dreariest theory of life that human mind could conceive—unintelligible to the brain, unsatisfactory to the heart. Far other is Evolution as we have learned it from the ancient books, as it has been traced for us by the Masters of Wisdom; for they tell us of that spirit, to a description of which we have just been listening, out of which springs a universe, the universe passing back, full of life, to expand into the Divine All-Consciousness. They tell us of an Involution which is the Source and the Fount of Life. Spirit involving itself in matter that it may become the mainspring of Evolution, and may gradually mould matter into a perfect expression of itself. And then this descent of Spirit into Matter—this expansion of Life from within, passing through stage after stage of evolution, reaches its lowest point in the Mineral Kingdom, thence begins the long climb upwards, thence, by expanding energy, we can pass onward, stage by stage to the early evolution of Man, Man as he appeared in the present phase of the earth's existence, first of all living things, the pattern of all forms, containing every possibility that that stage of the evolving globe was to produce. Passing from stage to stage, till the animal body was builded, till the astral form into which the physical was moulded was ready to gather the physical together and make a possibility of material human life. Then in that focused the life energy of the world, gathering to itself the forces which knit the molecules together and co-ordinated all into the astral and physical bodies. And then as the last touch of animal man, of this lower and transitory existence which was to be the garment of the soul, we find appearing the passional, the emotional, the instinctual nature, that which Man has in common with the brute, and out of which in course of evolution that part of the brute nature also took its rise. So that we come to a stage of human evolution where the animal side of Man is completely builded, the tabernacle of the flesh is ready for its tenant, the house of the soul ready for the incoming mind, and Man at this stage of his existence, nothing more than a beautiful animal, so to say, should appear in the possibilities of adaptation built into a similitude that would be able gradually to be moulded by the indwelling soul into a perfect instrument for expression on the lower plane of life; and then to that abode builded for the mind comes the thinking entity, that is, the real Man, Man whose very name comes from the root that means thought, Man whose very name in our own tongue is identical with the Sanscrit word which is the root of thinking; so that in our very title in the world we bear the impress of our special characteristics, that the human soul is the thinking energy, the thinker that makes the complete Man a possibility came not from the lower world, not given by material nature, not evolved from the astral plane, not given birth to by the lower life, not taking its origin in the passional, the emotional, the instinctual nature—Man's soul comes from above, not from below, not climbing upwards from the brute, but the focalized reflection of the Spirit.

That is the soul that came to Man as animal and took him into his charge, to build him up to the divine: for this thinker is the God in every man, the God who has evolved from Matter, the God who has descended that he may subdue to himself the lower nature and render every plane of existence translucent to a vehicle of the Divine. This God in Man is the teacher, the Guide, the instructor, the Helper, and also in his lower aspect the gatherer of experience out of which he shall build up character which he shall carry back with him to the higher work that lies before him in periods of existence yet unborn in the universe, that are still in the obscurity of eternity.

This thinker, this God descended into matter, has a dual aspect, one face turned to the Divine which is its source, the other face turned to matter which he has come to dominate and to subdue. These are the higher and the lower minds, the rational, and, in its union with the lower nature, the animal soul in Man: so that in its double nature you have the aspect that is turned to the brute to train it; you have the aspect turned to the spirit that strives ever upward towards union with the purely divine. And the whole life of man is the battle-field of that dual nature—the God struggling with the brute, in order that the brute itself may become divine. That is the way that Man evolves, that is the building up of the divine in the midst of the earth on which we live. Do you doubt that God is in every Man? Do you doubt that the essence of humanity is divinity itself? Men talk of others as sunk in evil. Men speak of their own race as corrupt, and by the very degradation they ascribe to it they make it more degraded than otherwise it would be; for we tend to reproduce the opinion that surrounds us. If we are evil and brutal, we tend then to take on, as it were, the character which is ascribed to us too often even by the religious faiths. But if Man be divine, if the very heart of Man be light, then you can appeal to the divine within the lowest, and know that answer will come, however muffled be the veil of flesh. Would you have proof that God in Man is present in the vilest, present in the most degraded, present in every son of man whose life seems that of the brute rather than of God? Come with me to one of our English villages far-away from the ordinary haunts of men— a village which, once all beauty, has been defaced by the greed of those who possess it and the carelessness of those who live in it. We have some mining villages in our country, I am ashamed to say, where the lives that are lived are lives of the lowest, of the most ignorant and most degraded. Not all of our mining population are thus. Some of them are strong and self-reliant men, but it is not of them I am thinking now. I am thinking of some villages I know where if you walk down the village street you would find gathered in front of the public house men whose language soils those ears that hear it, who speak foul words, who are gambling, betting, drinking, finding all pleasure in the senses, and you would say, " No light of the divine is there." 'Are you so sure? Wait and watch them as you wait, and as you are there, thinking how degraded men can be, how they seem to be nothing but the vilest of living creatures—listen to a sound there that makes every man spring to his feet, in order that with every sense alert he may hear the sound distinctly and understand what it means. There is a far-off rumbling that seems to shake the ground on which they stand. The far-off rumble that comes louder, louder, louder, till with a mighty clap as of a thunderbolt there is a crash, a roar, and a pillar of smoke that comes up from the earth, and from mouth to mouth the word flies, " Explosion in the mine below," and men are there, living or dead, one cannot tell. In a moment the whole village is alive, men, women, and children rushing to the mouth of the pit. There are cries of women who know not if they are wives or widows, wailings of children who know not if they be fatherless, and the strong men gather around the pit, the pit that is black with smoke, and unheeding that fiery death that is beneath,—there is a struggling at the mouth of the pit, men struggling with men, and struggling for what? Come near them and you will hear the words that flow from their lips. " Go back, you've got a wife or mother. Let me go down who have none to care if I die." And the men who were swearing, who were gambling, who were drinking, hearing that cry of men in agony, forget their brutehood and remember the God that is within, and they fight to go into the cage, they struggle for the chance to sacrifice their lives for their comrades ; and down they go, down into the hell of the burning mine, to see if some burning comrade be there still with the life within him and they can bring back to woman or to child the bread-winner of the family, the support and guardian of the home. Do you dare to tell me those men are not divine? Do you dare to say that where sacrifice is pleasant, the very source of sacrifice is absent from the heart of man? I tell you there is none however degraded, none however ignorant, none however vile, in whom the divine spirit has not His Sanctuary in the innermost heart, who shall not at length become pure as the little child with love that raises him from the mire of sin, and that energy of divine life which has in it the promise of triumph, however far off that day of triumph is. And Man evolving by this inner force, life after life, makes slow progression till a time comes in the life of the man when more rapid growth begins to be possible ; the time when the man by gradual evolution is beginning to understand the far-off possibility of reuniting, as it were, the higher and lower mind. When the upward striving of the lower mind is beginning to reach by aspiration that higher one of which it is the ray. When the higher mind, having worked for ages in human evolution, is beginning to be able to impress itself on the tabernacle so that that tabernacle is conscious of the indwelling of the God, and then there comes a time when the man thus evolving begins consciously to set before himself a definite aim to bend all his efforts in a definite direction, and there will be evil in the heart only or in the heart and lips as well, yet a conscious acceptance of Man's true goal in life, the service of his race and the giving of himself for Man. And then the man who has reached that point in evolution vows himself to the service of all that lives, and puts before him for all future lives that may come to him the one object of growing so that he may help others, of learning in order that he may enlighten their ignorance, of strengthening himself that his strength may be of help in raising the world of which he is a part, and then the lives consciously directed become more rapid in their evolving energy, life after life adds more and more rapidly to the vision of the soul, to the power of the lower mind to respond, till, stage by stage, the story grows deeper and higher, till step by step the life becomes purer and purer and fuller; and the last cycle of births is entered, which when completed will leave the man one of those who have triumphed over sin and death; and when these last lives are beginning, one lesson comes from those who have already achieved, one special direction is given to the disciple by which his life is to be guided, by which his safety on the path is to be secured. You may read it in the same book that I quoted this afternoon. Those fragments of the Book of the Golden Precepts, that are the very hymn book of every true disciple, and there you will find that the law of life must be compassion, that the law of life must be feeling and suffering and enjoying with others, that no tear must be allowed to fall till the effort has been made to wipe it from the sufferer's eye; but that every tear not wiped from the eye of a brother must remain burning on your own heart till that which caused it is removed. And then these lives of continual effort for others bring at last the evolved Man to the point where perfection is reached and triumph over death secured. They lead him to the point at which, once more to quote the same book, "He holdeth Life and Death in his strong hand." He is no longer a disciple, he stands complete in knowledge; he is no longer a combatant, the victory lies behind him and the spoils of victory are in his grasp. What shall he do with them? How shall he spend them? Weary with ages of struggle, what shall be his final choice? He stands on the threshold of that world, separated from ours by difference of condition, which no bridge is able to span. He stands on the threshold of that state of consciousness, so misunderstood in the West, called Nirvana, that mighty state of all consciousness and all knowledge which no words can syllable and no heart of Man conceive. He opens the door that leads to that sublime condition. It is his by right of struggle; it is his by right of conquest. His very foot is on the threshold of the doorway, and one moment he pauses ere he crosses the threshold. And as he stands there, Lo, a Voice, the Voice of Compassion itself, sounds in his hearing, and he pauses to listen. "Shalt thou escape while all that lives must suffer? Shalt thou be safe and hear the whole world cry?" And in the silence that follows, the cry of the world is heard. Across the abyss comes the sob of humanity, orphaned humanity, that is without guide and helper, and that sees one of its greatest passing out of sight. All the cries of men in agony, all the shrieks of women trampled under foot, all the wailings of little children in our world, make one mighty chord of anguish, and they cry to him to stop. What has his life been for many a life past? It has been a life hearkening to every cry of pain that comes to it. It has been a life that responds to every appeal for help that reaches its hearing. All the life has become divine compassion. Can it be deaf when help is needed by men? And in that silence, broken only by the sob of anguish, in that silence is made the great renunciation, the door of Nirvana is closed by the hand that opened it, from the threshold that might have been crossed the foot is withdrawn, and the Master turns back. He chooses the great renunciation, he chooses voluntarily to live in the world for the helping and the guidance of men. He brings back the strength he has conquered, the wisdom he has gained, the love that is his very nature, and he lays them all at the feet of humanity that he is willing to serve,—his knowledge for its guidance, his purity for its cleansing, his strength for its uplifting, his infinite compassion to have patience with its folly, forgiveness for its wickedness, endless endurance till it learn wisdom also by experience through which it passes. Those are the men that we call Masters. Those, the mighty souls to whom we give our heart's homage, not because they are wise so much as because they are loving; not so much because they are strong as because they are Compassion absolute. Those are the guides and the teachers, those the examples that stimulate us to work.

Behind the movement which we have been considering for the last two days stand those servants of men, inspiring all that is best and noblest in it. I do not mean guiding its policy, I do not mean driving it along every step of its life, for they let their servants learn by their own mistakes, desiring not mere puppets that they control, but men and women evolving toward perfection. That is the strength that lies behind our movement as behind every other great movement for the spiritual good of men, for it matters not whether we know the Masters—they know us. And they give their help to every one who works for Man, no matter whether his eyes be blinded or whether they be opened to the light they shed. That is the secret of our strength. What is it that in this Parliament of Religions has drawn crowd after crowd at all its sessions, to learn the truths that a few amongst us have here been employed in imperfectly setting forth? Youngest, you may say, of any movement as the world knows us, though in reality the oldest of all, what is it in this Theosophical Society, not yet in its twentieth year of life, which is making the eyes of all men turn towards it and making the hearts of all men ask what it has to give? Men are hungry for spiritual truth. Men are longing for spiritual knowledge. They ask for a knowledge of the soul which shall not be based only on faith; for a guidance in life clear and definite that may satisfy the heart and the reason alike. And this movement was started by those Masters of Wisdom to feed the hunger of the soul which the cycle of time had brought round again; and they sent into the world their messengers that they might make this movement possible. Who is its true founder so far as the material world is concerned? They selected, these great souls that stand beside this Society, a Russian woman, outcast from home and friends, Helena Petrovna Blavatsky, who went out from her Russian home, leaving wealth, rank, princely position behind her, eager only for knowledge of the truth and union with the divine life. Through many a land she travelled, through many a clime she wandered, one after another she examined the teachings of the world, till the eye of the soul was opened and the Master she served sent her out to do his work. Penniless she came back to the world. Told to go to America, she went to France—as far as her money took her —and there coming into possession of a few pounds, enough to land her in New York, but no more; yet nothing could stay her. She went with the word behind her; that word he gave her; and she came alone and friendless to your country to face the materialism of the West and to proclaim as alive again the true and ancient Wisdom-Religion. She was scoffed at and derided, laughed at and defamed. Every foul word that the malice of foul minds could image was heaped on her one head. They never thought she was a woman and had none to help her, and they did right, for that lion-heart asked no sort of consideration, and she would not use sex as defense against cruelty. She lived her life, she gathered round her men and women who got some glimpse of the strength that was within her, and the beauty of the divine life that she enshrined. They tried to crush her with calumny, tried to destroy her influence. What is the answer? The answer is that two years and a half after she passed away there are thousands of men and women scattered the world over to thank her for the life she lived, for the guidance that she gave to life. (Applause). They thought they had crushed her with their Hodgson babble; they thought that they could crush her with all their Psychical Research Society Reports, and the answer is that we are living to-day and we stand as testimony to her work, as witnesses to the life she has made possible for us. How has such a movement spread? How has such a Society been possible? Because of a spiritual life that lies behind it that no slander can wound and no power of man can touch. And to-day, to-day, those who made the movement possible glance over the Western world to see where some souls may be found willing to be helpers with them in the redemption of humanity, willing to share with them in the toil and triumph that lie beyond. Here and there there is some soul that catches glimpses of the light that shines from behind the veil, and gives itself in its pure measure as they had given themselves for men. Such are the helpers of the Masters. Such the co-workers that they are seeking, and not one of you but, if you chose to take the higher path, might make to-day your first step along the road, a step, it may be, feeble, uncertain, and halting, but if made out of love to Man and devotion to the spirit has in it the certainty of final success—is the beginning of the journey that shall lead you to be co-worker in the spirit. That, then, is the final appeal that from this platform comes to every man or woman ready to give himself for the helping and the saving of man. There are so many that want help, is there none to give it? so few to speak for the spiritual life among so many that are sunk in the flesh. And this I say to you, that no joy of earth, no hope that gilds an earthly future, and no delight that comes of earthly triumph; no such joy, no such happiness, no such ecstacy, bears any more proportion to the joy of the spiritual life than the fog that surrounds some mining village is radiant as the sunshine, or the pettiest joy of the gnat in the sunshine can emulate the power and delight of the intellect in man.

For greater than intellect is spirit, brighter than Mind is the Supreme Life; one joy, one peace inexhaustible. Such is the possibility that lies in front of you; for those who have got one glimpse of that, no earthly power has longer charm or desire. Before the radiance of that divine life, all glory of earth is poor and dim. This is not matter of faith, it is matter of knowledge; and every one whose vision is even partly opened will tell you that that only is the real life, and that the knowledge of the Divine is that which alone can satisfy the heart of Man. (Continued applause.)

Adjourned to Sunday at 8 p. m., in Hall of Washington.

EXTRA SESSION, SUNDAY EVENING AT 8 O'CLOCK, IN HALL OF WASHINGTON.

The Hall was crowded long before the hour for opening the session, and on the platform with the speakers were many members of the Society. Dr. J. D. Buck had the chair, and said:

This evening the session has been divided between several speakers who will each make short addresses upon subjects that are of interest to students of Theosophy. It was thought that this method would be more profitable and prove more satisfactory than any other.

I now beg to introduce to you again Brother William Q. Judge, who will speak on the subject of Cycles and Cyclic Law.

MR. JUDGE—Ladies and gentlemen: This is our last meeting; it is the last impulse of the Cycle which we began when we opened our sessions at this Parliament. All the other bodies which have met in this building have been also starting cycles just as we have been. Now, a great many people know what the word "cycle" means, and a great many do not. There are no doubt in Chicago many men who think that a cycle is a machine to be ridden; but the word that I am dealing with is not that. I am dealing with a word which means a return, a ring. It is a very old term, used in the far past. In our civilization it is applied to a doctrine which is not very well understood, but which is accepted by a great many scientific men, a great many religious men, and by a great many thinking men. The theory is, as held by the ancient Egyptians, that there is a cycle, a law of cycles which governs humanity, governs the earth, governs all that is in the universe. You may have heard Brother Chakravarti say the Hindus are still teaching that there is a great cycle which begins when the Unknown breathes forth the whole universe, and ends when it is turned in again into itself. That is the great cycle.

In the Egyptian monuments, papyri, and other records the cycles are spoken of. They held, and the ancient Chinese also held, that a great cycle governs the earth, called the sidereal cycle because it related to the stars. The work was so large that it had to be measured by the stars, and that cycle is 25,800 and odd years long. They claim to have measured this enormous cycle. The Egyptians gave evidence they had measured it also and had measured many others, so that in these ancient records, looking at the question of cycles, we have a hint that man has been living on the earth, has been civilized and uncivilized for more years than we have been taught to believe. The ancient Theosophists have always held that civilization with humanity went around the earth in cycles, in rings, returning again and again upon itself, but that at each turn of the cycle, on the point of return it was higher than before. This law of cycles is held in Theosophical doctrine to be the most important of all, because it is at the bottom of all. It is a part of the law of that unknown being who is the universe, that there shall be a periodical coming from and a periodical returning again upon itself.

Now, that the law of cycles does prevail in the world must be very evident if you will reflect for a few moments. The first cycle I would draw your attention to is the daily cycle, when the sun rises in the morning and sets at night, returning again next morning, you following the sun, rising in the morning and at night going to sleep again, at night almost appearing dead, but the next morning awaking to life once more. That is the first cycle. You can see at once that there are therefore in a man's life just as many cycles of that kind as there are days in his life. The next is the monthly cycle, when the moon, changing every 28 days, marks the month. We have months running to more days, but that is only for convenience, to avoid change in the year. The moon gives the month and marks the monthly cycle.

The next is the yearly cycle. The great luminary, the great mover of all, returns again to a point from whence he started. The next great cycle to which I would draw your attention, now we have come to the sun—it is held by science and is provable I think by other arguments—the next cycle is that the sun, while stationary to us, is in fact moving through space in an enormous orbit which we can not measure. As he moves he draws the earth and the planets as they wheel about him. We may say, then, this is another great cycle. It appears reasonable that, as the sun is moving through that great cycle, he must draw the earth into spaces and places and points in space where the earth has never been before, and that it must happen that the earth shall come now and then into some place where the conditions are different and that it may be changed in a moment, as it were, for to the eye of the soul a thousand years are but a moment, when everything will be different. That is one aspect of cyclic doctrine, that the sun is drawing the earth in a great orbit of his own and is causing the earth to be changed in its nature by reason of the new atomic spaces into which it is taken.

We also hold that the earth is governed by cyclic law throughout the century as in a moment. The beings upon it are never in the same state. So nations, races, civilizations, communities are all governed in the same way and moved by the same law. This law of cycles is the law of reincarnation that we were speaking of to-day: that is, that a man comes into the world and lives a day, his life is as a day; he dies out of it and goes to sleep, elsewhere waking; then he sleeps there to wake again the next great day; after a period of rest, he again enters life; that is his cycle. We hold in Theosophical philosophy it has been proven by the Adepts by experiment that men in general awake from this period of rest after 1,500 years. So we point in history to an historical cycle of 1,500 years, after which old ideas return. And if you will go back in the history of the world you will find civilization repeating itself every 1,500 years, more or less like what it was before. That is to say, go back 1,500 years from now and you will find coming out here now the Theosophists, the philosophers, the various thinkers, the inventors of 1,500 years ago. And going further back still, we hold that those ancient Egyptians who made such enormous pyramids and who had a civilization we cannot understand, at that dim period when they burst on the horizon of humanity to fall again, have had their cycle of rest and are reincarnating again even in America. So we think, some of us, that the American people of the new generation are a reincarnation of the ancient Egyptians, who are coming back and bringing forth in this civilization all the wonderful ideas which the Egyptians held. And that is one reason why this country is destined to be a great one, because the ancients are coming back, they are here, and you are very foolish if you refuse to consider yourselves so great. We are willing you should consider yourselves so great, and not think you are born mean, miserable creatures.

The next cycle I would draw your attention to is that of civilizations. We know that civilizations have been here, and they are gone. There is no bridge between many of these. If heredity, as some people claim, explains everything, how is it not explained why the Egyptians left no string to connect them with the present? There is nothing left of them but the Copts, who are poor miserable slaves. The Egyptians, as a material race, are wiped out, and it is so because it is according to the law of cycles and according to the law of nature that the physical embodiment of the Egyptians had to be wiped out. But their souls could not go out of existence, and so we find their civilization and other civilizations disappearing, civilizations such as the ancient civilization of Babylon, and all those old civilizations in that part of the East which were just as strange and wonderful as any other. And this civilization of ours has come up instead of going down, but it is simply repeating the experience of the past on a higher level. It is better in potentiality than that which has been before. Under the cyclic law it will rise higher and higher, and when its time comes it will die out like the rest.

Also religions have had their cycles. The Christian religion has had its cycle. It began in the first year of the Christian era and was a very different thing then from what it is now. If you examine the records of Christianity itself you will see that the early fathers and teachers taught differently in the beginning from that which the priests of to-day are teaching now. Similarly you will find that Brahminism has had its cycle. Every religion rises and falls with the progress of human thought, because cyclic law governs every man, and thus every religion which man has.

So it is also with diseases. Is it not true that fevers are governed by a law of recurrence in time; some have three days, some four days, nine days, fifteen days, three years and so on? No physician can say why it is so; they only know that it is a fact. So in every direction the law of cycles is found to govern. It is all according to the great inherent law of the periodical ebb and flow, the Great Day and Night of Nature. The tides in Ocean rise and fall; similarly in the great Ocean of Nature there is a constant ebb and flow, a mightier tide which carries all with it. The only thing that remains unshaken, immovable, never turning is the Spirit itself. That, as St. James said—and he doubtless was himself a wise Theosophist—is without variableness and hath no shadow of turning.

Now, this great law of periodical return pertains also to every individual man in his daily life and thought. Every idea that you have, every thought, affects your brain and mind by its impression. That begins the cycle. It may seem to leave your mind, apparently it goes out, but it returns again under the same cyclic law in some form either better or worse, and wakes up once more the old impression. Even the very feelings that you have of sorrow or gladness will return in time, more or less according to your disposition, but inevitably in their cycle. This is a law it would do good for every one to remember, especially those who have variations of joy and sorrow, of exaltation and depression. If when depressed you would recollect the law and act upon it by voluntarily creating another cycle of exaltation, on its returning again with the companion cycle of lower feeling it would in no long time destroy the depressing cycle and raise you to higher places of happiness and peace. It applies again in matters of study where we use the intellectual organs only. When a person begins the study of a difficult subject or one more grave than usual, there is a difficulty in keeping the mind upon it; the mind wanders; it is disturbed by other and older ideas and impressions. But by persistency a new cycle is established, which, being kept rolling, at last obtains the mastery.

We hold further—and I can only go over this briefly—that in evolution itself, considered as a vast inclusive whole, there are cycles, and that unless there were these turnings and returnings no evolution would be possible, for evolution is but another word for cyclic law. Reincarnation, or re-embodiment over and over again, is an expression of this great law and a necessary part of evolution.

Evolution means a coming forth from something. From out of what does the evolving universe come? It comes out from what we call the unknown, and we call it "unknown" simply because we do not know what it is. The unknown does not mean the non-existent; it simply means that which we do not perceive in its essence or fulness. It goes forth again and again, always higher and better; but while it is rolling around at its lower arc it seems to those down there that it is lower than ever; but it is bound to come up again. And that is the answer we give to those who ask, What of all those civilizations that have disappeared, what of all the years that I have forgotten? What have I been in other lives, I have forgotten them? We simply say, You are going through your cycle. Some day all these years and experiences will return to your recollection as so much gained. And all the nations of the earth should know this law, remember it and act upon it, knowing that they will come back and that others also will come back. Thus they should leave behind something that will raise the cycle higher and higher, thus they should ever work toward the perfection which mankind as a whole is striving in fact to procure for itself. (Applause.)

THEOSOPHY AND WOMAN.

MISS F. HENRIETTA MÜLLER.

The subject I have chosen for my address this evening is one which appears to be coming to the forefront and calling the attention of people in every country of the globe. I am not exaggerating when I say that the position of woman is attracting more attention in the country of America than in any other. The women in America occupy a position which the women in other lands look upon with envy and which may be regarded as unique. Why? Because we believe they are the forerunners of that which is to come. Here, indeed, it is true, and it is also true in other lands, that no religion and no philosophy presenting itself to the mind of the people for the first time to-day would be welcomed, or would secure any serious amount of attention, which did not accord to women a place of perfect equality with men. (Applause.) The time passed long since when a religion or a philosophy, placing men at the head of the universe and women at the bottom of it, would receive any serious consideration. And I wish to show you that that system of thought, that system of philosophy, that system of religion which to-day goes by the name of Theosophy, is just that one which accords to woman the place which the thinking and the advanced minds of to-day require that it shall accord to her.

When I first heard of Theosophy I was suspicious on this very point. Being one who had devoted many years of my life to the education, emancipation, and amelioration of the women of my country, I had for one to be satisfied that there did exist anywhere under the sun a system of religion that did justice to women. Therefore I was suspicious, and, when the time came that appeared to me suitable, I wrote to Madam Blavatsky asking her this question: Do women in the Theosophical Society enjoy equal rights, the whole way along the line, with men, or do they not? Her answer was: In the Society, which has Branches all over the world and which occupies itself with doing what is called the exoteric part of the work, beginning there and rising right up to the highest regions of the Masters, who are occupied in doing spiritual work in planes beyond our reach and beyond our ken, from the top to the bottom, that which is counted as the factor is not the personality; that which is the thing, that which receives the recognition is the work that is done; whether it is done by a woman or a man is not asked. It is virtue, it is struggle, it is the desire to help, it is the labor accomplished which counts as the factor, and not the person who does it. She then proved to me by illustration, by giving me names and by instances out of her own experience, that that was so. The point upon which I desired mostly to be reassured was, whether it was possible for a woman starting from the ordinary plane of life where you and I are dwelling, by her own efforts to reach to the development of the powers and to the condition of the highest adept. Upon this H. P. Blavatsky reassured me. For, she said, not only have there been women adepts known in the ancient history of India from time immemorial, but I myself enjoyed the personal acquaintance of such women in India and in the lands beyond India, in Thibet. She told me their names, she told me of their lives, she told me of the possibility of their still further developing themselves and reaching still greater heights of perfection and power.

I think that everyone here has heard, and possibly believes also, that the Christian religion has done a great deal for the emancipation of women in Christian lands. It has not pointed out to us those avenues of development which Theosophic teachings now offer, but I think you will agree with me when I say that it has plowed the land and prepared it for sowing the seed, that it has done all that the world was ready for in this direction by preparing the minds of women for self-development, for self-dependence, and by teaching them that through their own exertions, by the light of their own intelligence and their own consciousness, they must seek to emancipate themselves, not only from the thraldom of their own lower nature, but also from the subjection, from the social and personal subjugation they are under. But some of you will object: How about that wretched heretic Paul? I don't call him St. Paul, although some people do. Paul, you know, says, "Suffer not a woman to teach in the churches." And Paul seems to pepper all his Epistles with bitter and biting things about women, what they may do and what they may not do, how we may dress, sleep, and eat; I don't know what dreadful things he does not say touching us women; how we ought to live, according to his own way of thinking. That is not Christian, that is Paul, and I think I can prove it. Now, what a clever man he was when he said, "Suffer not women to teach in the churches," and when he took care not to say, "Suffer not women to work in the churches." If the women in America and England did not work in the churches and chapels,

I think in a month more than half of them would be shut, for although the women may not teach, they may work. (Applause.) For although we women may not teach the gospel with our lips, we may practice the gospel with our hands and our hearts ; there is nothing and no one to forbid us doing that. (Applause.) Why? Because, as said, St. Paul was too good to shut us out from doing that.

Well, then, he goes on to explain how and why it is that he says these things, and his explanation I think makes matters worse. (Applause.) He certainly does not speak as Christ did ; for compare the words, and still more the dealing, of Christ with women and you will find an enormous difference, you will find nothing in common between Paul and Christ. Christ never says a bitter or a biting thing : nor does he ever even speak a reproof during the whole of his life, with one apparent exception I shall refer to presently. In order to bring out the contrast I will relate one of the stories of Christ's life ; I take the story of the woman of Samaria. The disciples had all gone away to buy food, and Christ sits down by the well and the woman of Samaria comes to draw water. She is a strange woman, uneducated, unknown to him, belonging to the lower class, belonging, moreover, to the class that was looked down upon by the Jews as outcast. Jesus talks out to that woman and begins forthwith to disclose to her not merely the simple, practical, ethical Christian teaching, but the deepest mysteries of the Christian religion He considers her worthy to receive them and her alone, for no one else was there. To her he teaches the truth that he is the life, that he can feed her, that she is to come to him for the living waters of life. He not only teaches her this, but I believe there is some foundation for the opinion that this woman was the first one to hear from that profound mystical teacher that God is to be worshipped in spirit and in truth; and then he proceeds to explain to her the meaning of that saying. Upon this the disciples come back from the city where they have been, and, quite characteristic of Paul and the other disciples, they marvelled that Christ should have been speaking to a woman. Now, here comes out in strong contrast the attitude of the two. For women to-day are urged by the more developed teachings of Theosophy, as regards the possibilities of their development ; it is not because, but in spite of, the teachings of Paul, but it is and because of the teachings of Christ himself. And before I sit down I would recommend everyone of you here to read the writings of Paul and to read the history of Christ with that sole end in view, to bring out that point and to satisfy yourselves upon it. It will bring to you a flood of light and it will be to you a revelation of new beauty and truth in the character and teachings of Christ. My time is now up and I am very sorry I am not able to say something more. I should like to have said something more upon the subject of Theosophy and women, but I hope to do so upon some other occasion.

THEOSOPHY AND OUR CIVILIZATION.

DR. JEROME A. ANDERSON.

It were useless for me, dear friends, to attempt to tell you all about the message of Theosophy in the brief time which has been allotted to me, and I therefore will not waste your nor my time in any attempt to go over any large amount of territory or ground. I would rather go directly to the point and show you in a few words a few points in which I think the message of Theosophy is of great import to the Western world. Now, if a man be a man and not a child, he will recognize his best friend in one who shows him his faults. It is well enough for us to constitute ourselves a mutual admiration society and tell how great we are. That does us no good ; it does us harm. He is our true friend who points out our weaknesses, who shows us those apertures in the citadel of our very existence, through which the enemies of our lives are liable to penetrate and do us harm. Therefore I will endeavor to point out to-night some defects of this Western civilization of ours and in what manner Theosophy remedies or offers a remedy for those defects.

In the first place let me say that in the teachings of Theosophy, as I understand them, there is no evil in the universe. All that we think to be evil and recognize under the forms of evil is due to ignorance alone (applause), and therefore you will see how important it is that we do have light upon the problems of life, and in this way how important, because the message of Theosophy is giving light to the Western world. Now, let us examine our civilization and we will find that upon both the material and the intellectual planes we are in the habit of wrong thinking, that we are going in wrong directions. I don't say this in any spirit of carping criticism, or assuming higher ideas for myself as a Theosophist or for those on the stage with me. We are simply earnest students of human nature and the problems of life, and we want to know what is true and to avoid error, and on this line simply do I point out to-night what seem to me grave errors in our modes of thought, which lie at the very bottom of our civilization.

Upon the material plane the great curse of our Western thought and idea is in the individualism or separateness of man from man. We are separate in every possible way throughout our whole existence ; we separate ourselves from each other by caste, by color, by creed, by race, by country, and not only do we separate ourselves throughout all our lives, but when the last hour comes, when death approaches, then we separate ourselves eternally in death. What a fearful idea is this, that we must not only be separate here, but also be separate in the great beyond. For this idea of a separation both here and in the beyond, I believe we can in all justice charge it upon, certainly we cannot charge it upon a lack of philosophy, I was going to say upon the Christian religion, but I will not say so. It is religion by which the great mass of mankind live and die; and it is religion which teaches us to pray for ourselves, to work out our own salvation with fear and trembling. We have a couplet, out here in the West, at least, which expresses the idea, and that is this:

> "Oh Lord! have mercy upon me and my wife,
> My son John and his wife,
> Us four,
> And no more."

That is the very essence of our religion, and, thinking that way, you must see how it will penetrate down through the strata of our thinking, perverting all our ideas, giving us wrong conceptions all along upon the many duties of our life. We are taught to consider ourselves, to feel ourselves in this civilization to be Ishmaels, each one with his hand raised against his fellow man, climbing over each others' bodies, succeeding only because another fails. That is the attitude of the Western civilization upon the material plane of our existence.

Now, Theosophy comes in and shows us that because of the shortness and the unreality of this existence we ought not to place our hearts here, that we ought not to live here in our ideas or anything of that kind. It seems to me there is no other way of killing out this immense selfishness, because the fact is we have been taught to believe we have but one life and no more after going from this life forever, and, that being so, it almost becomes our duty to take each other by the throats and get all out of life we can. Don't you see that if we have to live but once and wont come back any more, it makes it philosophical, reasonable, and logical to try to get all we can. But when Theosophy comes with the doctrine of many lives, with these lives under the law of cause and effect, teaching that the life in the present is the result of the life in the past, we begin to think and to consider that any evil we do in this life will return to ourselves in those to come, and so we begin to be careful, if for no other reason but selfishness only, in order to live happily in the next life. So we do right if only for the most selfish motive. Then the teaching of Theosophy in regard to the many lives which one must live upon this earth has a most wonderful effect upon the selfishness and individualism of this Western civilization.

Our concepts of duty are all awry and wrong. We are taught to believe that we owe only duty to ourselves, or at most that duty only extends to our own immediate circle; we work entirely in the sense of separateness, we work for ourselves alone, strive for ourselves alone. Yesterday in the other hall you heard a most beautiful metaphor from our Brother Chakravarti, wherein he pointed out to you the Brahmanical conception of duty. It seems to me that if we in the West can hardly rise to that ideal, we can rise to other ideals. I wish to point out to you to-night that which seems to me the conception of duty which Theosophy teaches to the Western world. It will be best given by relating a fable, and that fable is this: It is said that at one time there was a legend, or a story, or a belief in a beautiful city, one of the most wonderful of which the human mind could conceive, and in that city was to be found all that could delight the human heart in every way, and it is further told that there were three men who started out to find that beautiful city. One departed to the right and pushed gradually on. He was heard of no more. Another started to the left and pushed gradually on, for no one knew in what direction to go for this beautiful city. He likewise was heard of no more. The third started out as gradually as the other two, but before he had gone very far he found a suffering man and he stopped to relieve him; he passed a little further and found another man suffering and relieved him also; and so on, step by step he went, ever stopping to relieve the suffering he found on every hand. At last he came to the determination that he would not seek the beautiful city but would spend his life in relieving the want and suffering which lay immediately before him. (Applause.) But, mark you! no sooner had he made this resolution, that he would spend his life in the amelioration of misery, when lo! before him lay the open gates of that beautiful city he had started out to find. That is the teaching of Theosophy, that our duty lies to those nearest to us, it lies right directly in front of us, that it is dangerous for us to attempt to do the duty of another. We must not attempt to go out in far directions, to reach here and there, but to do that which lies directly in front of us. That is our conception of duty. It has enabled us as Theosophists to do that work which lies immediately before us and to endeavor to benefit humanity. In this way it is a conception to which we can all rise.

Passing on from the material plane to that of intellect, the one great defect also upon this plane is that of not recognizing our own responsibilities for our own acts. In the religion of the West also, which I am sorry thus to seem to attack, we have had to depend upon another for our salvation; we have been told that all the acts of our life could be forgiven away. This civilization can never advance and take its true position among the civilizations of the earth until all this is done away with. The law of cause and effect is a universal law and cannot be violated on any plane. If I put my hand in the fire it will burn me on the material plane. If I commit a vice or crime upon the higher one, my soul will be tainted, for effect follows cause upon one plane just as surely as upon any other. There is not one law for one plane and another for another. We must become philosophical, we must recognize the fact that that which happens by law upon the material plane must also happen by law upon the mental plane, and that we alone are responsible for our acts, and that no vicarious atonement can relieve us from that responsibility, and that there is no power in the universe which can set aside an effect when the cause has once issued into action.

DEVOTION.

MRS. ISABEL COOPER-OAKLEY.

It is sometimes said, and said untruly, that in Theosophy there is no devotional life. This comes only from the lips of those who have made no deep study of the subject. There is in Theosophy a devotional life, as deep, as true, and as fervent as was ever taught in any religious system that has been known throughout the world. Now, I will divide my subject into two portions, the first, the general aspect, and then the particular application of it to us as Theosophists.

You have all of you heard of occultism, and occultism is the very centre of Theosophy. Now, the word "occultism" in itself wants definition. There is a good occultism, and there is what is called black magic; the first is white; it is that which is good, wise, unselfish, pure, true. Black magic or occultism is that which is selfishness, in which persons try to gain for themselves only and try to develop themselves for their own personal benefit. Now, when I am speaking of occultism I am not talking of black occultism. H. P. Blavatsky in a very fine article draws a very strong distinction between true occultism and what she calls occult frauds. I am not speaking of a little clairvoyance, or a little clairaudience, or a little thought-transference, or a great many other little dabblings in what people call occultism. I am speaking of the real development of the soul life which belongs to that school of occultism that lies at the very centre of Theosophy. In India there are many schools of occultism. At the back of the Theosophical Society there is one school of occultism which is based on the very highest, most unselfish, and most devoted line of teaching. It is one of the inner schools which is taught by those Masters whom we know to be at the back of the Theosophical Society, and therefore, when I am speaking of occultism, I am not referring to any other school, any Western school, or any Eastern school except this one form of development of the divine light within man.

Now Theosophy, as you know, is a philosophy and a science and religion, and therefore when it comes to deal with the very deepest part of the soul's life, it has not only the fervent aspirations of the religious systems which you know, it has not only the devotion which you see in so many other religions, but it has absolutely the scientific method by which the soul of man may be developed, by which the soul of man may come into touch with the divine soul, which is the very life-principle of the whole universe. What is termed Yoga in India means the method by which the soul of man, the divine spirit and mind of man, may link itself with that divine spirit and life from which man comes, from which he is only divided by his material senses, of which spirit he is only a little shadow for the time being during his short earthly career. Now, in speaking of the teaching that we have in the Theosophical Society there is one book, one priceless little book, which has been left to us by Helena Petrovna Blavatsky, which was written for those whom she termed "The few." Why? because she knew that it was only the few in the hurry and the press of the everyday life, it was only the few who would really stand aside from the stream of life and try to give some thought and some time to the soul within. She translated this book from one of those priceless treasures then in the possession of the Eastern teachers of Theosophy. It is called the *Book of Golden Precepts*, and from it she has gathered some few of the precepts which those who really desire to develop their spiritual life will take up and study. Dedicated as it is to the few, it is the few only who really find benefit in it. It is called *The Voice of the Silence*. The name is in itself paradoxical, but the name in itself is a volume of teaching. Is is the Voice of the Silence because it is only when the silence and the hush come over the material part of man's life that the real Voice of the Silence can speak. It is only when man will take some little time to still his worldly life, to still his worldly thoughts, that the true small voice which really lives in the heart of every man may make itself heard. And therefore Helena Petrovna Blavatsky gave us this book, leaving it to the few who would listen in the silence to the voice that would speak, and she gave it to us as the guide, the prayer book, and the very basis of our daily life.

The book itself is divided into three portions; it is divided into The Two Paths, the two paths which are spoken of, and preached of, and talked of in every religious system in the world. Jesus Christ in speaking of the life of the soul spoke of the broad path, and said that broad was the way that led to destruction and narrow the gate that leads to life eternal. Narrow is the gate also that leads to this life eternal. The gate is the narrowing down and crushing out of all the lower principles of man. It is, if we may so call it, the toning down of all the lower principles and making them one with that vibrating chord which is the keynote of that inner life. And when a man starts upon that narrow way, then there lies before him another work to be done. Putting our foot forward only, and making our choice of the narrow way, does not clear up for us all the work we have to do. Then comes the taking of ourselves in hand, then comes all the struggling with our selfish natures, the putting away of the selfish desire for life, the putting aside of all material wishes of this world; and then we come face to face with what is termed in this book The Seven Portals. The Seven Portals are seven gateways which should be opened by every man and woman as they pass onward and upward into the devotional life in Theosophy. You have all of you heard of the Seven Deadly Sins in the Roman Catholic church. Now the seven deadly sins are exactly those sins that stand in our way; those are the very seven deadly sins which bar our pathway; they are analogous to the seven principles of man; and those portals have to be opened one by one, just as the principles have to be crushed out, the lower principles, one by one; and it is only as we open those portals in front of us that the development of the true divine life within really takes place. When the six portals are opened and we stand in front of the seventh portal, when the lower principles of man are all under control and we stand in the light within and it is trying to make its vibrating impulse heard within our hearts, then are we getting some little way upon that path which every great teacher of the world has talked about.

Now, when the seven portals are open, when all these lower principles are stilled, then comes what H. P. Blavatsky speaks of as The Voice of the Silence. She speaks here, making the same division always made in Theosophical teachings, the distinction between the higher and the lower self : " The self of matter and the self of spirit can never meet; one of the twain must disappear; there is no place for both." There is no place, friends, for the self of our lower natures if we want to live according to the highest and the purest of Theosophical teachings. " Kill out desire, but if thou killest it take heed lest from the dead it should again arise " That means, even when getting onwards in this path, even when by means of daily crushing out our most besetting faults, even when by daily meditation and daily aspiration we are trying to get some little way upon that pathway, we have to keep a watch over this hydra-headed monster of our lower natures, trying ever hard to crop up again into life, trying ever to crush down this gentle voice which is trying to make itself heard. " Kill out the love of life; but if thou slayest *Tanha*, let this not be for thirst of life eternal, to replace the fleeting by the everlasting."

The fundamental teaching in Theosophy is this : All this work is not to be done for ourselves alone; the fundamental teaching of the devotional life is not to seek our own salvation, is not to get a place in that heaven for ourselves, but to perfect ourselves in this work, to purge ourselves of this lower nature, so that when the Voice of the Silence can be heard in our hearts we are then better instruments for those teachers to work through, we are better helpers for those who are teachers, to make the Voice of the Silence heard in the heart of every man and every woman around us. Why not, friends, take some time in your daily life, every one of you, give up some little, some little time in which you may try to listen to the Voice of the Silence. Down through the ages those reproachful words of Christ, when coming out of his agony in the garden, when coming out of the agony he was going through for all humanity, he turned around to Peter and said : " What! could ye not watch with me one hour ?" And in the heart of every man there is that note of reproach ringing from the Voice of the Silence within: " What ! in this material civilization, can ye not watch one hour, can ye not give up a few moments of your daily life and think of that life we are crushing out here ? Can ye not put out for a few moments all earthly desires, acts, and wishes, and give some few moments for the Voice of the Silence to be heard in your hearts ?" Look at it from what point you will, look at it how you can, that is the thing you will have to arrive at sooner or later. If you will not make it willingly now, you will have to make it sometime in this life, or if not in this life, at some future time. If you are going to live your life for yourself only, if you are going to live to help the material civilization to go on in the way it is now going, then you should give up your life to the material world and crush out that voice if you will, but you yourself in your next lives will pay the penalty, according to the Theosophical teaching. We can lay no burden on humanity by selfishness which we shall not come back and bear ourselves. For the sake of humanity what is the reason you cannot give up some time of your daily life? Every moment of your daily life that you put aside to think, even ten minutes, about this Voice of conscience within, even if you take but ten minutes to let the spiritual side of your nature speak, you are helping all humanity, you are helping the whole world in a way that no material work you can do can help; because just so far as we develop our spiritual nature, Helena Petrovna Blavatsky taught us that just so far as we develop this spiritual side, we are helping the whole world upward, we are helping the spiritual cycle upward. That it is only when the Voice of the Silence speaks in our hearts that we add to the Voice of the Silence that is speaking in the hearts of every man and woman that that work can harmonize with the divine life in the material world in which we live. And these are the messages she left to us, this was the book and teaching she put into our hands for all those who really want to listen and to learn the devotional side of Theosophy. It gives you step by step the way in which your devotional life should be led, it gives you step by step the thoughts, the work, the methods by which the Voice of the Silence can be arrived at. And with this message given to us by her to hand down to humanity, I say that it is not true when people say to us that there is no devotional life in Theosophy. It is there, it is there for every man and woman to learn if they choose to find it. For the Voice of the Silence lives in the heart of every man and every woman, and it is our fault, and it is a fault for which we shall have to pay if we do not let it teach us at some time or another.

BUDDHISM.

HEVAVITARANA DHARMAPALA.

I am always ready to speak to an American audience. I love the American people, they are so good, so hospitable, and their voices I should say are so sweet. I like the American people very much. I am asked to-day to speak on Buddhism. I think we Buddhists as a whole love the American people. Individually I love you, but the whole Buddhist population in Ceylon, Burmah, Siam, they love you very much indeed. Buddhism is just now attracting the attention of the West, of Europe's greatest thinkers in England, France, and Germany.

Well, you will be surprised to hear it when I say that in 1824 Buddhism was simply unknown to the thinking people of Europe. Dr. Marshman in 1824 said: "Well, Buddha, he must be the Egyptian Apis. There is no mention made," he said, "in any Indian philosophy about Buddha." So the only possible conclusion he could arrive at was that Buddha was Apis. Then Sir William Jones, the Orientalist, examined Brahminical literature and he found mention made here and there of Buddha. Well, he could not see anything beyond that he was an Avatar of the god Vishnu. He says, "Surely this must be the Scandinavian Wodin." He proved Buddha to be the Scandinavian Wodin. So matters were in that state until 1837, when Mr. James Prinsep and William Turner, both Oriental scholars, Mr. Turner was in Ceylon and Mr. James Prinsep was in India, examining into antiquarian remains in India; he had come across an inscription on a stone somewhere in a deep jungle; it was an inscription written on a stone in a character he could not at the time translate, and he thought it was an Egyptian hieroglyphic. He worked and at last he found that it was an inscription written in the Pali character, sculptured some twenty-one centuries ago. He went to work and found something very startling. Just at the same time Mr. Turner examined Pali literature in Ceylon, and he found an immense subject, a large subject for study. It was a curious coincidence—Mr. Turner contributing his researches in the society of Asia, in the society of Bengal, and in the very month Mr. James Prinsep disclosed this Pali inscription and published his researches in The Journal. In almost the same month a great flood of light was turned upon a subject just then attracting the attention of the greatest minds of the day. It was the discovery of a great religion, and that was Buddhism.

Well, in 1837 the great discovery was made, and to-day you find scientists, philosophers, and theologians, and all great men studying this great religious system. It was in the early days that Buchner said, if there was a materialism, it was Buddhism; it is full of materialism; and so the verdict was that it was a material system; and Max Müller examined into its teachings and found that this Nirvana is annihilation, and he said Buddhism is nihilistic. Then came a deeper study of the subject, and Profs. Davids and Childers, great men, translated some religious scriptures in Pali and they proved it was not a materialistic system. Mr. Buchner thought Buddhism was surely nothing more than a system of Pantheism of the German type, and he said not only every Pantheist, but also every theologian, should study Buddhism. It is identical with the German thought. Then came the agnostics, and they found in Buddhism a system of agnosticism; and Dr. Davids said in 1881, Buddhism is nothing but a system of agnosticism, and he called Buddha the great agnostic philosopher of India. Then the study of pessimism began, and the students of pessimism, especially the followers of Schopenhauer, they said "Surely this is a pessimistic system," and they said Buddha was a pessimist. Now comes the last of all, the great Prof. Huxley. He says this is nothing but a system of idealism, and now he says that Gautama Buddha has gone deeper into the subject than all the modern idealists, and he says Buddhism supplies nearly one-half of the basis of idealism.

So we are just now in a confusion. It is found that materialism, that pantheism, that agnosticism, that pessimism, that idealism, are Buddhism, and yet I think we shall wait, because the subject has not yet been profoundly treated ; this is superficial thought. Of course that is the verdict of those great scholars, and if I go to say the verdict is not right, they will say, " You cannot contradict those great scholars ; they are absolutely right." Of course they say, Buddha says, " I have no esotericism in my philosophy, I don't keep anything close fisted ; I give to all." Yes, but then we have to examine, and before you examine Buddhism examine the other religions, and then you will find that the esotericism of Brahminism is made public property in Buddhism. Those who have read the Upanishads will find a certain great teacher called Yagnabalkya. The man was asked by his wife Maitrya some questions which he did not reveal to her. It was only revealed in the secrecy of the chamber. And again when asked the same question, Why are we born, and why do we die ? the reply was given in secrecy between you and me ; no more, and it was given in privacy. All that was esoteric in the other philosophy, in Brahminism, Buddha gave out to the world. I may say that the Buddhist philosophy, or you may call it a religion, or a system, has two aspects, one a purely social aspect, and the other a complete system of esoteric, you also call it a transcendental, psychology, and the whole body of the writings mentions the associates of the blessed one. It is the school of the Initiates. In that sense the whole of this association is one compact school of Initiates, aud to enter into that school you have to renounce all the world and its pleasures, and you have to take up a life of active altruism, and love study, and love thought, and to live a life, so to speak, a life, a pure life, absolutely pure. And then he says you will get truths. Buddha says not to bind yourself into any system ; if you do, if you have any preconceived ideas, he says you will not get truth.

So get rid of everything you have got, all isms. If you have got pessimism, throw it overboard ; if you have idealism, throw it overboard. Let us be free, as free as crystal. The mind must be pure. He says : Don't have love to me ; if you have the love to me and you commence to study, you will not get truth. So first of all leave off all personality ; and he says accept truth for its own sake. If you are hurt when anybody scolds you, don't be offended or you will not then get truth ; you will not get truth if you are offended. So you must be entirely free from personalities ; and he says that through that pure life man will be that ideal, that consummation, so to speak, of all good Buddhists. That Nirvanic life, that eternal time, that possession, so to speak, of human understanding in this life ; and he says you can realize that state, but you must be prepared to sacrifice all you hold good and beautiful. If you love your watch, he says you cannot then get truth ; anything you love you must be prepared to sacrifice that ; then and then alone truth will dawn upon you. (Applause.)

"THE HIGHER AND LOWER SELF."

PROF. G. N. CHAKRAVARTI.

In the rush and stir of your daily life, in the ceaseless turmoil of activity of physical life, it is only natural that people should be perfectly unconscious that there is any self besides the self that is created by the sensation given rise to by the five senses of the body.

And yet sometimes when you retire from the rough rubbing of the world, sometimes when you are listening to the sweet melodies of a babbling stream, sometimes when you are looking with admiration upon the silvery blue of the starry firmanent, you seem to forget the life of the world ; the daily marketable life recedes in the background. All consciousness of the struggle with the various temptations and trials of this world leaves the plane of your consciousness, and you seem to sink into the vast profundity of some power, of some world behind you. You realize then that you are not the ignoble, mean, and grovelling creature, fighting and elbowing your way in the keen struggle of life against life ; you realize in the presence of that spirit that your capacities are infinite, that your future is limitless, and that you are the very angel of paradise thrust out from your birthright.

It is not, however, always that people in the West have opportunities to realize such a state of being. There is such a high-pressure life in the West, such feverish struggle for that which I cannot understand, that it is seldom, almost never, that you can retire into a sanctuary which is behind the external consciousness. Every one in the West seems always to be occupied with some occupation which is to deal with the physical relations of man to the world, or at best he merely works the lower aspects of one's intellect. Seldom therefore can he realize what lies beyond the mind in the Western nations. His life is like the remorseless giant, the Rakshasha, the giant in the deep ocean who extorted the promise from the person who raised him that he must always give him work—the moment he was unable longer to find him some work, "that moment," said the giant, "I will swallow up your whole being into my stomach." The mind which you have been given has been pursued on this physical plane, and is now that hydra-headed monster which demands from you work, work, ceaseless and constant ; and the moment you do not give him work he threatens you with annihilation. You stand aghast at what lies beyond. There is a gap indeed between the mental plane and the plane of the soul, and you look at that chasm and your head reels, for you cannot look beyond.

But allow me to tell you that if you look deep enough into that chasm you can find the living immortal waters of life which can make you happier, nobler, sublimer beings than you can ever be if you are occupied as you are on the plane of the mind. You are familiar, ladies and gentlemen, with that phenomenon in objects which is called total reflection. As long as the proper angle is not reached, a ray of light passing through a medium becomes distorted, and you have an inaccurate picture of the object; but only give the perfect angle to the ray of light, let it come to the point of the critical angle, and lo and behold! the distortion and refraction give place to the most beautiful reflection—perfect and total reflection, as it is technically called. So is it with the mind. At first when you withdraw from the mental plane you feel a depression, a desolation, a despair, a longing for something upon which you can stand. But only go one step further, only try to extort from nature the richness, the wealth which it holds in store for you, and that feeling of depression will be driven away, the giant which once threatened to swallow you up will fall at your feet, and you will rise triumphant with the knowledge of having conquered, the knowledge of having acquired the birthright of the spiritual possession.

In the East, however, where there is not such a keen struggle for life, men can oftener retire from the plane of mental consciousness. In fact it is ordained in the daily religious duties of the Hindus that they should spend at least half an hour twice a day in reflection on the Divine; and the conditions under which this has to be done are laid down. It is recommended that he should sit, if possible, on the banks of a silent stream at a time when day joins hands with night, when the stars are just disappearing or just appearing, and then there will flow into him an ineffable calm. He puts his soul *en rapport* with the soul of the great nature which is the true source of all happiness. He instils into his mind the real poetry of existence, the real romance of the universe. Hence it is that in all the great religious systems poetry and prophecy have meant the same thing; and I need hardly remind you that the Latin word *vates* means both a prophet and a poet; and in the majestic language of the Sanscrit philosophies one of the names of the highest Divine Being himself is Kavin Paranim, the ancient poet. Yes, by withdrawing himself from the outer consciousness in which man has crystallized his will being, and by throwing himself on the bosom of mother nature, he realizes that there is some essence, some portion of himself which is the true essence of his being, and in whose light alone he can find peace and comfort. This is the higher self of which I am to talk to you to-night; this is the real self of the man, which decayeth not, which is the primitive portion of his being, not that which but appears and disappears in forms clothed in incarnation and reincarnation, but that higher self which is not touched by external changes, which has on it to-day a fresh garment and to-morrow casts it off in order to have a better and more suitable one. So it is this higher self which to-morrow passes on to a more suitable habitation—so says the Bhagavad Gita, this immortal self of yourself is not burned by fire, is not drowned by water, is not slain by the slayer's knife, but all defies the various effects that can be produced by anything physical. It is the aim of every human being, therefore, to bring his lower self into consonance with the higher.

We know so little about the higher self because the lower self is not prepared to receive any vibrations that are evoked in the higher. You are aware that it is a law of acoustics, in order that a string may catch the vibration of any sound it must be tuned in order to be moved by that sound. Similarly it is with the brain consciousness. Your brain is so materialized, so ossified, so deadened to all that is subtle, ethereal, and noble, that it no longer vibrates in response to the waves that emanate from the higher self. It is the duty of every man, therefore, if he is to learn anything of this higher life, to so train his brain, so to train his lower consciousness, that he may be able to catch these vibrations of the higher self. This is what is meant by self-control. The very word self-control shows that there is a higher self which has to control the lower. This is the great moral principle of which Kant speaks as one of the two things which fill him with awe. This reunion of the lower self with the higher is the great truth, the mystical verity that is represented in all the great religious systems of the world by beautiful allegories and fables. This is the meaning of the fall of Adam from his paradise, and the regaining of the paradise through Christ who represents the higher self. This is the meaning of Proserpine gathering flowers, being carried away by Pluto who represents the lower self, and of being regained almost by her husband. This great truth is also represented by many, I think hundreds, of beautiful allegories in the great Sanscrit literature of the East. I shall take the liberty, with the permission of the chairman, to narrate to you one which appears to me to be one of the most beautiful that can be found in any literature existing on the face of the earth.

My object in quoting this one to you is to show how in the East they make a harmonious blending of higher spiritual truths with instruction for the common people who cannot follow the real esoteric side of things. In the story you will find ordinary duties of life, ordinary virtues which every man has to observe and possess, brought out in resplendent beauty, and at the same time below the surface it conceals one of the deepest and grandest spiritual mystical truths that you can learn. Another object is to show to you by the help of one illustration that our books teem with literature which has an esoteric aspect to it. Max Müller, as my brother Dharmapala has told you, denies that in the East there is an esotericism. No greater mistake, no more preposterous, no more disgraceful injustice to the sacred literature of the East can be perpetrated than by the assertion that there is no esoteric side to the teachings of the East. I shall go on now to narrate the story that I have in mind, and I shall leave it to you to judge whether the esoteric side which I shall present to you of that story is forced or is natural.

In olden days there lived a princess, the daughter of a great king. Her beauty was well known throughout the world, and she was endowed with all the virtues recounted in the Shastras which should adorn the female sex. There also was in the neighborhood another king who had lost all his kingdom and had retired with his wife and son into a dreary dense jungle, living a life of misery, of desolation, and of discomfort, and, what is more, he was blind also. Nature could afford to him not one moment of delight or of beatific vision.

This princess when she attained the age of marriage was consulted by her father as to whom she was going to marry, for in ancient India the girl was allowed to make her own choice quite as much as now in the West. The girl replied that she had set her heart upon the son of the blind and exiled king living in the wilderness. The son's name was Satya Ram. In the ancient times nothing was done by the princes without consulting the great Rishis of old. The king therefore invoked Narada and asked him if the choice of his daughter was well and was likely to bring happiness to her. The sage with his vision prophetic looked into the future and said that no person wandered the earth who was nobler or more virtuous than the son of the exiled king, but that there was one great objection to the choice—that he would die within three months after the marriage. The king, the father of the princess, at once made up his mind and said, "This one defect is quite enough to outweigh all the load of virtues that you have recounted," and asked his daughter what she thought of the position. In India you must remember that a person can marry once alone. And the daughter said, "I have mentally made my choice. I have given my heart to my intended. Not more than once can a woman marry. I shall stick to my resolution. I shall be loyal to my thought, I shall be devoted to my future husband ; come what might, I shall marry the man whom I have fixed upon."

The father knowing the virtuous character of his daughter allowed her to have her choice. She was duly married and brought to the exiled home of her husband. There with her many virtues of charity, loving kindness, and devotion she soon won the affections of her husband and of her father-in-law. Time went on happily enough until near came the prophecied day of the husband's death. Three days before the appointed day, the wife, whose name was Savitree, began to fast—made a rigid vow for the welfare of her husband. The father-in-law knew her to be delicate and said that she was not capable of making such a long fast—a fast of three days and performing such a rigid vow of abstinence. But she was determined ; she asked permission to go on, and she was allowed to undertake the vow.

On the third day, the day appointed for the death of her husband, she prayed that she might be allowed to go with her husband into the wilderness where he went daily to fell wood for the use of the family.

This startled both the father-in-law and the mother-in-law. They said "Child, thou art too delicate to wander thy way through the thorny paths of this jungle, thou must stay home. No such proposition can be entertained." But she insisted upon following him. She said, "This day I must go with him, I cannot stay back," and she who never made any request was allowed to have her way in this particular.

Away both of them went into the jungle, the husband and wife, till they reached the appointed spot where the wood was to be felled, and immediately after the husband got a throbbing pain in the head and very soon fell senseless in the lap of his wife. The wife nursed him in her bosom till the last wave of life seemed to be ebbing away from the frame of the husband. Then appeared, after the life was gone, Yama, King of Death, to take away the life of the husband. Seeing Yama, Savitree, the wife, said, "Why, the Lord of Death, why come you yourself from your mighty throne to take this man away, and did not send one of your ministers?" The reply was, "The magnetic purity of the devoted wife is too strong to allow any of my subordinates to approach within miles of its presence. It therefore required the King of Death himself to come down from his throne to perform this work."

When Death began to take the life away, this devoted wife followed Death as he carried her husband through the wilderness, and she was asked "Why followest thou now? Thy duties to thy husband are over, wend back thy way home." But she persisted, said such words of wisdom, saying that no duties to her were greater than serving her lord. Nothing that the home could give her back by returning would make up for the loss of her husband. She persisted in following Yama. Yama, attacked by her sweet words and her unflinching devotion, said, "You may ask, save the life of your husband, any boon, and I will give it to you." She said, "My father is deprived of his kingdom. The first boon that I ask of you is that he shall return to his kingdom and regain his wealth."

"Granted," said Yama. "Now you shall go back."

Still she pursued Yama, still she refused to go back, again she used such sweet words of wisdom, poured forth such expressions of unflinching devotion to her husband into the ears of Yama, that he was induced to grant her a second boon, and she said, "My father-in-law has lost the power of sight. My prayer is that sight be given back to him."

"It shall be so," again said Yama, "now go thou back."

Yet she pursued. She was not to be sent away without having accomplished her end. She prayed that she might have a hundred beautiful and strong children from her womb.

The Death, forgetting for the moment in the sweetness of her voice, said, "Granted is thy prayer." Immediately the next moment turns around this ideal of chastity and says to Yama, "Lord of Death, knowest thou what thou hast just now granted? Knowest thou that a Hindu wife can never go to a second husband? Knowest thou that my prayer cannot be granted unless my husband comes back to life? Thou art the minister of justice. Thou canst not speak untruth, therefore my last boon is the life of my husband."

Startled, confused beyond all comprehension, the mighty Death shook down his head and said, "Take thy husband back. Thy chastity has taken back from the very home of death the life which has already become its own. Thy chastity will remain the ideal for generations and generations for women to follow."

Returned she back home with the life of her husband. They all regained their lost kingdom, the father-in-law regained his lost sight, and once more they reigned peacefully.

This is the exoteric story; this outside aspect of it is enough to offer an ideal of devotion, of purity, of chastity, to any civilized community that has existed on the face of the earth. But there is an esoteric aspect which is even sublimer than this.

Savitri in the Sanscrit language means the daughter of Savarta, which means the spiritual sun. Savitri therefore means the spiritual soul of man which emanates from the great spiritual sun of which I spoke to you last night. Marriage of this spiritual daughter to Sakravan represents the marriage of a spirit to the lower self, to the personality of the man. Sakravan was the son of the king who had lost country and sight. What does it represent? That the personality of man is the creation of the human mind which has lost all its kingdom of paradise which has flown from it. It has also lost all its sight which allows it to look into that heaven from which it has fallen. The marriage of the spiritual soul with this lower self then brings about the happiness of life, and at the very moment when the destruction of the lower self might have been achieved by its devotion to matter, comes the help of the higher self, the spiritual self, the daughter of the spiritual sun, to save man, the personal man; and not only to save him but to regain for the human mind all the wealth and all the kingdom that it has lost, and that spiritual insight which it had been deprived of. This, then, is the real meaning of this grand allegory, and this the meaning of all the various other allegories that the different systems of religion are found teeming with. The great object therefore of your life must be to direct your gaze inward, bend down your ears to the voice of the divine mother which ever crieth in mellifluous strains to be heard by you, but whose sweet voice you hear not. If you once but catch those sweet strains, if you kneel at her feet and say "Mother, save me," she will take you in her lap, wash all the thousand wounds that your self has been penetrated by, and lull you into gentle sleep in her bosom, and then you can go on through the trials and turmoils of life with a peace abiding in your breast that can be found nowhere save in the bosom of that Great Mother.

THE SUPREME DUTY.

ANNIE BESANT.

I speak to-night on the supreme duty. I proclaim to-night the universal law of life; for only by service is fulness of life made possible, to the service of man the whole of the universe to-day is yoked. For under the name of man, man past, present, and future, man evolving up to the divine man, eternal, immortal, indestructible, that is the service to which every individual should be pledged, that the object of life, that the fashion of evolution; and I shall try to put for you to-night in few words something of the elements of this service, something of its meaning in daily life, as well as something of the heights whereto the daily practice may at length conduct the human soul, for poor indeed is that religion which cannot teach the men and the women of the world the duty of daily life, and yield to them inspiration which shall aid them in their upward climbing to the light.

Great is philosophy which moulds the minds of men, great is science which gives light of knowledge to the world; but greater than all is religion which teaches man his duty, which inspires man with strength to accomplish it; greatest of all is that knowledge of the human soul which makes daily service the path of progress and finds in the lowest work the steps that lead to the highest achievement.

According to the philosophy which we stand here to represent, we have in the universe and in man various planes of being, sevenfold in their full enumeration. A briefer classification will serve me for the hints which alone I can throw out to-night. Let us take the plane of the physical man and see what on that plane the service of man may connote. First of all, the service of man implies what was called by the Buddha right livelihood, that is, right fashion of gaining ordinary life, honest way of gaining the means of ordinary existence. Not a livelihood based on the compelled service of others, not a livelihood which takes everything and gives nothing back, not a livelihood which stretches out its hands to grasp and closes its fists when gift is asked instead of gain. Right livelihood implies honesty of living, and honesty implies that you give as much as you take, that you render back more than you receive, that you measure your work by your power of service, not by your power of compulsion. That the stronger your brain the greater your duty to help, that the higher your position the more imperative the cry to bend that position to the service of human need. Right livelihood is based on justice. Right livelihood is made beautiful by love, and if there is to be a reckoning between the giving and the taking, then let the scale of giving weigh the heavier, and give to man far more than you take from him.

But on the material plane more is asked of you than the discharge of this part of duty, right livelihood, that injures none and serves all. You have also a duty of right living that touches on the plane of the body, by which I include to-night the whole of the transitory part of man, and right living means the recognition of the influence that you bring to bear upon the world by the whole of your lower nature as well as by the higher. It implies the understanding of the duty that the body of each bears to the bodies of all, for you cannot separate your bodies from the bodies amidst which you live, since constant interchange is going on between them. Tiny lives that build up you to-day help to build up another to-morrow, and so the constant interaction and interweaving of these physical molecules proceed. What use do you make of your body? Do you say " It is mine. I can do with it as I will. Shall not a man do as he will with his own?" Even so. But there is nothing a man has that is his own, for all belongs to that greater man, the aggregate humanity, and the fragments have no rights that go against the claim of service to the whole. So that you are responsible for the use that you make of your bodies. If when these tiny lives come into your charge you poison them with alcohol, you render them coarse and gross with over-luxurious living and send them out into the community of which you form a part, and send them out to other men and women and children, they sow there the seeds of the vices they have learned from you, of the gluttony, of the intemperance, the impurity of living that you have stamped on them while they remained as part of your own body. You have no right to do it. No excuse can bear you guiltless of the crime. There are drunkards amongst us. Granted they are responsible for their crime, but also every human being is responsible for them who helps to spread the poison in a community which is focalized in those miserable creatures. And so every atom that you send out alcohol-poisoned from yourself helps to make drunkenness more permanent, helps to make its grip tighter upon the victims already in its grasp, and you are guilty of your brother's degradation if you do not supply pure atoms of physical life to build up others who in very truth are one with yourself.

And so you have something of what service of man means on this lowest plane, and another service that you, above all, richer people in this land and in others, could set an example of, so that others from your voluntary action may learn to follow in the same path, you should simplify the physical life, you should lessen the physical wants, you should think less of luxury and more of the higher life, less labor wasted to minister to the artificial wants of the body, and more time for the souls of men to grow less encumbered with the anxieties of life. If you take such teaching to the poor, true as the teaching is, one hardly dares to put it to them on whom the iron yoke of poverty presses, and who find in so much of physical suffering one of the miseries of their life. You should set the example, because with you it is voluntary action. You should set the ideal of plain living and high thinking instead of the ideal of senseless luxury, of gross materialistic living on every side. Can you blame the poor that they think so much of earthly pleasure, that they desire so passionately material ease? Can you blame them if in every civilized country discontent is growing, threats are filling the air, when you set the ideal which they copy in their desire, and when you, by the material pleasure of your lives, tell them that man's aim and object is but the joy of the sense, is but the pleasure of the moment? This also is your duty in the service of man on a material plane, so that, lessening the wants of the body, he may learn to feed the soul, and making the outer life more nobly simple may give his energies rather to that which is permanent and which endures.

But not only on the physical, the lowest plane, is the service of man to be sought. We rise to the mental plane, and there too must man be served far more efficaciously than he can be served on the physical plane. Do you say that at least I cannot do service on the mental plane? That the mental plane is all very well for the great thinker that publishes some work that revolutionizes thought? That it is all very well for the speaker who reaches thousands where I can reach but units? It is not so. The great thinker, be he writer or be he speaker, has not such enormous over-plus of impulse as you, judging by the outer appearance, may imagine. True, his work is great, but has it never struck you in what lies the power of the speaker, whence comes the strength with which he moves a crowd? It does not lie in himself; it lies not in his own power, but in the power he is able to evoke from the men and women he addresses, from the human hearts he wakes. It is their energy and not his in the tide of his speech. The orator is but the tongue that syllables out the thoughts in the hearts of the people; they are not able to speak them, they are not able to articulate them. The thoughts are there, and when some tongue puts them into speech, when the other inarticulate sense takes the force of the spoken word, then they think it is oratory. It is their own hearts that moves them, and it is this voice, inarticulate in the people, which from the lips of the speaker makes the power that rings from land to land.

But that is not all. Every one of you in your daily thinking, every one of you has thoughts that you pour out to the world. You are making the possibilities of the morrow, you are making or marring the potencies of to-day. Even as you think, the thought burning in your brain becomes a living force for good or for evil in the mental atmosphere just as far as the vitality and the strength that are in it may be able to carry it on in its work in this world of mind. There is no woman, however weak, there is no man, however obscure, who has not in the soul within him one of the creative forces of the world. As he thinks, thoughts from him go out to mould the thoughts and lives of other men. As he thinks thoughts of love and gentleness, the whole reservoir of love in the world is filled to overflowing; and as he contributes to them, so every day is formed that public opinion which is the moulder of men's ideas more than sometimes we are apt to dream. So that in this everyone has share, so that in this all men and women have their part. Your thought-power makes you creative

Gods in the world, and it is thus that the future is builded, it is thus that the race climbs upward to the divine.

Not alone in the physical nor alone in the mental sphere is this constant service of man to be sought; but of the service of the spiritual sphere, no words of platform oratory can fitly describe its nature or its sacredness. That is the work that is done in silence, without sound of spoken word, of clatter of human endeavor. That work lies above us and around us, and we must have learned the perfection of the service in the lower ere we dare aspire to climb where the spiritual work is done. What, then, is the outcome of such suggestion, what the effect in life of such philosophy applied to the life of each as it is made or met in the world to-day? Surely it is that we should think nobly. Surely it is that our ideals should be lofty. Surely it is that in our daily life we should ever strike the highest keynote, and then strive to attune the living to the keynote that at our noblest we have struck. According to the ideal the will is lifted. In the old phrase, the man becomes that which he worships. Let us see, then, that our ideals be lofty. Let us see that what we worship shall have in it the power that shall transform us into the image of the perfect man; that shall transmute us into the perfect gold of which humanity shall finally consist. If you would help in that evolution, if you would bear your share in that great labor, then let your ideal be truth; truth in every thought and act of life. Think true, otherwise you will act falsely. Let nothing of duplicity, nothing of insincerity, nothing of falsehood soil the inner sanctuary of your life, for if that be pure your actions will be spotless, and the radiance of the eternal truth shall make your lives strong and noble. Not only be true, but also be pure, for out of purity comes the vision of the divine, and only the pure in heart, as said the Christ, shall see God. That is true. In whatever phase you put it, that is true, whatever words describe it. Only the pure in heart shall have the beatific vision, for that which is itself absolute purity must be shared in by the worshipper ere it can be seen.

And then add to these ideals of truth and of purity one that is lacking in our modern life, the ideal of reverence for what is noble, of adoration for that which is higher than one's self. Modern life is becoming petty because we are not strong enough to reverence. Modern life is becoming base, sordid, and vulgar because men fear that they will sink if they bow their heads to that which is greater than they are themselves. I tell you that worship of that which is higher than yourself raises you, it does not degrade you. That the feeling of reverence is a feeling that lifts you up, it does not take you down. We have talked so much about rights that we have forgotten that which is greater than a man's right with himself. It is the power of seeing what is nobler than he has dreamed of, and bowing in the very dust before it till it permeates his life and makes him like itself. Only those who are weak are afraid to obey; only those who are feeble are afraid of humility. Democrats we are in our modern phrase, and with the world of to-day as we have it democracy in the external world is the best fashion of carrying on the outer life. But if it were possible that as in the days of old in Egypt and India the very gods themselves wandered the earth as men and taught the people the higher, trained the people in the higher truth, conveyed to the people the higher knowledge, would we claim that we were their equals, and that we should be degraded by sitting at their feet to learn? And if you could weave into your modern life that feeling of reverence for that which is purest, noblest, grandest ; for wisdom, for strength, for purity, till the passion of your reverence should bring the qualities into your own life—Oh, then your future as a nation would be secure. Then your future as a people would be glorious, and you men and women of America, creators of the future, will you not rise to the divine possibilities which every one of you has hidden in his own heart? Why go only to the lower when the stars are above you? Why go only to the dust when the sun sends down his beams that on those beams you may rise to his very heart? Yours is the future, for you are making it to-day, and as you build the temple of your nation, as you hope that in the days to come it shall rise nobly amongst the peoples of the earth and stand as pioneer of true life, of true greatness, lay you the foundations strong to-day. No building can stand whose foundations are rotten, no nation can endure whose foundations are not divine. You have the power. Yours is the choice, and as you exercise it the America of centuries to come will bless you for your living or will condemn you for your failure ; for you are the creators of the world, and as you will so it shall be. (Applause.)

DR. J. D. BUCK, Chairman : Speaking on behalf of our foreign delegates, of our associates on this platform, and of the Theosophical Society in this grand Convention, we do not feel that we can adjourn without expressing, as I now have the honor to do, to the managers of the Parliament of Religions our sincere appreciation of the courtesy, the kindness, the great fairness and liberality which have been extended to the Theosophical Society during all of its sessions. The Congress stands adjourned *sine die.*

APPENDIX.

CREDENTIALS OF EUROPEAN DELEGATES.

These are to be found in resolutions passed by the Convention of the European Section in July, 1893, at London. The delegates were Annie Besant, Miss F. Henrietta Müller, Mrs. Isabel Cooper-Oakley.

SPECIAL CREDENTIALS TO PROF. CHAKRAVARTI.

Three Brahmanical bodies in India gave him credentials which are printed in English below. As he was called to act by the whole Thesophical Society, every Section contributing to the expense, no credentials for that purpose were needed.

[Written in English.]

WE, THE UNDERSIGNED members of the CAWNPORE HARI BHAKTI PRODAYINI SABHA, do hereby appoint Babu Gyanendra Nath Chakravarti, M.A., L.L. B., F. T. S., as our delegate for the purpose of expressing the views and tenets of this Brahminical Society in the Parliament of Religions at Chicago. Signed,

KALI NATH BANERJI,
KASHISHWAR CHAKRAWARTY,
NARAIN CHUNDER BANERJII,
SHIBCHUNDER BUTTACHARJEE,
SHUNGALUND,
BESHUMVHER NATH,
BEHARILAL KAPUR,
BRAJALAL CHAKRAVARTI,
LALTA PERSHAD BAJPAI,
HARI RAM,
GYANENDRA NATH GHOSAUL,
KHETTER CHUNDER DASS,
GOOROO N. MOOKERJEE,
DHARMADAS MUKERJEE,
PUNDIT BISESWAR MISSER,
PUNDIT RAMDULARE DUBEY,
PUNDIT SITA RAM,
DEVI PODA ROY,
JOGENDRO NAUTH CHATTEJI,
PURNA CHANDRA MUKERJI,
HARAN CHANDRA BHADJA,
AGHORE NATH MUKERJEE,
THACOOR DASS MOOKERJEE,
TRAYLOKYA NATH BANERJEE,
NAGENDRA NATH BANERJEE,
JOGENDRA NATH BANERJEE,
BEJOY GAPAL NANDI,
SIDHESHWAR MUKERJEE,

SARAT CH. BANERJI,
JATENDRA NATH MOOKERJEE,
LALIT MOHAN MUKERJEE,
HURRYDAS DUTT,
SARAT CHANDRA BANERJEE,
RAJANDRAN CHAKRAVARTI,
SHIVA KRISHNA ROY,
SREENATH DASS,
HARISH CHUNDER MUKERJEE,
SHAMAN C MOOKERJEE,
UMAPUDO ROY,
M. M. GHOSE,
JOGENDRA NATH BASU, L.M.S.
ABANI SANKER ROY,
SURENDRO NAUTH BANERJEE,
POORNA CHUNDRA BHADURI,
M. N. GANGULI,
G. N. GANPATI.
RAMA KISSEN BANERJEE,
OTOOL CHUNDER MOOKERJEE,
J. N. OULTO,
M. D. SINGHA,
HERA LAL GHOSH,
HARA MOHAN CHAKRAVARTY,
NUGENDRONATH GHOSAL,
BEHARY LAL GHOSH,
K. L. MUKERJEE,
I. N. CHATTERJEE,
BIDHU BHUSAN BHATTACHARJI.

[In Sanscrit.]
MAY PROSPERITY ATTEND YOU.

AT A MEETING OF THE VARNASHRAMA DHARMA SABHA
PUNDIT KASHINATH SASTRI.

As there is going to sit in the Western land of America a grand Convention of all the different religions of the world, it is desirable that somebody should represent this Sabha at its sittings. We therefore hereby depute Sri Pundit Ganendra Nath Chakravarti to represent us at the Congress, and we hope that prosperity may attend the Sabha of ours.

[In Hindustan.]
DELHI, India (Indraprastha.)

AT A MEETING OF THE SANATAN DHARM RAKHSHANEE SABHA,
MEERUT.

As there is going to sit in America a Parliament of the different religions of the world, to be attended by men of learning, intelligence, and religious training, this Sabha requests Sri Pundit Ganendra Nath Chakravarti that he would kindly represent the Brahmanic doctrines at its sittings.

AUSTRALASIAN CREDENTIALS.

To MRS. ISABEL COOPER-OAKLEY,
Fellow of the Theosophical Society:
MADAM: The Victorian Theosophical League, being hereunto authorized by the various Branches of the Theosophical Society throughout the Australasian Colonies and Tasmania, hereby appoint you as Delegate to represent the Thesophists of Australia and Tasmania at the Congress of Religions to be held in connection with the World's Fair at Chicago, U. S. A., in the month of September, 1893.
Dated this 31st day of July, 1893.
Victorian Theosophical
League Headq'rs, H. W. HUNT, F. T. S., President.
Collins St., H. B. LEADER, F. T. S., Secretary.
Melbourne.

NEW ZEALAND, July 26, 1893.
To MRS. COOPER-OAKLEY:
MADAM: We, the undersigned officers of the Theosophical Society, as representing the North and Middle Islands of New Zealand, respectively hereby appoint you to act as our delegate to the

forthcoming Congress of Religions to be held at Chicago (U. S. A.) during September proximo. In doing so we desire to express our keen sense of the eminent services rendered by you to the cause of the most ancient Wisdom Religion during your recent tour through Australasia. We have the honor to remain, Madam,
Your obedient servants,
LILIAN EDGER, President,
W. H. DRAFFIN, Hon. Sec.
Auckland T. S.
GRANT P. FARQUHAR, President,
A. W. MAURAIS, Hon. Sec.
Dunedin T. S.

CEYLON CREDENTIALS.

HEADQUARTERS
THEOSOPHICAL SOCIETY,
COLOMBO, CEYLON, 19th July, 1893.

That at a meeting of the Colombo Theosophical Society held at its Headquarters on the 19th July, 1893, the following resolution was proposed by Brother D. J. Subasinha and séconded by Brother I. Gunawardana, and unanimously carried :

"That Brother H. Dharmapala do represent the Colombo Theosophical Society at the Theosophical Congress to be held at Chicago on the 15th and 16th September, 1893, in connection with the World's First Parliament of Religions."

D. J. GUNAWARDANA, President.
C. P. G. GOONIWARDEN, Secretary.

THE THEOSOPHICAL SOCIETY.

General Information.

The Society is not a secret or political organization; it is an international body; its constitution is founded on the principles of perfect autonomy and non-interference; it is wholly without a creed or dogma; the sole doctrine to be accepted is that of Universal Brotherhood. Its stated objects are:

First.—To form the nucleus of a UNIVERSAL BROTHERHOOD OF HUMANITY, without distinction of race, sex, creed, caste, or color.

Second.—To promote the study of Aryan and other Eastern literatures, religions, and sciences, and demonstrate the importance of that study.

Third.—To investigate unexplained laws of nature and the psychical powers latent in man.

As a condition precedent to membership, belief in and adherance to the first of the above named objects is required; as to the other two, members may pursue them or not, as they see fit. The act of joining the Society, therefore, carries with it no obligation whatever to profess belief in either the practicability of presently realizing the brotherhood of mankind, or in the superior value of Aryan over modern science, or in the existence of occult powers latent in man. It implies only intellectual sympathy in the attempt to disseminate tolerant and brotherly feelings, to discover as much truth as can be uncovered by diligent study and careful experimentation, and to essay the formation of a nucleus of a Universal Brotherhood.

Officers and Offices.

General Headquarters at Adyar, Madras, India, where the Society has a property and buildings, where the Oriental Library is and where the President at present resides.

President, Col. H. S. Olcott; *Vice-President*, William Q. Judge, New York; *Secretary* and *Treasurer* subject to appointment.

European Headquarters at 19 Avenue Road, Regent's Park, London, England. General Secretary of European Section, George R. S. Mead.

American Headquarters, 144 Madison Avenue, New York. General Secretary of American Section, William Q. Judge.

Indian Section Headquarters at the Society's building, Adyar. General Secretary Indian Section, Bertram Keightley.

For administrative purposes Sections are formed when the number of Branches in a territory warrants it. At the date of this report the Sections are India, America, Europe.

Annual Conventions of Sections.

Indian Section in December-January; European Section in July; American Section in April.

Joining the T. S. and Membership.

Applicants become members by joining a Branch or by being admitted as at large (or unattached) by any proper officer. In all cases the application has to be signed by the applicant and endorsed by two active members in good standing. The application is handed to a Branch if made thus, or to the president of a Branch who, as such, has the right to admit members as at large or unattached ; the General Secretary has also the right to admit members as at large or unattached. In each case the application is sent to the General Secretary of the Section for registering and issuing diploma. The President of the T. S. of course may admit members at all times and places, but Secretaries have no such right outside their Sections. Members at large may affiliate at any time with a Branch if mutually agreeable. It is understood that any member may attend any meeting of any Branch wherever he may be.

Dues for entrance are fixed by each Section according to its constitution. Annual dues of Branches are fixed by the by-laws of the Branch.

WHAT MEMBERS RECEIVE.

In America all members receive the yearly report, such documents as issue from time to time from the office of the General Secretary, and also a copy of the *Forum*, which is an occasional (monthly as near as may be) pamphlet consisting of questions and answers on Theosophical topics. Issues of the Oriental Department when printed are also sent to each member. Branches receive each month or so a Branch paper upon some Theosophical subject.

The Circulating Library at Headquarters is also open to members under its rules.

A CORRESPONDENCE CLASS is carried on from Headquarters, open to all members. In this questions are sent out at stated intervals upon Theosophical subjects, answers examined and returned with comments, lines of study indicated, references given, and now and then summaries of the subject studied forwarded to the members. Any member of the American Section in good standing can join by applying to the *Secretary Correspondence Class, 144 Madison Ave., New York*.

In Europe the *Vahan* takes the place occupied in America by the *Forum*, and the same system is otherwise pursued.

In India the *Prasnottara* is their question and answer publication, and they also have Branch papers.

PERIODICALS.

The Theosophist, Adyar, Madras, India, $5.00 per year.
Lucifer, London, 19 Avenue Road, N. W., $4.25 per year.
The Path, 144 Madison Avenue, New York, $2.00 per year.
Theosophical Siftings, London, 7 Duke St., Adelphi, W. C., $1.25 per year.
New Californian, Los Angeles, Cal., $1.50 per year.
Pacific Theosophist, 1504 Market St., San Francisco.
Others in various Oriental languages.

AMERICAN SUB-CENTRES.

San Francisco, 1504 Market St.; Chicago, 26 Van Buren St.

www.ingramcontent.com/pod-product-compliance
Lightning Source LLC
Chambersburg PA
CBHW020842160426
43192CB00007B/757